Sprachkurs *Premium*

Englisch

Lernbuch

Anthony Fitzpatrick
Leah Fitzpatrick

Sprachkurs Premium Englisch
von Anthony Fitzpatrick, Leah Fitzpatrick

Konzept und Koordinierung: Anthony Fitzpatrick
Redaktion: Sigrid Janssen
redaktionelle Mitarbeit: Tina Harnischfeger
Projektleitung: Rebecca Syme
Layout und technische Umsetzung: sign, Berlin
Umschlaggestaltung: Cornelsen Verlag Design
Umschlagfoto: Purestock/Alamy; Blue Jean Images/Alamy

Weitere Lextra Englisch-Titel:
978-3-589-01539-9 Lextra Großes Themenwörterbuch Englisch
978-3-589-01561-0 Lextra Grund- und Aufbauwortschatz Englisch
978-3-589-22264-3 Lextra Lerngrammatik Englisch + CD-ROM

www.cornelsen.de
www.lextra.de

Die Links zu externen Webseiten Dritter, die in diesem Lehrwerk angegeben sind, wurden vor Drucklegung sorgfältig auf ihre Aktualität geprüft. Der Verlag übernimmt keine Gewähr für die Aktualität und den Inhalt dieser Seiten oder solcher, die mit ihnen verlinkt sind.

Dieses Werk berücksichtigt die Regeln der reformierten Rechtschreibung und Zeichensetzung. Bei den mit ® gekennzeichneten Texten haben die Rechteinhaber einer Anpassung widersprochen.

1. Auflage, 1. Druck 2010

Alle Drucke dieser Auflage sind inhaltlich unverändert und können im Unterricht nebeneinander verwendet werden.

Druck: CS-Druck CornelsenStürtz, Berlin

ISBN 978-3-589-01571-9

 Inhalt gedruckt auf säurefreiem Papier aus nachhaltiger Forstwirtschaft.

INHALTSVERZEICHNIS

Lextra Sprachkurs Premium Englisch

Einleitung

Dieser Selbstlernkurs besteht aus drei Elementen:
* Lesebuch
* Lernbuch
* Audio-MP3-CD

Das Lesebuch und die Audio-MP3-CD bilden die zentrale Grundlage des Kurses.

Das Lesebuch

Die **36 Units** des Lesebuchs bestehen aus Gesprächen und bilden eine fortlaufende Geschichte. Mit den Hauptpersonen und ihren Stimmen auf der **Audio-MP3-CD**, einem zentralen Bestandteil des Kurses, werden Sie schnell vertraut: Peter, ein junger Deutscher, der ein Praktikum in einer britischen Firma macht, fährt nach Manchester, England. Während seines Aufenthalts in Großbritannien reist er nach London und Edinburgh, wo er verschiedene Aspekte der britischen Kultur und Lebensweise erlebt. Auf seiner Arbeitsstelle wird er mit einem schwierigen Fall konfrontiert.

Die Gesprächstexte führen Sie durch verschiedenste Situationen in Großbritannien, im privaten Alltag wie in beruflichen Zusammenhängen. Der Kurs ist also kein einfacher „Touristensprachführer", sondern bereitet Sie ebenso auf berufliche Alltagssituationen vor.

Die Geschichte beginnt mit sehr einfachen Äußerungen und überfordert Sie nicht durch schwierige Strukturen. Die Fortschritte ergeben sich fast unbemerkt …

Jede Unit ist übersichtlich auf zwei Seiten dargestellt: links steht der englische Text, rechts die deutsche Übersetzung. Der englische Sprechtext und die deutsche Übersetzung sind so in Zeilen unterteilt, dass sich sprachliche Sinneinheiten ergeben. Durch die gegenüberliegende Übersetzung können Sie sehen, wie ein deutscher Ausdruck auf Englisch wiedergegeben wird und was ein englischer Ausdruck auf Deutsch bedeutet. Sie lernen keine isolierten Wörter, sondern sinnvolle Ausdrücke. Das erleichtert den Einstieg ebenso wie die Wiederholung.

Vokabular

Am Ende des Lesebuchs finden Sie ein englisch-deutsches und ein deutsch-englisches Verzeichnis aller im Kurs vorkommenden Wörter. So können Sie die Bedeutung eines Wortes rasch nachschlagen. Falls Sie sich nicht an den inhaltlichen Kontext des Wortes erinnern können, finden Sie im Wörterverzeichnis einen Hinweis auf die Unit, in der das Wort vorkommt.

Sprache und Ausdrucksfähigkeit als Ziel

Die Auswahl der grammatischen Strukturen und des Wortschatzes bietet Ihnen eine solide Grundlage, um Ihr Hör- und Leseverstehen, sowie Sprechen und Schreiben einfacher Sätze zu verbessern. Die Zeit zur Erreichung dieses Ziels hängt von Ihrer persönlichen Veranlagung und Ihrer verfügbaren Zeit ab.

Der Lextra Sprachkurs Premium wurde nach modernsten Erkenntnissen der Sprachwissenschaft entwickelt. Der Kurs berücksichtigt die Lernzielbeschreibungen des Gemeinsamen europäischen Referenzrahmen für Sprachen. Diese Zielbeschreibungen enthalten eine umfangreiche Empfehlung, die Spracherwerb, Sprachanwendung und Sprachkompetenz für Lernende bedarfsorientiert, transparent und international vergleichbar macht. Der Referenzrahmen spricht von den Stufen A1, A2, B1, B2, C1 und C2. Bei intensiver Nutzung des Lextra Sprachkurs Premium erreichen Sie am Ende die Stufe B1-B2. Aber auch weniger ehrgeizige Lerner werden aus dem Kurs und seinen am Gemeinsamen Referenzrahmen orientierten Angeboten großen Gewinn ziehen.

Die Audio-MP3-CD

Die Audio-MP3-CD bildet einen zentralen Bestandteil dieses Kurses und enthält zu jeder Unit die Tonaufnahmen, die Sie brauchen. Hier wurde das Audiomaterial von bis zu sechs CDs komprimiert für Sie auf einer Audio-MP3-CD zusammengefasst. Die Tracknummer, mit der Sie die Texte und Übungen auf der Audio-MP3-CD ansteuern können, ist jeweils im Buch angegeben, z. B. ▶
014
Die Audio-MP3-CD enhält:

- Die Aufnahme der Gespräche, zu Beginn etwas langsamer, da Sie sich zunächst in die Sprache einhören sollen. Die Aufnahmen dienen Ihnen gleichzeitig als Modell für die Aussprache. Allmählich gehen die Aufnahmen in ein natürliches Sprechtempo über, damit Sie sich an ein normales Tempo gewöhnen.
- Die Aufnahme der Gespräche mit Nachsprechpausen, die Ihnen Gelegenheit geben, das Gehörte selbst sprechend zu erproben.
- Hinweise auf vielfältige Übungen im Lernbuch, zu denen Sie die Audio-MP3-CD brauchen. Das sind Übungen zur Unterscheidung einzelner Laute oder zum Hörverstehen der Gespräche. Dabei geht es nicht um unwichtige Details, sondern darum, ob Sie die wichtigen Informationen der angegebenen Situation verstanden haben.

Die Sprecher der Audio-MP3-CD sind Engländer. Nur in einzelnen Übungen wird auf grammatikalische und orthografische Unterschiede zum amerikanischen Englisch hingewiesen. Nichtsdestotrotz ist dieser Kurs auch für Lerner zu empfehlen, die Interesse über das britische Englisch hinaus haben. Ein einheitliches Englisch gibt es nicht. Bereits in Großbritannien kommen es viele regionale Unterschiede vor und amerikanisches, kanadisches oder australisches Englisch weist vor allem in Aussprache und Vokabular Besonderheiten auf, die wir in diesem Kurs nicht darstellen können. Aber Englisch ist eine gemeinsame Weltsprache für Millionen von Sprechern und dieser Kurs wird Sie befähigen, sich mit ihnen verständigen zu können.

Das Lernbuch

Zu jeder Unit gibt Ihnen das Lernbuch mit den Übungen einige Erklärungen zur Sprache, Sprachanwendung und Landeskunde, die am Anfang jeder Unit stichwortartig gelistet werden. Sie erläutern:

- Einzelheiten der im Text vorkommenden sprachlichen Formen. Diese Hinweise sind allgemeine Erläuterungen zur Grammatik.
- Hinweise zur Sprachanwendung, d. h. wie und wann man einen Ausdruck verwendet, und zur Sprechabsicht, d. h. wie man einen Ausdruck versteht.
- Erläuterungen zu spezifischen kulturellen Eigenheiten Großbritanniens und Unterschiede zu Deutschland. Die landeskundlichen Informationen sind mit einer englischen Fahne gekennzeichnet.

Im Lernbuch finden Sie ebenfalls Querverweise auf die Kurzgrammatik (ab Seite 192), z. B.
→ **G** Grammatik 6, sowie auf andere Kapitel und Dialoge, in denen relevante Inhalte behandelt werden, z. B. → **U** Unit 5.2., → **D** Dialog 14.

Die Querverweise bieten die Möglichkeit, weitere Grammatikformen eines bereits bekannten Wortes oder einer grammatikalischen Struktur nachzuschlagen. Haben Sie z. B. vom Verb *be* die Form *am* kennengelernt, können Sie weitere Formen des Verbs in der Kurzgrammatik finden. Das einfache Nummernsystem hilft Ihnen dabei.

Übungen

Zu jeder Unit finden Sie eine Reihe von Übungen.
Zielsetzungen der Übungen sind:
- Wiederholung und Festigung von Wörtern und Ausdrücken.
- Die richtige Verwendung grammatikalischer Formen von Wörtern.
- Bewusstmachung der Sprachanwendung, sowie Realisierung von Sprechabsichten.
- Trainieren von Hören und Verstehen (in Verbindung mit der Audio-MP3-CD).

Tests

Nach den Units 12, 24 und 36 kommt ein umfassender Test, welcher die verschiedensten Inhalte aller bisher behandelten Units wiederholt.

Lösungen

Die Lösungen zu den Übungen und Tests ermöglichen Ihnen die Auswertung und Kontrolle Ihrer Leistungen. Sollten Sie feststellen, dass Sie eine größere Zahl von Antworten nicht richtig gegeben haben, können Sie die Übung zu einem späteren Zeitpunkt wiederholen.

Kurzgrammatik

In der Kurzgrammatik finden Sie die Grundelemente der englischen Grammatik. Sie stellt keine komplette Grammatik der englischen Sprache dar, sondern bietet Ihnen einen Überblick über die wichtigsten grammatischen Regeln, die Sie für die Beherrschung der Alltagssprache benötigen.

Weitere Tipps für ein effektives Englischlernen finden Sie in der Einleitung des Lesebuchs.

Wir wünschen Ihnen viel Spaß und Freude bei der Verwendung dieses Kurses.

Ihr Sprachkurs Premium Team

Empfehlungen für das Lernen

Wir empfehlen Ihnen folgende Arbeitsschritte im Rahmen einer Unit:
1 Lesen Sie den deutschen Dialog im Lesebuch, um den Inhalt zu erfassen.
2 Hören Sie den englischen Dialog, ohne mitzulesen. So bekommen Sie einen Gesamteindruck.
3 Hören Sie mehrfach den englischen Dialog und lesen Sie mit. Wenn Sie an einer Stelle Fragen bezüglich der Bedeutung haben, springen Sie in die gleiche Zeile des gegenüberliegenden deutschen Textes.
4 Hören Sie wieder den englischen Dialog, ohne mitzulesen. So konzentrieren Sie sich voll auf das Verstehen und Aufnehmen des englischen Gesprächs.
5 Hören Sie den Dialog in der Pausenversion und sprechen Sie nach. Sie gewöhnen sich an Aussprache, Betonung, Intonation und Rhythmus.
6 Lesen Sie nun die Erläuterungen zu Sprache und Sprachanwendung im Lernbuch. Dabei werden Ihnen verschiedene sprachliche Inhalte und Strukturen besser verständlich und klarer bewusst. Nutzen Sie dabei die Querverweise auf die Grammatik im Lernbuch, wenn Sie das, was in den Erläuterungen zu Sprache und Sprachanwendung erklärt wird, in einem vollständigeren grammatischen Zusammenhang sehen wollen.
7 Machen Sie die angebotenen Übungen im Lernbuch und auf der Audio-MP3-CD und kontrollieren Sie Ihre Ergebnisse mit dem Lösungsschlüssel im Lernbuch.
8 Hören Sie abschließend noch einmal oder mehrmals den englischen Dialog.

1

On the plane

- Artikel
- Positive und negative Aussagesätze
- Ja/Nein-Fragen

- Kurzantworten
- Pronomen (*it*)
- Nationalitäten

1 Der bestimmte Artikel *the*

Im Gegensatz zum Deutschen gibt es im Englischen nur eine Form für den bestimmten Artikel:

der, die, das = *the*

Auch die einzelnen Fälle des bestimmten Artikels im Singular und im Plural (z. B. des, dem, den, die) heißen im Englischen immer *the: the car* (des Autos, dem Auto).

Aussprache: Vor Konsonanten   [ðə] *the newspapers, the travellers …*

→ **G** Grammatik 9

2 Positive (bejahende) und negative (verneinende) Aussagesätze

Im Englischen wie im Deutschen ist die Wortstellung in Aussagesätze Subjekt + Verb. Das Subjekt nennt die Person, die Sache, das Thema, über die bzw. das etwas im Satz gesagt wird. Das Verb bezeichnet, was geschieht oder was ist:

Subjekt   Verb
I   am   German.

In positiven Aussagesätzen gleicht die Wortstellung der des Deutschen:

I am German.
This is row 10.
My company is in London.

Negative Aussagesätze werden gebildet, indem man *not* hinter das Verb stellt:

No, I am not (American).

→ **G** Grammatik 44, → **G** Grammatik 47

3 Ja/Nein-Fragen mit dem Verb *be*

Wie im Deutschen steht das Verb vor dem Subjekt:
>   *Is this row 10, seat G?*

→ 🅖 Grammatik 55

4 Kurzantworten

Auf Ja/Nein-Fragen erwartet man im Englischen eine Kurzantwort:
>   *Are you from America? – No, I am not.*
>   *Is this row 10, seat G? – Yes, it is. / No, it is not.*

Eine Antwort nur mit *Yes* oder *No* wird als unhöflich erachtet.

→ 🅖 Grammatik 56

5 Pronomen

Das Pronomen *it* steht im Englischen für ‚es‘, ‚er‘ oder ‚sie‘ (Subjektform).

→ 🅖 Grammatik 1

6 Kurzform und Langform

In der gesprochenen Sprache und in persönlichen Briefen wird die Kurzform, in der formellen Schriftsprache die Langform benutzt. Im *Lextra Sprachkurs Premium Englisch* wird bei den Audio-Aufnahmen immer die Kurzform gesprochen, in den Büchern aber die Langform verwendet. Wir meinen, dass dieses Verfahren Ihnen die normale Aussprache vermittelt, aber gleichzeitig die Formen des Sprachsystems besser zeigt.

Sie hören:	*No, I'm not. I'm Canadian. I'm from Toronto.*
Lesen aber:	*No, I am not. I am Canadian. I am from Toronto.*
Sie hören:	*But it's true.*
Lesen aber:	*But it is true.*

Die Langformen werden dann verwendet, wenn man die Verneinung besonders betonen will oder wenn der Satz mit einem Hilfsverb endet:
>   *Is this row 10, seat G? – Yes, it is.*

 7 Nationalitätsbezeichnungen
004

Die folgende Liste enthält die Namen der Länder und der jeweiligen Bezeichnungen der Nationalität, die Sie wahrscheinlich am häufigsten brauchen werden.

Land	Nationalität	Land	Nationalität
Austria	Austrian	Germany	German
Belgium	Belgian	Greece	Greek
Britain	British	Ireland	Irish
Great Britain	British	Italy	Italian
England	English	Luxembourg	Luxembourger

Land	Nationalität	Land	Nationalität
Northern Ireland	Irish/British	Portugal	Portuguese
Scotland	Scottish	Spain	Spanish
Wales	Welsh	Switzerland	Swiss
Canada	Canadian	the Netherlands	Dutch
Denmark	Danish	the USA/America	American
France	French		

Anders als im Deutschen werden Nationalitätsbezeichnungen großgeschrieben: *I am German.*

8a   Der unbestimmte Artikel *a*

Der unbestimmte Artikel bezeichnet eine nicht näher bekannte Person oder Sache: *a company.*

→ **G** Grammatik 10

8b   Der unbestimmte Artikel bei Berufsbezeichnungen

Bei Berufsbezeichnungen verwendet man im Englischen immer den unbestimmten Artikel:
  *I am **a** trainee.*

9   What about …?

  What about your English course? – Was ist mit deinem/Ihrem Englischkurs?

ÜBUNGEN

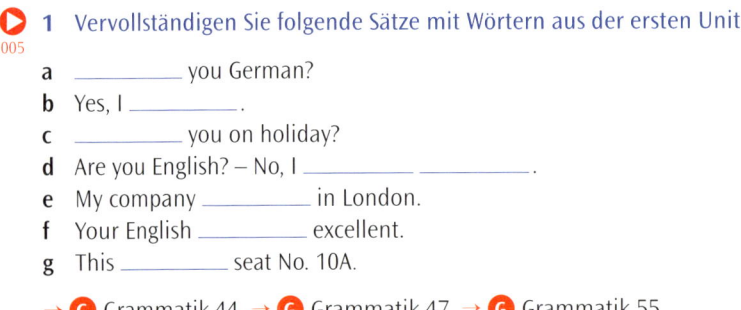

1 Vervollständigen Sie folgende Sätze mit Wörtern aus der ersten Unit.

005

a _____ you German?

b Yes, I _____ .

c _____ you on holiday?

d Are you English? – No, I _____ _____ .

e My company _____ in London.

f Your English _____ excellent.

g This _____ seat No. 10A.

→ **G** Grammatik 44, → **G** Grammatik 47, → **G** Grammatik 55

2 Verbinden Sie die deutschen Sprechabsichten mit einem passenden englischen Ausdruck.

a	Jemanden ansprechen		**1**	Yes, it is.
b	Sagen, woher man kommt		**2**	I see.
c	Etwas bestätigen		**3**	That's very kind of you to say so.
d	Sich bedanken		**4**	I am from Frankfurt.
e	Auf ein Kompliment reagieren		**5**	Excuse me.
f	Fragen, woher jemand kommt		**6**	Are you from America?
g	Sagen, dass Sie etwas verstehen		**7**	Thanks.

▶ 006

3 Wortstellung im Satz. Bringen Sie die Wörter in die richtige Reihenfolge.

a this Row 10 is _____?
b I German am _____.
c you here on holiday are _____?
d kind very you of is that _____.
e improve to English my am here I _____.

→ **G** Grammatik 44, → **G** Grammatik 55

4 Wie viele Wörter aus der ersten Unit können Sie in dieser ‚Buchstabensuppe' wiederfinden?

T	U	A	M	E	X	Y	N
H	W	I	G	Y	O	U	S
R	S	C	E	E	Q	M	T
T	H	A	N	K	S	X	W
K	H	O	L	I	D	A	Y
G	J	N	H	E	R	A	K
V	E	R	Y	Z	A	R	E

In dieser Unit haben Sie gelernt, wie Sie …

jemanden ansprechen. . . . . Excuse me.
sagen, woher man kommt. . . . . I am from Frankfurt.
sagen, dass Sie etwas verstehen. . . . . I see.
etwas bestätigen. . . . . Yes, it is.
sich bedanken. . . . . Thanks.
auf ein Kompliment reagieren. . . . . That's very kind of you to say so.
fragen, woher jemand kommt. . . . . Are you from America?

2

During the flight

- Lautzeichen
- Wortstellungen
- Artikel
- Personalpronomen (*you*)
- Possessivbegleiter (*my, your*)
- Plural-*s*

1 Das Alphabet

009

Das englische Alphabet, nach Lautgruppen geordnet:

[eɪ]	[iː]	[e]	[aɪ]	[juː]	[əʊ]	[ɑː]
A	B	F	I	Q	O	R
H	C	L	Y	U		
J	D	M		W		
K	E	N				
	G	S				
	P	X				
	T	Z				
	V					

2 Wortstellung in Sätzen mit modalen Hilfsverben

Die Wortstellung ist im Fragesatz wie im Deutschen. Im Aussagesatz steht das Hauptverb hinter dem modalen Hilfsverb.

> ***Can** I help you?*
> *I **can read** my book.*

Die englischen modalen Hilfsverben haben nur eine Form.

> *I/You/We etc. can …*

→ **G** Grammatik 26–28

3 Der unbestimmte Artikel

Vor einem Wort, das mit einem gesprochenen Konsonant beginnt:

a $\begin{cases} newspaper \\ magazine \end{cases}$

Vor einem Wort, das mit einem gesprochenen Vokal beginnt:

an $\begin{cases} English\ magazine \\ American\ newspaper \end{cases}$

> **Merke:**
> Nicht die Schreibweise, sondern die Aussprache des Anfangslautes entscheidet darüber,
> ob *a* oder *an* verwendet wird.

→ **G** Grammatik 10

4 Das Personalpronomen *you*

Im Englischen unterscheidet man nicht zwischen ‚du', ‚Sie' und ‚ihr'; das Personalpronomen *you* (Subjektform) steht für alle drei Formen.

→ **G** Grammatik 1

5 Die Possessivbegleiter *my* und *your*

Possessivbegleiter (auch als adjektivische Possessivpronomen bekannt) stehen immer vor einem Nomen (sie werden von einem Nomen ‚begleitet'). Der Gebrauch von Possessivbegleitern entspricht weitgehend dem im Deutschen. Die Formen *my* und *your* verändern sich nicht und entsprechen im Deutschen den Formen ‚mein/e' bzw. ‚dein/e'; ‚Ihr/e'; ‚euer/eure'.

→ **G** Grammatik 2

6 Substantiv: Bildung des Plurals mit *-s*

Der Plural des Substantivs wird durch das Anhängen von **-s** gebildet:
*The newspaper**s** are only for business class traveller**s**.*

→ **U** Unit 15.1, → **G** Grammatik 11

ÜBUNGEN

1 Ergänzen Sie die Äußerungen in der linken Spalte mit einer passenden Äußerung in der rechten Spalte.

a	Excuse me.		1	Yes, it is.
b	Is this your ticket?		2	Yes, I am.
c	Can I have a drink?		3	Yes, certainly.
d	Would you like a newspaper?		4	Yes, a 'Times', please.
e	Are you Ms Sue Johnson?		5	Yes?

▶ 2 Schreiben Sie den folgenden Dialog den Anweisungen entsprechend auf Englisch.

010

a Fragen Sie, ob Sie jemandem behilflich sein können.

_____?

b Bedanken Sie sich und bitten Sie um eine Zeitung.

_____?

c Bitten Sie Frau Johnson nach vorne (ins Flugzeug) zu kommen.

_____?

d Fragen Sie, ob dies Frau Johnsons Buch ist.

_____?

e Bejahen Sie die Frage und bedanken Sie sich.

_____.

▶ 3 Wortstellung im Satz. Bringen Sie die Wörter in die richtige Reihenfolge.

011

a am, Sue Johnson, morning, I, good

_____.

b Ms, name, your, is, Johnson

_____?

c this, your, seat, is

_____?

d sorry, business, seat, is, for, class, travellers, this

_____.

e like, would, this, you, book

_____?

→ **G** Grammatik 44, → **G** Grammatik 55

4 Wie viele Wörter aus der zweiten Unit können Sie in dieser ‚Buchstabensuppe' wiederfinden?

T	N	O	R	F	W
R	A	P	U	N	O
A	C	T	O	I	U
V	E	R	Y	M	L
E	T	A	E	S	D
L	H	A	V	E	N
L	I	K	E	R	S
E	S	A	E	L	P
R	E	H	T	O	B

5 Welches Wort gehört hierhin?

a _____ I help you?

    Are   Is   Can   Would

b Excuse me, _____ your name Mr Brown?

    are   is   can   am

c We _____ looking for a seat.

    are   is   can   am

d _____ you like an American magazine?

    Are   Is   Can   Would

→ **G** Grammatik 44, → **G** Grammatik 55

6 *a* oder *an*?

a He is _____ English trainee.
b It is _____ Canadian newspaper.
c Are you in _____ American company?
d Alitalia is _____ Italian company.
e Is the Fokker _____ German or _____ Dutch plane?
f Is Hoffmann _____ English or _____ German name?

→ **G** Grammatik 10

In dieser Unit haben Sie gelernt, wie Sie …

jemanden begrüßen.	Good morning.
jemandem Hilfe anbieten.	Can I help you?
sich jemandem vorstellen.	Hello. My name is Peter Hoffmann.
über Besitz reden.	Is this your ticket?
sich höflich bedanken.	Thank you very much.
ein Angebot ablehnen.	No, thank you.
sich entschuldigen.	I'm sorry.
etwas anbieten.	Would you like a …?
Überraschung ausdrücken.	Oh, really?

3

Arrival

- Begrüßung I
- 's-Genitiv I
- this – that; these – those
- Pronomen (*one*)
- there is; there are

🇬🇧 Begrüßung I

How do you do? gilt als höfliche, formelle Begrüßungsformel zwischen unbekannten Personen. Die Erwiderung lautet ebenfalls *How do you do?* Dies ist eine der seltenen Situationen, in der ein Engländer jemandem die Hand gibt, was ansonsten in England bei der Begrüßung nicht üblich ist.

Nice to meet you gilt als neutrale Begrüßungsformel, die in allen Situationen verwendet werden kann.

Ansprechen mit dem Vornamen

Heutzutage spricht man in Großbritannien und Amerika Personen, mit denen man beruflich oder persönlich zu tun hat, fast immer mit dem Vornamen an. Dies bedeutet aber nicht, dass diese Form der Anrede mit dem deutschen ‚du' gleichzusetzen ist.

1 Der besitzanzeigende 's-Genitiv I

Den s-Genitiv bildet man, indem man 's an das Substantiv hängt:
> I am the personnel director**'s** assistant.

→ **G** Grammatik 15

▶ 2 this – that; these – those
014

This (dieses hier) bezieht sich auf Personen oder Sachen in der Nähe des Sprechers.
That (dieses dort) weist auf Personen oder Sachen in größerer Entfernung vom Sprecher hin.

These ist der Plural von *this*; *those* ist der Plural von *that*:
> this suitcase – these suitcases   that suitcase – those suitcases

→ **G** Grammatik 3

3 Das Pronomen *one*

Um zu vermeiden, dass Substantive wiederholt werden, verwendet man die Ersatzform *one*:

> *These are my suitcases; this one and that one.*

→ **G** Grammatik 8

4 *there is* und *there are*

There is und *there are* entsprechen dem Deutschen ‚Es ist/sind …‘ oder ‚Es gibt …‘ und drücken allgemein aus, dass etwas vorhanden ist.

There is bezieht sich auf einen Gegenstand oder eine Person.
There are bezieht sich auf mehrere Gegenstände oder mehrere Personen.

In Fragesätzen steht *is*/*are* vor *there*:

> *Is there a trolley around?*

ÜBUNGEN

1 Ergänzen Sie den nachfolgenden Dialog.

015

a   Are you Mr Hoffmann?
b   No, _____ .
c   Oh, I am sorry.
d   _____ .
e   Excuse me, are you Mr Hoffmann?
f   Yes, _____ .
g   My name is John Bull.
h   _____ ?
i   How do you do?

→ **G** Grammatik 55, → **G** Grammatik 56

2 Wortstellung im Satz. Bringen Sie die Wörter in die richtige Reihenfolge.

a   me, you, excuse, are, Mr Hoffmann

_____ ?

b   meet, nice, you, to

_____ .

c   do, you, how, do

_____ ?

d   lots, there, over, are, there

_____ .

e   Sue, me, please, call

_____ .

f   you, help, luggage, your, I, can, with

_____ ?

3   Kreuzen Sie die jeweils richtige Reaktion an.

a	**Oh, sorry.**	**b**	**Please call me Peter.**	**c**	**Excuse me.**
1	That is all right.	**1**	Yes, thanks.	**1**	Sorry. I am English.
2	That is that.	**2**	Fine.	**2**	No, thank you.
3	No, I am not.	**3**	Great.	**3**	That's all right.
4	Oh, really?	**4**	Yes?	**4**	I am from Canada.

016

4   Ja/Nein-Fragen: Vervollständigen Sie die Fragen und Kurzantworten.

a   _____ from Germany?   – Yes, I _____ .
b   _____ your name Peter Baker?   – Yes, it _____ .
c   _____ they here on holiday?   – No, they _____ here on business.
d   _____ there a trolley around? – No, there _____ _____ .
e   _____ my books over there?   – No, your books _____ here.

→ **G** Grammatik 55, → **G** Grammatik 56, → **U** Unit 1.4

017

5   Ergänzen Sie die Äußerungen in der linken Spalte mit einer passenden Äußerung aus der rechten Spalte.

a	Excuse me.	**1**	No, I am all right, thank you.
b	Is this your book?	**2**	Yes, there are two over there.
c	Are you from Canada?	**3**	No, thank you. I would like a newspaper.
d	Would you like a magazine?	**4**	Yes?
e	Can I help you?	**5**	No, I am not.
f	Is there a trolley around?	**6**	No, that is my book there.

In dieser Unit haben Sie gelernt, wie Sie …

jemanden ansprechen. . . . . Excuse me, are you …?
jemanden formell begrüßen. . . . . How do you do?
sagen, dass Sie sich freuen, jemanden kennenzulernen. . . . . Nice to meet you.
jemanden auffordern, Sie mit Vornamen anzusprechen. . . . . Please call me Jack.
jemandem Hilfe anbieten. . . . . Can I help you?

4

In the car park

- Artikel
- Possessivbegleiter
- Possessivpronomen

- *so*
- *have got*
- Fragen mit Fragewort + *to be*

▶ 1 Der unbestimmte Artikel nach *what*
020

Der unbestimmte Artikel steht nach *what* nur vor zählbaren Begriffen in Ausrufen.

> What *a* fantastic car!

→ **G** Grammatik 10

2 Possessivbegleiter

Die Verwendung von Possessivbegleitern entspricht weitgehend der im Deutschen. Die Formen bleiben stets unverändert und entsprechen im Deutschen: mein/e; dein/e; Ihr/e, sein/e; ihr/e; unser/e; euer/eure; ihr/e.

> my
> your
> his, her, its } brother / sister / parents
> our
> their

Im Englischen unterscheidet man nicht zwischen ‚dein/e‘, ‚Ihr/e‘, ‚euer/eure‘ oder ‚ihr/e‘; der Possessivbegleiter *your* steht für alle Formen.

→ **G** Grammatik 2

3 Possessivpronomen

Die Possessivpronomen stehen im Gegensatz zu den Possessivbegleitern immer allein, d. h. ohne Substantiv. Sie lauten:

> *mine – yours – his / hers – ours – theirs*

Possessivpronomen werden verwendet, um Zugehörigkeit auszudrücken:

> *Is this book **mine** or **yours**? = **my** book or **your** book*
> *Neither (weder noch). It's **hers**. = **her** book*

Man kann diese Pronomen auch wie folgt verwenden:

> *They are friends **of mine**. = **my** friends*
> *They are friends **of his**. = **his** friends*

→ **G** Grammatik 2

4 *so*

So verwendet man nach einigen Verben, um die Wiederholung eines Satzteils zu vermeiden:

> *Your English is very good, Peter.*
> *That is very kind of you to say **so**.*

5 *have got*

Man kann entweder *have* oder *have got* verwenden, um Besitz auszudrücken. Im gesprochenen Englisch ist jedoch *have got* gebräuchlicher:

> *I **have (got)** a friend in Frankfurt.*

6 Fragen mit Fragewort + *be*

Die Form des Verbs *be* steht zwischen Fragewort und Subjekt:

> *Where **are** you from in Germany, Peter?*

→ **G** Grammatik 52

ÜBUNGEN

1 Beschriften Sie die Gegenstände mit den folgenden Wörtern.

newspaper • hand luggage • magazine • trolley • car

a _____ b _____ c _____ d _____ e _____

2 Setzen Sie die fehlenden Wörter ein.

021

there • British • friend • German • programme • sister • car • Frankfurt • name

a Is that your _____?
b No, my car is over _____ .
c Here is the _____ for your first day.
d Thank you. Are you _____?
e Yes, I am. And you are _____?
f That is right. I come from _____ .
g Oh, I have a _____ in Frankfurt. His _____ is Peter Reilly.
h Really? I know his _____, Susanne Reilly.

3 Wortstellung im Satz. Bringen Sie die Wörter in die richtige Reihenfolge.

022

a great, a, what, car

_____ !

b very, you, say, that, so, is, to, kind, of

_____ .

c for, letter, there, a, you, is

_____ .

d is, problem, a, there

_____ .

e director, meet, first, the, we

_____ .

→ **G** Grammatik 44

4 Was passt nicht? (Mehrere Antworten sind möglich!)

a	My car is …	**c**	Here is the … for your first day at Winthrops.
1	over there	**1**	newspaper
2	over here	**2**	plan
3	not there	**3**	programme
4	over that	**4**	ticket
b	What a … car!	**d**	It is very kind of you to say …
1	fantastic	**1**	me
2	fine	**2**	so
3	great	**3**	this
4	sure	**4**	that

5 Hören Sie sich den Dialog an. Sind die folgenden Aussagen richtig (*True*) oder falsch (*False*)?

023

a Gerd is from Berlin.
b Gerd's family lives in Frankfurt.
c Gerd's sister lives in Berlin.
d Gerd would like to live in Charlottenburg.
e Gerd lives with a friend in Zehlendorf.

		True	False
a	Gerd is from Berlin.		
b	Gerd's family lives in Frankfurt.		
c	Gerd's sister lives in Berlin.		
d	Gerd would like to live in Charlottenburg.		
e	Gerd lives with a friend in Zehlendorf.		

6 Welches Wort gehört hierhin?

024

a They are friends of _____ .
   my   mine   you   your

b First, you meet the human resources director. _____ name is Mrs Brown.
   His   My   Her   She

c Her name is Martina Glass. _____ has one sister and one brother.
   Her   She   He   His

d Yes, their father is my _____ best friend.
   father   fathers   father's   fathers'

→ **G** Grammatik 1, → **G** Grammatik 2

In dieser Unit haben Sie gelernt, wie Sie …

sich bei jemanden bedanken dafür, ...	I am grateful that you
dass (er Sie abholt).	(are here to pick me up).
etwas bewundern.	What a fantastic car!
Interesse bekunden, um ein Gespräch.	That is interesting.
in Gang zu halten.	
Überraschung ausdrücken.	What a coincidence!

5

At Winthrops' headquarters

- Begrüßung II
- Wortstellung in Nebensätzen
- Verben mit *-ing*-Form
- Zahlen 1–10

- 's-Genitiv II
- Toilette
- *no* = kein
- *Would you …? / Could you …?*

Begrüßung II

Hi gilt als informelle Begrüßung unter Freunden oder guten Bekannten.
Hello ist dagegen völlig neutral.
Pleased to meet you ist eine eher distanzierte Begrüßungsformel. (Vgl. *Nice to meet you.*)

→ **U** Unit 3

1 Wortstellung in Nebensätzen

Die Wortstellung in englischen Nebensätzen ist die gleiche wie in Hauptsätzen:
> *Can I tell Mr X that **you are here**?*
> ***You are here** to meet Mr X, I assume.*

2 Verben mit *-ing*-Form

Auf bestimmte Verben wie *mind* folgt eine *-ing*-Form (Gerundium):
> *Would you **mind** waiti**ng** a moment?*

→ **G** Grammatik 42, → **U** Unit 9.6, → **U** Unit 36.1

▶ 3 Die Zahlen 1–10
027

	Kardinalzahlen	Ordinalzahlen		Kardinalzahlen	Ordinalzahlen
1	one	(the) **first**	6	six	(the) six**th**
2	two	(the) **second**	7	seven	(the) seven**th**
3	three	(the) **third**	8	eight	(the) eigh**th**
4	four	(the) four**th**	9	nine	(the) **ninth**
5	five	(the) **fifth**	10	ten	(the) ten**th**

4 's-Genitiv II

Endet ein Substantiv auf -s, wird nur ein Apostroph angehängt (s'):
> Winthrop**s'** headquarters

Dies gilt auch, wenn der Plural eines Substantivs auf -s endet:
> The passenger**s'** newspapers

→ **G** Grammatik 15, → **U** Unit 3.1

 Toilette

In den USA gilt es als unschön, das Wort *toilet* zu verwenden. Dort sind die Ausdrücke *bathroom* oder *restroom* üblich.
In Großbritannien fragt man normalerweise nach *the Ladies, the Gents* oder *the loo*.

5 *no* = kein

> It's no problem.

6 *Would you …? / Could you …?*

> … verwendet man, um eine (höfliche) Bitte auszusprechen.

ÜBUNGEN

1 Ergänzen Sie den nachfolgenden Dialog.
028

a Good afternoon.
b _____ .
c Can I help you?
d _____ .
e How do you do, Mr Bond? Pleased to meet you.
f _____ .
g Can I tell Ms Johnson you are here?
h _____ .
i Oh, the line is engaged. Would you mind waiting a moment?
j _____ .
k Ah, she can see you now. Please go over there to the lift.
l _____ .

2 Verbinden Sie die Sprechabsichten auf Deutsch mit einem passenden englischen Ausdruck.

a	Jemanden um einen Moment Geduld bitten	1	Would you like a drink?
b	Sagen Sie, dass er gerade telefoniert	2	Yes, please do.
c	Jemandem ein Getränk anbieten	3	He is on the phone at the moment.
d	Auf eine Anfrage positiv reagieren	4	Would you mind waiting a moment, please?

3 Schreiben Sie den folgenden Dialog den Anweisungen entsprechend auf Englisch.

029

a Stellen Sie bitte Herrn Peter Hoffmann vor.

_____ .

b Sagen Sie, woher er kommt.

_____ .

c Sagen Sie der Rezeptionistin, dass Herr Hoffmann mit Herrn Baker verabredet ist.

_____ .

d Bitten Sie den Gast, sich einen Moment lang zu gedulden.

_____ ?

e Antworten Sie, dass es Ihnen nichts ausmacht zu warten.

_____ .

f Bieten Sie dem Gast einen Tee/Kaffee an.

_____ ?

g Lehnen Sie ab.

_____ .

h Sagen Sie dem Gast, dass Herr Baker nun bereit ist, ihn zu sehen.

_____ .

4 Wortstellung im Satz. Bringen Sie die Wörter in die richtige Reihenfolge.

030

a tell, are, can, you, I, Peter, here

_____ ?

b mind, moment, would, a, you, waiting

_____ ?

c all, is, problem, it, at, no

_____ .

d me, where, could, toilets, you, the, tell, are

_____ ?

e engaged, line, is, the

_____ .

→ **G** Grammatik 44, → **G** Grammatik 55

5 Bitte ankreuzen, was Sie *nicht* antworten können.

a	Would you like a drink?
1	Yes, please.
2	No, thank you.
3	That would be nice.
4	That is fine.

b	Where are the toilets?
1	Over there.
2	Oh, really?
3	Over here.
4	On the right.

c	Is Mr Jackson here?
1	No, he isn't.
2	Yes, he is.
3	He is over there.
4	Yes, please.

d	Thanks for the lift.
1	That's all right.
2	OK.
3	It's a pleasure.
4	No, fine.

6 Richtig *(True)* oder falsch *(False)*?
031

		True	False
a	Es ist vormittags.		
b	Der Besucher möchte Herrn Carlsson treffen.		
c	Der Besucher heißt Smith.		
d	Herr Carlsson kann heute keinen Besuch empfangen.		
e	Der Besucher möchte nicht warten.		
f	Der Besucher möchte gern Tee trinken.		

In dieser Unit haben Sie gelernt, wie Sie …

jemanden vorstellen und sagen, ... This is Peter Hoffmann from Germany.
    woher er/sie kommt.
etwas anbieten. . . . . Would you like (a drink)?
einen Vorschlag unterbreiten. . . . . Let's …
sagen, dass Sie erfreut sind, ... Pleased to meet you.
    jemanden kennenzulernen.
sagen, dass die Leitung besetzt ist. . . . . The line is engaged/busy.
jemanden bitten, sich zu gedulden. . . . . Would you mind waiting a moment?
sagen, dass jemand gerade telefoniert. . . . . He/She is on the phone at the moment.
sagen, dass es Ihnen nichts ausmacht. . . . . It is no problem at all.
ein Gespräch kurzerhand und . . . . Excuse me.
    ohne Erklärung beenden.

Introductions

- Imperativ
- Betonung mit *do*
- *present perfect*
- *all the*

1 Der Imperativ

Der positive Imperativ entspricht dem Infinitiv des Verbs:

> **Come in.**
> **Have** a seat.

Ein Imperativ wird mit einer Form des Hilfsverbs *do* verneint:

> Please **don't** hesitate to call me.

→ **G** Grammatik 45

2 Betonung mit *do*

Um etwas zu betonen oder Nachdruck zu verleihen, verwendet man *do* vor dem Hauptverb:

> **Do** come in.

3 *present perfect* (Perfekt)

Bei regelmäßigen Verben wird das *present perfect* aus *have* + *-ed*-Form des Vollverbs gebildet.

> We **have** look**ed** at almost all the offices.
> As soon as we **have** finish**ed** here.

Bei unregelmäßigen Verben wird das *present perfect* aus *have* + entsprechende Form des Partizips (vgl. die Liste der unregelmäßigen Verben im Lesebuch) gebildet.

> I am sure I **have seen** him before.

Verneinung   I **have** not **had** any problems so far.

Frage   **Has** Jack **shown** you around yet?
        Have you **been** to Manchester before?
        (Sind Sie schon einmal [im Leben] in Manchester gewesen?)

Das *present perfect* wird für Handlungen verwendet, die zu einem Zeitpunkt in der Vergangenheit begonnen haben und bis in die Gegenwart andauern:

> This is the first time I **have been** to the North of England.

→ **G** Grammatik 33

Das *present perfect* kommt besonders häufig in Fragen vor, die sich auf einen Zeitraum von der Vergangenheit bis hin zur Gegenwart beziehen. Die Adverbien **already**, **before**, **ever**, **just**, **never**, **since** und **yet** werden häufig mit dem *present perfect* verwendet.

→ **G** Grammatik 21

4 *all the*

all the offices – alle Büroräume; *all the family* – die ganze Familie

→ **G** Grammatik 7

ÜBUNGEN

▶ **1** Wortstellung im Satz. Bringen Sie die Wörter in die richtige Reihenfolge

034

a there, here, lift, building, is, a, in, the

_____ ?

b matter, what, the, is

_____ ?

c enjoy, here, hope, stay, your, I, you

_____ .

d been, London, to, have, you, before

_____ ?

e need, you, if, please, me, help, call

_____ .

→ **G** Grammatik 36, → **G** Grammatik 41

2 Verbinden Sie die Sprechabsichten auf Deutsch mit einem passenden englischen Ausdruck.

a	Jemanden fragen, was los ist		**1**	That is very kind of you.
b	Überraschung ausdrücken		**2**	Have a seat.
c	Jemandem einen Stuhl anbieten		**3**	Really?
d	Eine Aussage bestätigen		**4**	Call me if you need my help.
e	Jemandem seine Hilfe anbieten		**5**	What is the matter?
f	Sich für ein Angebot bedanken		**6**	Yes, you are right.

3 Bitte kreuzen Sie an, was Sie *nicht* antworten können.

a **What is the matter?**

1 Nothing.

2 I have lost my ticket.

3 I am surprised.

4 The lift is not working.

b **Have you been to Liverpool before?**

1 Yes, I have.

2 No, I have not.

3 Yes, for the first time.

4 Yes, in 1996.

c **Has John shown you around yet?**

1 No, he hasn't.

2 No, he is not.

3 Yes, he has.

4 Yes, thanks.

d **Call me if you need my help.**

1 Thank you.

2 Thanks.

3 That is very kind of you.

4 Thanks. That is right.

e **Have a seat.**

1 Thank you.

2 Yes, please.

3 No, thank you.

4 No, thanks, not now.

4 Schreiben Sie den folgenden Dialog den Anweisungen entsprechend auf Englisch.

035

a Fragen Sie, was mit Ihrem Freund los ist.

_____?

b Beteuern Sie, dass es eigentlich nichts ist.

_____.

c Bieten Sie Ihrem Freund an, Sie anzurufen, falls er Ihre Hilfe braucht.

_____.

d Bedanken Sie sich für dieses Hilfsangebot.

_____.

e Verabschieden Sie sich.

_____.

5 Ergänzen Sie den nachfolgenden Dialog.

036

a Good morning Mr Smith. My name is Robert Lowe.

_____.

b And this is my colleague Jack Russell.

_____.

c Nice to meet you, too.

_____?

d Yes, we have been to Manchester before.

_____?

e No, not on business. We are here to see Manchester United play.

_____?

f Yes, I would like a drink, please.

6 Vervollständigen Sie die Fragen.

a Have you _____ to London before?
b _____ Jack shown you around yet?
c What is the _____? You look surprised.
d Is _____ a telephone here at the production site?
e I have been to Glasgow, but _____ it really got a lot of industry?

7 Setzen Sie die richtige Form des _present perfect_ in die Lücken ein.

a _____ you _____ to Glasgow before? (be)
b Jack _____ me the production line. (show)
c Where _____ the Canadian _____? (go) To the toilet?
d Peter _____ his ticket. (lose)
e We _____ Mr Hoffmann _____ from the airport. (pick up)
f They (not) _____ Mr Jackson in his office this morning. (see)

→ **G** Grammatik 33, → **U** Unit 6.3

In dieser Unit haben Sie gelernt, wie Sie …

jemanden fragen, was los ist.	What is the matter?
Überraschung ausdrücken.	Really? I am surprised.
jemanden auffordern, sich hinzusetzen.	Have a seat.
eine Aussage bestätigen.	Yes, you are right.
sich für ein Angebot bedanken.	That is very kind of you.
jemanden fragen, ob er eine Stadt	Have you been to (Manchester) before?
bereits besucht hat.	
jemandem einen schönen Aufenthalt	I hope you enjoy your stay here.
vor Ort wünschen.	

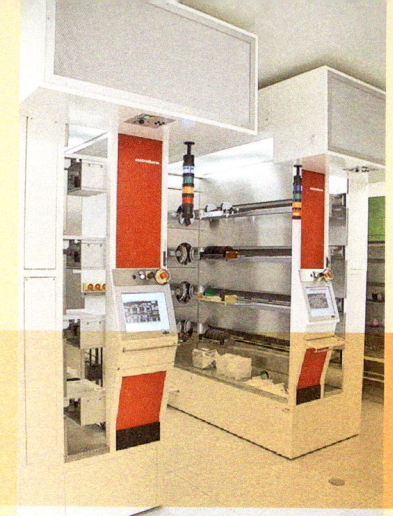

A tour around the factory

- *going to-future*
- Steigerung von Adjektiven I
- Fragen mit *do*

- *simple present*
- Längenmaße
- *What size…?*

1 *going to-future*

Im Englischen kann man auf verschiedene Art und Weise über zukünftige Ereignisse sprechen.
Going to wird häufig verwendet, um über Absichten und Pläne zu sprechen.

> We **are going to sell** the idea to American investors.

Wenn das Verb des Satzes **go** ist, kann man beim *going to-future* auf dieses *go* verzichten.

> We **are going (to go)** down to the production line now.

2 Die Steigerung von Adjektiven I

Bei der Steigerung von Adjektiven wird an kurze Adjektive **-er** angehängt:

> tall   –   tall**er**

Ein Konsonant nach kurzen, unbetonten Vokalen wird beim Schreiben verdoppelt:

> big   –   bi**gg**er

Ein stummes **e** entfällt: *fin**e**   –   finer*

Ausnahmen: good   –   better   –   best
                  bad   –   worse   –   worst
                  a lot   –   more   –   most

→ **G** Grammatik 16

3 Fragen im *simple present* (einfaches Präsens) mit *do*

Fragen, die ein Vollverb enthalten, bildet man mit dem Hilfsverb *do*:

> **Do** you **see** those metal rods?

→ **G** Grammatik 53

Auf solche sogenannte Ja/Nein-Fragen sind im Englischen Kurzantworten üblich:

> Yes, I/you/we/they **do**.
> No, I/you/we/they **do not**.

→ **G** Grammatik 56

4 simple present (einfaches Präsens)

Mit Ausnahme der 3. Person Singular lauten alle Verformen im *simple present* wie der Infinitiv:

I	**remember** his name.
You	**come** from Canada.
We	**go** to London.
You two	**live** in Manchester.
They	**know** my parents.

In der 3. Person Singular wird ein **-s** an den Infinitiv angehängt:

	Aussprache des -s-Lautes
*The computer oper**ates** the machine.*	Wenn der Laut auf einen stimmlos gesprochenen Konsonanten [p, t, k, f] folgt, ist der Laut auch stimmlos [s].
*He li**ves** in Manchester.* *He kno**ws** my sister.*	Der Laut ist stimmhaft [z], wenn er auf die stimmhaft gesprochenen Konsonanten [b, d, g, l, m, n, v] oder auf einen Vokal folgt.
*The machine produ**ces** rivets.*	Wenn -es auf einen Zischlaut [s, ʃ, tʃ, dʒ, z] folgt, wird es [ɪz] ausgesprochen

→ **G** Grammatik 29

5 Längenmaße

1 inch			=	*2,45 cm*
1 foot	=	*12 inches*	=	*0,3048 m*
1 yard	=	*3 feet*	=	*0,9144 m*
1 mile	=	*1760 yards*	=	*1,6093 km*

In Großbritannien ist zwar das metrische System eingeführt, es wird aber nur zögernd von der Bevölkerung angenommen.
Einige adjektivisch gebrauchte Maße müssen im Plural keine Pluralform annehmen:

> *A six foot man.*

6 What size …?

> *What size are you?* = Welche Größe haben Sie / hast du?

ÜBUNGEN

▶ **1** **Bitte beantworten Sie die Fragen. Benutzen Sie dabei die Vorgaben in Klammern.**
039

a What is Peter going to read during the flight?

_____ . (He / a book)

b Where is Peter going to put his luggage?

_____ . (He / under his seat)

c What is Jack going to help Peter with?

_____ . (He / his luggage)

d Where are Jack and Peter going to go now?

_____ . (They / production line)

e Are you going to go to England on holiday?
No, _____ . (we / Ireland)

f Where is Mr Jackson going to go in the morning?

_____ . (He / Liverpool)

→ **G** Grammatik 30

▶ **2** **Schreiben Sie bitte Vergleichssätze. Verwenden Sie dabei die Vorgaben in Klammern.**
040

Beispiel: (Bonn / Berlin / small) Bonn is smaller than Berlin.

a (plane / car / big)

_____

b (your thumb *[Daumen]* / finger / thick)

_____

c (Canada / Germany / big)

_____

d (Peter / Jack / tall)

_____

e (Peter's English / Jack's German / good)

_____

f (single / double room / small)

_____

g (Italian clothes / English clothes / nice)

_____

→ **G** Grammatik 16

3 Setzen Sie die richtige Form des Verbs in die Lücken ein.

to feed • to measure • to operate • to use • to wear

a I _____ a protective helmet on the production line.
b They _____ the lift to go up to Mr Jackson's office.
c I think you _____ about 6'1". Is that right?
d The worker _____ the metal rods into the machine.
e The computer _____ the machine.

→ **G** Grammatik 29

4 Setzen Sie die richtige Form des Verbs in die Lücken ein.

come • have (2x) • help • hope • improve • know • live • look • meet •
pick (up) • put • read • say • see • think

a Jack _____ the morning papers at breakfast.
b Peter _____ the human resources director in his office.
c Suzie _____ where the toilets are.
d I _____ you have a nice stay in London.
e We _____ in Germany.
f We _____ from Germany.
g She _____ her luggage on the trolley.
h Can you _____ my car?
i Jack _____ Peter up from the airport in the company car.
j _____ Mr Jackson been to Glasgow before?
k I can _____ you with your luggage.
l Peter _____ been to Britain before.
m He _____ my English is excellent.
n Suzie _____ that the line is engaged.
o I want to _____ my English.
p He _____ like the Canadian from the plane.

→ **G** Grammatik 29, → **G** Grammatik 33, → **G** Grammatik 53, → **U** Unit 7.4

5 Bilden Sie Fragen mit *Do* + Vollverb.

041

a _____?
– Yes, I like London very much.
b _____?
– No, I haven't any sisters, but I have got two brothers.
c _____?
– No, they don't operate flights to Liverpool.
d _____?
– No, you don't have to wear a helmet here.
e _____?
– No, we leave for London in an hour, not for Edinburgh.
f _____?
– Yes, I (do) know Peter Berg. He is a friend of my father's.
g _____?
– No, they don't live in Manchester, they live in Chester.

→ **G** Grammatik 40, → **G** Grammatik 45

6 Schreiben Sie die folgenden Sätze den Anweisungen entsprechend auf Englisch.

042

a Sagen Sie, dass sie nun die Fertigungsstraße besuchen werden.

_____.

b Sagen Sie, dass sie Schutzanzüge anziehen müssen, weil es Firmenvorschrift ist.

_____.

c Fragen Sie, wie groß Ihr Bekannter ist.

_____?

d Bieten Sie Ihrem Bekannten einen Schutzanzug an.

_____.

e Sagen Sie, dass Sie nun angekommen sind.

_____.

f Bitten Sie Ihren Bekannten, den Schutzhelm jetzt aufzusetzen.

_____.

7 Beantworten Sie folgende Fragen auf Englisch.

a Where are we going? (production line)

_____.

b How tall are you? (5'6")

_____.

c Do you see that woman over there? (next to, trolley)

_____.

d Who operates the machine? (computer)

_____.

In dieser Unit haben Sie gelernt, wie Sie ...

jemanden nach seiner Größe fragen.	How tall are you?
Erstaunen und Anerkennung ausdrücken.	That is clever.
Dinge vergleichen.	You are taller than Jack.
Zeit gewinnen, um das Wort nicht . . . . abgeben zu müssen.	Let me see ...
Körpergrößen in englischen Maßen ausdrücken.	1,90 m = 6'3"six foot three inches

8

At the estate agent's

- **Begrüßung III**
- *will-future*
- *Bed & breakfast*
- **Straßennamen I**

 Begrüßung III

 Folgende Begrüßungsformeln sind je nach Tageszeit üblich:

Good morning.	=	Guten Morgen.
Good afternoon.	=	Guten Tag. (12.00 bis etwa 17.00 Uhr)
Good evening.	=	Guten Abend.

1 *will-future*

Die Zukunftsform mit *will* drückt oft eine spontane Entscheidung aus:
> *Just give me the number and I'**ll phone**.*

… oder auch ein Versprechen:
> *I **will call** immediately.*

Das *will-future* wird gebildet aus dem Hilfsverb *will* + Infinitiv des Vollverbs:
> *I **will check**.*

Verneinung: *The flat **will not (won't) be ready** until tomorrow.*

→ **G** Grammatik 35

 Bed & breakfast

Übernachtung mit Frühstück, kurz „B&B" genannt, gibt es in Städten, Ferienorten und Dörfern in ganz Großbritannien. Einige B&B sind Privathäuser, traditionelle Landgasthäuser oder Bauernhöfe. Überall werden Sie freundlich aufgenommen, und Sie erhalten Gelegenheit, die Briten in ihren eigenen vier Wänden kennenzulernen.

Pensionen sind hauptsächlich in Städten am Meer und in anderen Touristenzentren zu finden. Sie sind etwas teurer als B&B, haben aber mehr Zimmer und Bäder.

2 Kein Artikel vor Straßennamen I

Straßennamen stehen ohne Artikel: *It is a large house in King Street.*

ÜBUNGEN

1 Bitte ankreuzen, was man *nicht* sagen kann.

a	**How may I help you?**
1	No, thank you.
2	I believe you have a reservation for me.
3	Have you got an apartment for me?
4	Can you give me the number of the hotel, please?

b	**I am afraid there is a small problem.**
1	Oh, dear.
2	Oh, no!
3	Oh, really?
4	Oh, you are not good.

c	**Can we offer you accommodation in a hotel?**
1	Yes, please.
2	Yes, I know it.
3	No, thank you.
4	No, I would like a bed & breakfast place.

d	**I will call and book you in.**
1	That is very kind of you.
2	Thank you.
3	Yes, you do that.
4	No, thank you. I will phone.

▶ 2 Schreiben Sie den folgenden Dialog den Anweisungen entsprechend auf Englisch.

046

a Begrüßen Sie den Makler. (Es ist 10 Uhr.)

_____ .

b Sagen Sie, wie Sie heißen. (Herr Brown)

_____ .

c Sagen Sie, dass Sie eine Reservierung für ein Apartment in Castle Heights haben.

_____ .

d Der Makler sagt, dass es ein Problem gibt.

_____ .

e Sie sind erstaunt.

_____ ?

f Fragen Sie, ob der Makler ein Hotel empfehlen kann.

_____ ?

g Bedanken Sie sich und bitten Sie um die Telefonnummer.

_____ ?

h Sagen Sie, dass Sie anrufen werden.

_____ .

3 Hören Sie sich die Aufnahme an. Ergänzen Sie dann den nachfolgenden Dialog.

047

a Good afternoon.

_____ .

b How may I help you?

_____ .

c Yes, we have a reservation for you, Mr Samson. I'm afraid that there is a small problem.

_____ .

d Well, the single room is not ready, but we can offer you a double room.

_____ .

e A double room is £85, but we can offer it to you for £45.

_____ .

f I will call immediately and book you in.

_____ .

4 Welches Wort passt *nicht* zu den anderen?

a apartment – bed & breakfast – hotel – reservation
b Excuse me. – Good morning. – Good afternoon. – Hello.
c immediately – just a minute – now – two rooms
d big – much – tall – small
e fine – good – nice – unfortunate
f offer – produce – recommend – room

In dieser Unit haben Sie gelernt, wie Sie …

jemandem Hilfe / einen Dienst anbieten.	How may I help you?
Bedauern ausdrücken.	We are very sorry.
jemanden um einen Moment Geduld bitten.	Just a minute.
jemanden um eine Empfehlung bitten.	What can you recommend?
jemandem eine Unterkunft anbieten.	We can offer you accommodation in a hotel.

9

A phone call

- Am Telefon I
- Wochentage / Monatsnamen / Datum
- How much is / are …?

- Zahlen 11–101
- to look forward to … -ing
- Personalpronomen

 ## Am Telefon I

In Großbritannien meldet man sich gewöhnlich am Telefon nicht mit dem Namen, sondern mit *Hello* oder mit der Telefonnummer.

Die Ziffern der Telefonnummer werden, anders als im Deutschen, einzeln angegeben, wobei die ersten drei Ziffern eine Einheit bilden:

496 32578 = *four – nine – six* (pause) *three – two – five – seven – eight*

Doppelziffern werden normalerweise mit *double* angegeben:

496 32577 = *four – nine – six* (pause) *three – two – five – double seven*

▶ **1** Die Wochentage
050

Monday	Montag	*Friday*	Freitag
Tuesday	Dienstag	*Saturday*	Samstag
Wednesday	Mittwoch	*Sunday*	Sonntag
Thursday	Donnerstag		

▶ **2** Die Monatsnamen
051

January	Januar	*July*	Juli
February	Februar	*August*	August
March	März	*September*	September
April	April	*October*	Oktober
May	Mai	*November*	November
June	Juni	*December*	Dezember

3 Das Datum

052

Das Datum wird wie im Deutschen geschrieben, allerdings ohne Punkt:
26 September 1999

An die Tageszahl in der Kurzform wird **th** angehängt:
26th September 1999

Die Tageszahl kann auch nachgestellt werden:
September 26(,) 1999 oder *September 26th(,) 1999*

4 *How much is/are …?*

… heißt ‚Wie viel kostet/kosten …?'
How much is the room?   *How much are the rooms?*

 5 Die Zahlen 11–101

053

Kardinalzahlen				Ordinalzahlen	
11	eleven	21	twenty-one	eleventh	twenty-first
12	twelve	32	thirty-two	twelfth	thirty-second
13	thirteen	43	forty-three	thirteenth	forty-third
14	fourteen	54	fifty-four	fourteenth	fifty-fourth
15	fifteen	65	sixty-five	fifteenth	sixty-fifth
16	sixteen	76	seventy-six	sixteenth	seventy-sixth
17	seventeen	87	eighty-seven	seventeenth	eighty-seventh
18	eighteen	98	ninety-eight	eighteenth	ninety-eighth
19	nineteen	100	one hundred	nineteenth	one hundredth
20	twenty	101	one hundred and one	twentieth	one hundred and first

6 *to look forward to … -ing*

Die Formulierung *We look forward to (meeting) you* wird sehr häufig verwendet, auch in Briefen
(… *hearing from you*). Achten Sie darauf, dass hier die **-ing-Form** verwendet wird und nicht der
Infinitiv.

→ **G** Grammatik 42

7 Liste der Personalpronomen

Subjektform				Objektform			
I	ich	*we*	wir	*me*	mir, mich	*us*	uns
you	du; Sie	*you*	ihr; Sie	*you*	dir, dich; Ihnen, Sie	*you*	euch; Ihnen, Sie
he	er	*they*	sie	*him*	ihm, ihn	*them*	ihnen, sie
she	sie			*her*	ihr, sie		
it	es; er; sie			*it*	ihm, es; ihm, ihn; ihr, sie		

→ **G** Grammatik 1

ÜBUNGEN

1 Verbinden Sie die Sprechabsichten auf Deutsch mit einem passenden englischen Ausdruck.

a	Sich telefonisch nach einer Nummer erkundigen	**1**	Have you any rooms free for tonight?
b	Jemanden am Telefon verlangen	**2**	When will you arrive?
c	Fragen, ob noch Zimmer frei sind	**3**	Is that 496 32571?
d	Fragen, wann jemand ankommt	**4**	How much are the rooms?
e	Fragen, wie viel eine Übernachtung kostet	**5**	Can I speak to Mrs Baker, please?

2 Wählen Sie bitte *there is* oder *there are* für die Lücken in den nachstehenden Fragen und Sätzen.

a _____ four single rooms on the first floor.
b _____ a bath in three of the rooms.
c Yes, _____ a telephone over there.
d Sorry, _____ no bath in the single room, but _____ a bath in the double room.
e _____ a newspaper for Mr Jackson, please?
f _____ morning papers for hotel guests?
g _____ estate agents in Green Street.

→ **G** Grammatik 57, → **U** Unit 3.4

3 Hören Sie sich den Dialog an und vervollständigen Sie dann die Sätze mit den vorgegebenen Pronomen.

054

I • you • he • our • their • my • your (2x) • his • they (2x) • we

a – Good afternoon. _____ would like to book a room for _____ father for the 22nd of April, please.
b – Does _____ father want a single or a double room?
c – _____ girlfriend is with him so I think _____ would like a double room, please.
   – Fine. One double for the 22nd of April.
d – When will _____ arrive?
e – _____ plane lands at 7 p.m. so _____ will be here at about 8.30 p.m.
f – That is fine. Is there a telephone number where I can phone _____ if I need to check anything with you?
g – Yes, _____ office number is 896 53274.
h – And could I have _____ private number, please?
i – Oh, _____ haven't got a phone at home at the moment.

→ **G** Grammatik 1, → **G** Grammatik 2, → **U** Unit 9.7

▶ 055 **4** Ordnen Sie den Ziffern die ausgeschriebenen Zahlen zu.

3	5	50	6	60	99
13	15	8	16	45	100
30		80		87	

forty-five = _____   six = _____   eighty = _____
eight = _____   three = _____   five = _____
ninety-nine = _____   eighty-seven = _____   thirty = _____
sixteen = _____   fifteen = _____   sixty = _____
fifty = _____   thirteen = _____   one hundred = _____

→ **U** Unit 5

5 Ergänzen Sie den nachfolgenden Dialog.

How much • calling • will • any • speaking • have • Just a moment (2x) • speak • bed & breakfast

a Can I _____ to Mrs Bambridge, please?
b Certainly. _____ , please.
c Hello, this is Mrs Bambridge _____. Who is _____?
d Hello. My name is Peter Hoffmann. Do you have _____ rooms free on 30th March.
e _____. Yes, I _____.
f _____ is the single?
g It is £35 for _____.
h Fine. I _____ take that.

▶ 056 **6** Hören Sie sich den Dialog an. Richtig *(True)* oder falsch *(False)*?

		True	False
a	The man's name is London.		
b	He wants a double room for two nights.		
c	The hotel has a reservation for him for a single room.		
d	For the night of 21st September he has to take two single rooms.		
e	He can have a double room on 22nd September.		
f	He will have to pay £194 (2 x £97) on 21st September.		
g	The price of a double room is £135.		

7 Hören Sie sich folgende Datumsangaben an und sprechen Sie nach. Schreiben Sie dann die Datumsangaben in die rechte Spalte.

057

a 03.03.   the third of March
b 12.01.   _____
c 18.10.   _____
d 01.05.   _____
e 31.07.   _____
f 13.02.   _____

8 Wortstellung im Satz. Bringen Sie die Wörter in die richtige Reihenfolge.

a rooms, are, much, please, how, the

_____ ?

b speak, can, to, I, Mrs Thompson

_____ ?

c calling, who, is

_____ ?

d single, want, you, or, do, double, a, room

_____ ?

e would, I, please, prefer, think, room, the, I, double

_____ .

f please, that, can, spell, you

_____ ?

In dieser Unit haben Sie gelernt, wie Sie ...

sich am Telefon verhalten.	Hello.
	Is that 496 32572?
	No, this is 496 32571.
	Oh, sorry. Wrong number.
	Speaking. Who is calling, please?
jemanden am Telefon verlangen.	Can I speak to ..., please?
nach Zimmern in einer Pension /	Have you any rooms free for tonight?
einem Hotel fragen.	
den Preis eines Zimmers erfragen.	How much is a single/double room?
Namen buchstabieren.	Certainly. H–O–FF–M–A–NN.
eine Präferenz / Vorliebe ausdrücken.	I think I would prefer the double room.
ein Datum angeben.	(the) 26th September

10

At the boarding house

- Stellung des Adverbs
- Uhrzeit

- Fragen mit *do, does* und Fragewort + *do, does*
- *could/couldn't*

1 Die Stellung des Adverbs

Adverbien wie *usually, always* usw. stehen vor dem Vollverb:

> I **usually** have breakfast at seven o'clock.
> He **always** goes to work at 7.45.
> I don't **usually** eat breakfast.

→ **G** Grammatik 18

▶ 2 Die Uhrzeit

060

It's …

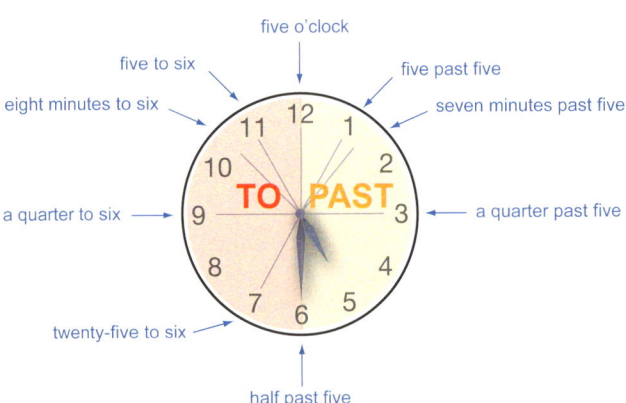

In der Alltagssprache verwendet man kaum die 24-Stunden-Uhrzeit. Sie wird fast ausschließlich für offizielle Zeitangaben (z. B. bei Auskunft über Fahrpläne) verwendet. Will man zwischen Zeitangaben am Vormittag oder am Nachmittag unterscheiden, sagt man *a.m.* für Zeitangaben zwischen Mitternacht und Mittag und *p.m.* für Zeitangaben zwischen Mittag und Mitternacht.

> 08.15 *(a) quarter past eight (in the morning); 8.15 a.m.*
> 20.15 *(a) quarter past eight (in the evening); 8.15 p.m.; twenty fifteen*

Wenn die Minutenangaben nicht durch fünf teilbar ist, fügt man meisten minutes hinzu:
> *It's eight minutes to five.*

3 Ja/Nein-Fragen mit Vollverben

Fragen, die ein Vollverb enthalten, werden im *simple present* mit dem Hilfsverb *do* gebildet;
in der 3. Person Singular folglich mit der Form *does,* wenn nicht nach dem Subjekt gefragt wird:
> *Does she speak English?*

→ **G** Grammatik 49, → **G** Grammatik 50, → **U** Unit 7.3

Wie bei modalen Hilfsverben steht das Vollverb im Infinitiv (hier: *speak*). Das *-s* der 3. Person wird somit nicht an das Hauptverb, sondern quasi an *do* angehängt.

→ **G** Grammatik 53

4 Fragen mit Fragewort und *do, does*

Wie bei Ja/Nein-Fragen verwendet man eine Form des Hilfsverbs *do* zur Bildung von Fragen, die mit einem Fragewort eingeleitet werden und ein Vollverb enthalten. Die Form von *do* steht zwischen Fragewort und Subjekt.

Fragewort	do/does	Subjekt (Person/en, Sache/n)	Verb
When	do	you	eat breakfast?
When	does	he	leave?
How	do	your friends	like Germany?
Where	do	you	live in Switzerland?
What	do	they	produce?
	verändert sich		**verändert sich nicht**

→ **G** Grammatik 53

5 *could/couldn't*

Die englischen modalen Hilfsverben (*can, could, may, might, must, will, would,* etc.) haben keine unterschiedlichen Endungen:
> *Can/Could you tell me where the toilets are?*
> *He can/could help you.*
> *They might help you.*

→ **G** Grammatik 26–28

ÜBUNGEN

1 Welche Wörter verstecken sich hier?

a G O D R B A I N   _____
b F R A B S T E A K   _____
c T O N I C L A N T E N   _____
d Y A L U L U S   _____
e S T E U G   _____

2 Hören Sie die Information über Patricia Jenkins und kreuzen Sie an, was sie morgens macht.
061

		always	usually	often	sometimes
a	starts her day early				
b	gets up at 7 a.m.				
c	reads the morning papers				
d	eats a Continental breakfast				
e	only has coffee				
f	walks to work				
g	takes the bus at 8.30 a.m.				
h	starts work at 9 a.m.				

Schreiben Sie nun ganze Sätze über Patricia Jenkins' Routine.

→ **G** Grammatik 18

3 Vervollständigen Sie die Sätze, indem Sie die vorgegebenen Verben einsetzen.

**to eat • to fly • to get up • to go • to have • to jog • pick up • to play •
to read (2x) • to take (2x) • to walk**

a He usually _____ at 6.45.
b He always _____ breakfast at 7.15.
c He sometimes _____ the bus to the airport at 9.15.
d He often _____ to Manchester.
e Jack _____ Peter _____ in the company car.
f He _____ lunch with Jack and his new colleagues.
g He always _____ through the park to the B & B.
h I usually _____ squash on Saturday morning.
i We sometimes _____ through the park.
j I usually _____ The Times, but sometimes I _____ The Guardian.
k We often _____ to the theatre.
l Do you always _____ the number 7 bus?

→ **G** Grammatik 18, → **G** Grammatik 29

4 Stellen Sie Fragen mit *Do*.

062

a Fragen Sie Herrn Brown, ob er um 7.30 frühstücken möchte.

b Fragen Sie, ob er Tee oder Kaffee zum Frühstück möchte.

c Fragen Sie, ob er ein englisches oder kontinentales Frühstück haben möchte.

d Fragen Sie, ob er Englisch spricht.

e Fragen Sie Peter Hoffmann, ob er sein Zimmer sehen möchte.

→ **G** Grammatik 49

5 Stellen Sie der Rezeptionistin Fragen. Schreiben Sie Fragen mit *Do* + Vollverb.

a _____? – Yes, I do speak English.

b _____? – Yes. We have four rooms free for tonight.

c _____? – Yes. All our single rooms have baths.

d _____? – Yes, we offer English and Continental breakfast.

e _____? – No, sorry. We get English newspapers, not German.

→ **G** Grammatik 49

6 Setzen Sie die richtigen Fragewörter in die Satzlücken ein.

Who • When • How • Where • Why • What

a _____ does the next bus to London leave?

b _____ do you get there? By plane? By train?

c _____ do you want to eat today? At a restaurant?

d _____ do you think of Mozart?

e _____ do you like London?

f _____ do you want to see? Mr Jackson or Mr Brown?

→ **G** Grammatik 53

7 Herr Brown unterhält sich mit Peter. Er möchte Folgendes wissen.

063

a where he works in Germany: Where do you _____?

b how he travels to work there: _____?

c when Peter usually starts work in Germany: _____?

d what he does for lunch: _____?

e when Peter usually gets home: _____?

f how many foreign languages he speaks: _____?

g what he thinks of his job in Germany: _____?

h why he likes Winthrops: _____?

→ **G** Grammatik 53

8 Streichen Sie in jeder Reihe das Wort durch, das *nicht* zu den anderen passt.

a any – sometimes – usually – always

b first – one – second – fifth

c good – nice – kind – unfortunate

d Continental – eat breakfast – drink tea – drink beer

e bus – car – plane – walk

9 Ordnen Sie die Uhrzeiten links den Uhrzeiten rechts zu.

a	6.30 a.m.	**1**	twenty-four minutes past five (in the afternoon)
b	3.45 p.m.	**2**	five to eleven (in the morning)
c	22.29	**3**	a quarter past seven (in the evening)
d	19.15	**4**	half past six (in the morning)
e	17.24	**5**	twenty-nine minutes past ten (in the evening)
f	8.31 a.m.	**6**	a quarter to four (in the afternoon)
g	10.55 a.m.	**7**	twenty-nine minutes to nine (in the morning)

10 Hören Sie sich die Aufnahme an und zeichnen Sie die Uhrzeiten ein.

064

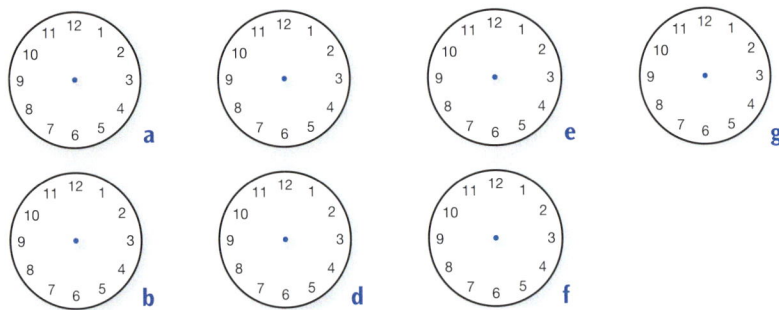

a   b   d   e   f   g

11 Schauen Sie sich den Dialog von Unit 10 nochmals an. Wie viele Zeiten werden genannt?

→ **D** Dialog 10

12 Stellen Sie Fragen, die zu den vorgegebenen Anworten passen.

a _____? – The restaurants open at 6.30 p.m.
b _____? – I usually have breakfast at 8 a.m.
c _____? – Peter leaves the house at 8.15.
d _____? – Work at Winthrops starts at 9 a.m.
e _____? – Peter can see Mr Jackson at 10 a.m.

In dieser Unit haben Sie gelernt, wie Sie …

jemanden bitten, Ihnen zu folgen.	This way, please.
fragen, wann jemand frühstücken möchte.	What time would you like breakfast?
jemanden fragen, ob er/sie etwas bevorzugt.	Do you prefer …?
sagen, dass Sie etwas liebend gerne möchten.	I would love to have …
um Wiederholung des Gesagten bitten.	I beg your pardon?
auf Dank reagieren.	You're welcome.

11

What a beautiful day!

- *simple present* mit „Signalwörtern"
- Fragen mit *did*

1 *simple present* mit „Signalwörtern"

Das *simple present* wird oft mit Ausdrücken wie ***always**, **every** (**every few minutes**; **every day**/ **morning**/**evening**/**week**), **never**, **often**, **sometimes**, **usually*** verwendet.

> He ***always*** goes to work at 7.45.
> I ***usually*** have breakfast at seven o'clock.

2 Fragen mit *did* im *simple past*

Wie im *simple present* werden Fragen im *simple past,* die ein Vollverb enthalten, mit einer Form des Hilfsverbs *do,* im *simple past* also mit *did* gebildet, wenn nicht nach dem Subjekt gefragt wird:

> ***Did*** you sleep well?

→ **G** Grammatik 49, → **U** Unit 7.3

ÜBUNGEN

1 Die folgenden Wörter helfen ihnen, die Lücken im Text zu schließen.

20 minutes • November • weekend • Monday • 9 p.m. • 25th

a   Please reserve a double room for September _____ .
b   The bus takes _____ to the city from here.
c   The bus leaves at _____ .
d   The film is on at the Rex cinema on _____ .
e   _____ is not a nice month to go to the park.
f   We would like to stay at home at the _____ .

2 Streichen Sie in jeder Reihe ein Wort, das nicht zu den anderen passt.

a lovely – wonderful – beautiful – a pity
b a quarter of an hour – half an hour – ten minutes – September
c breakfast – live – do – think
d eat – drive – walk – fly
e at – on – of – in

3 Stellen Sie Fragen mit *do, does* und antworten Sie darauf.

067

a _____ Jack, Suzie and Peter _____ for Winthrops? (work)
– _____ .

b _____ Suzie _____ on Saturdays? (work)
– _____ .

c _____ they _____ on Sundays? (work)
– _____ .

d _____ Peter _____ a foreign language? (speak)
– _____ .

e _____ Suzie _____ a foreign language? (speak)
– _____ .

f _____ Suzie _____ Australia? (come from)
– _____ .

g _____ they all _____ the atmosphere at Winthrops? (like)
– _____ .

h _____ Jack and Peter _____ playing squash? (like)
– _____ .

i _____ Suzie _____ playing squash? (like)
– _____. She likes playing badminton.

→ **G** Grammatik 49, → **G** Grammatik 50

4 Bitte formulieren Sie die Fragen und antworten Sie, indem Sie die Vorgaben beachten.

a Ask when Mr Hoffmann would like to have breakfast. (7.30)
b Ask Jack when he goes to work. (8.30)
c Ask when the bus leaves. (8.32)
d Ask Mr Jackson when **your** working day at Winthrops starts. (9 a.m.)
e Ask at what time the plane leaves. (11.53)

→ **G** Grammatik 53

5 Bitte ankreuzen, was Sie *nicht* antworten können.

a	**You can take the bus.**
1	Good idea!
2	Yes, you are right.
3	Where is the car?
4	Can I?

b	**Has she got a sister?**
1	No, she hasn't.
2	Yes, she has.
3	No, she has a brother.
4	Yes, one brother.

c	**Can you tell me how to get to the bus stop, please?**
1	No, sorry. I'm from Germany.
2	Yes, certainly.
3	Yes, just a moment.
4	I do.

d	**You take bus number 17.**
1	Where is he?
2	Is that the bus there?
3	Thank you.
4	Great.

6 Setzen Sie die Verben in den Klammern in der richtigen Form ein.

a He always _____ (to get up) at 7 o'clock.
b Peter sometimes _____ (to play) squash on Saturdays.
c We _____ (to use) the car to drive to work.
d They _____ (to drink) coffee for breakfast, but prefer tea in the afternoon.
e I _____ (to see) there are three passengers at reception.
f Mrs Bambridge always _____ (to make) breakfast for her guests.
g Suzie _____ (to work) at the reception desk of Winthrops'.

→ **G** Grammatik 29

In dieser Unit haben Sie gelernt, wie Sie …

jemanden um Rat bitten.	Is it better to … or to …?
fragen, wie oft etwas geschieht.	How often do the buses run from here?
sagen, wie oft Verkehrsmittel fahren.	They run frequently.
jemandem recht geben.	I think you are right.

12

The machines are operating slowly

- *present continuous*
- *have to / must / need*

1 *present continuous* (Verlaufsform des Präsens)

Das *present continuous* verwendet man, um eine Handlung zu beschreiben, die zum gegenwärtigen Zeitpunkt vor sich geht, von der wir aber wissen, dass sie vorübergehend stattfindet und bald enden wird.

> *Are you settling in?*
> *They are operating a little slowly.*
> *They are working on the machine at the moment.*

Formen

Das *present continuous* wird aus einer Form von *to be* + *-ing*-Form des Vollverbs gebildet.

Aussage

I	are	
You, We, They	are	*working* on the machine at the moment.
He, She, it	is	

Verneinung

I	am **not**	
You, We, They	are **not**	*working* on the machine at the moment.
He, She, it	is **not**	

Frage

Am	I	
Are	you, we, they	*working* on the machine at the moment?
Is	he, she, it	

→ **G** Grammatik 30

Schreibregeln

Man verwendet in den meisten Fällen den unveränderten Infinitiv + -ing (work + -ing = working).
Endet der Infinitiv jedoch auf ein geschriebenes, aber nicht gesprochenes -*e*, so fällt dieses weg:

settl*e* – settl**ing**, operat*e* – operat**ing**, tak*e* – tak**ing**, leav*e* – leav**ing**

Ein Konsonant wird im Englischen verdoppelt, wenn der Infinitiv auf einen kurzen, betonten
Vokal + Konsonant endet:

get – ge**tt**ing

2 *have to / don't have to – must / must not – need / need not*

Will man eine Verpflichtung oder ein Gebot ausdrücken, kann man im Präsens sowohl *must* als
auch *have to* verwenden.

We { *must* / *have to* } *inspect the machines this morning.*

Mit allen anderen Zeitformen verwendet man aber *have to.*

He had to go home.   *You will have to come next weekend.*

In der Umgangssprache wird *have to* häufiger verwendet als *must*. *Must* wird wie alle anderen
modalen Hilfsverben gebraucht, *have to* jedoch meistens zusammen mit einer Form des Hilfsverbs *do.*

Must we / *Do we have to* } *wear protective overalls?*

Die Verneinung einer Frage mit *have to* lautet *do/does not have to:*

We don't have to hurry because we have plenty of time. (= nicht müssen)

Die Verneinung einer Frage mit *must* lautet *need not:*

We needn't come to work on Monday. It's a holiday. (= nicht brauchen)

Der Ausdruck *must not* hingegen drückt ein Verbot aus und bedeutet ‚nicht dürfen':

You mustn't speak to the men when they are operating the machines. (= nicht dürfen)

Need / Need not verwendet man, wenn etwas nicht als notwendig oder zwingend erachtet wird:

I need to call him before he goes home.   *You needn't tidy up.*

→ **G** Grammatik 28

ÜBUNGEN

1 Setzen Sie die richtige *-ing*-Form ein.

a I _____ through the park because it is a lovely day. (to walk)
b Jack and Suzie _____ French. (to learn)
c Come to our house. We _____ a party. (to have)
d She _____ to Berlin by plane. (to travel)
e Jack _____ Peter _____ at Manchester airport right now. (to pick up)
f _____ you _____ in Germany at the moment? (to live)

→ **G** Grammatik 30

2 Schreiben Sie Sätze im *present continuous*.

a Jack – operate – the machine – today

_____

b Peter – settle in – well

_____

c We – work – in London – at the moment

_____

d They – eat – Chinese food

_____

→ **G** Grammatik 30

3 Hören Sie die Wörter. Stellen Sie Fragen mit *Do you like …?* oder *Would you like …?*, in denen
070 die folgenden Wörter Gegenstand der Frage sind.

a Chinese food   **d** computer games
b a dessert   **e** a drink
c jazz music   **f** to visit the British Museum

→ **G** Grammatik 27, → **G** Grammatik 49

4 Lesen Sie den Dialog in Unit 12 noch einmal. Sind die folgenden Aussagen richtig *(True)* oder
falsch *(False)*?

→ **D** Dialog 12

		True	False
a	Peter is not settling in very well.		
b	Jack has to inspect the machines.		
c	They are going to the factory floor.		
d	Peter likes Chinese food.		
e	There is an Indian restaurant near Winthrops.		

5 Bringen Sie die Wörter in die richtige Reihenfolge.

dislike • like • love • hate (hassen)

best   1 _____

         2 _____

         3 _____

worst   4 _____

6 Beantworten Sie die Fragen unten mit den folgenden Ausdrücken.

☺☺ = love   ☺ = like   ☹ = dislike   ☹☹ = hate

a Do you like jazz, Jack?
Yes, I _____ . I _____ . ☺☺

b Peter, do you like Indian food?
No, I _____ . I _____ . ☹

c Would you prefer tea or coffee?
Tea, please. I _____ . ☹☹

d Would you like bacon and eggs for breakfast?
Yes, I _____ . I really _____ bacon and eggs. ☺

▶ **7** Hören Sie den Dialog. Tragen Sie dann ein, ob die Sätze richtig *(True)* oder falsch *(False)* sind.
071

		True	False
a	Frank sometimes watches programmes on television.		
b	Today he is going to work by car.		
c	He usually goes to France on holiday.		
d	He uses his computer regularly.		
e	He never plays squash.		

→ **G** Grammatik 29, → **G** Grammatik 30

▶ **8** Jack sagt Peter, was sie an Peters erstem Arbeitstag tun werden. Hören Sie zu und kreisen
072   Sie ein, was Peter zu tun hat.

see Mr Jackson   bring packed lunch   wear a tie

wear a protective overall   shake hands with everyone   write a report

→ **G** Grammatik 28

In dieser Unit haben Sie gelernt, wie Sie …

jemanden fragen, wie es ihm/ihr geht. . . . . How are you?
auf eine Frage nach dem Wohlbefinden reagieren. . . . . And what about you?
sagen, dass Sie etwas tun müssen. . . . . I have to (inspect the machine).
sagen, dass Sie gerne mitgehen. . . . . I will be pleased to come along.
sagen, dass Sie etwas nicht so gern mögen. . . . . I am not so fond of …
sagen, dass Ihnen etwas gut passt. . . . . (That) Suits me fine. Sounds perfect.

Test 1

Hier haben Sie die Möglichkeit zu überprüfen, wie gut Sie den Inhalt der ersten zwölf Units beherrschen.

Kreuzen Sie die richtigen Antworten an und vergleichen Sie Ihre Angaben mit dem Lösungsschlüssel.

1 Setzen Sie die folgenden Verbformen richtig ein.

am • are • can • is

a _____ this your car?
_____ you German?
I _____ here as a trainee.

b _____ I ask you a question?

c Peter Hoffmann and the Canadian _____ not English.

d You _____ go to the front of the plane.

e You _____ here for the English course.

f We _____ from Germany.

2 Setzen Sie die richtigen Personalpronomen ein.

my • his • her • your • our • their

a Is this your car, Jack? – No, it is not. _____ car is over there.

b Is this Jack's car? – No, it is not. _____ car is in the car park.

c Is it _____ car? – No, it is not. My car is a VW.

d Peter and Jack work for Winthrops. _____ company is in Manchester.

e Are _____ names Jack and Peter?

f Jack and Peter: "_____ company is in Manchester."

g Martina is from Germany. _____ name is Glass.

3 Welche Wörter fehlen hier?

a My English is not very good. I am here to _____ it.

b Can I _____ you with your luggage?

c Potsdam is _____ Berlin, isn't it? – Yes, it's only 36 kilometers away.

d Can I ask you _____ questions?

e My French is not very good. What _____ you? Do you speak French?

f Thank you. It is very _____ of you to help.

g Tom and Jo are very good friends of _____. I know their parents very well, too.

4   Bringen Sie die Wörter in die richtige Reihenfolge, um Sätze zu bilden.

a   your, name, what, is

_____ ?

b   Jean-François, French, is

_____ ?

c   to, front, come, ask, plane, of, I, the, can, you, the, to

_____ ?

d   can, get, I, where, newspaper, German, a

_____ ?

e   Park Road, in, is, there, an, pub, Irish

_____ ?

f   not, is, there, no

_____ .

g   London, you, arrive, when, do, in

_____ ?

h   you, live, where, in, Germany, do, Peter

_____ ?

i   Spanish, Jack, speak, does

_____ ?

j   Jack, Peter, and, do, work, where

_____ ?

5   Ordnen Sie die Aussagen und Fragen in der rechten Spalte den richtigen Reaktionen in der linken Spalte zu.

a	Your English is very good		1	That's all right.
b	Hello. My name is Peter Hoffmann.		2	What a coincidence!
c	Would you like a newspaper?		3	No, I'm all right, thank you.
d	Oh, sorry.		4	That's very kind of you to say so.
e	Can I help you?		5	No, thank you. I would like a magazine.
f	Martina is a very good friend of Peter's and of Jack's.		6	How do you do?
g	Can I speak to Mr Smith, please?		7	I'm sorry, but he's on the phone at the moment.
h	Call me if you need my help.		8	You're welcome.
i	How may I help you?		9	I'd like to speak to Mrs Jones, please.
j	Single or double?		10	I think you're right.
k	Thank you very much.		11	That's very kind of you.
l	I think the buses run every ten minutes.		12	I think I would prefer a double room.

13

What would you like to start with?

- Bei Tisch
- Unbestimmter Artikel nach *half*
- Mengenangaben
- Speisen

Bei Tisch

‚Guten Appetit' zu wünschen und das Anstoßen mit Gläsern sind in Großbritannien nicht üblich.

1 Der unbestimmte Artikel nach *half*

Bei Mengenangaben steht der unbestimmte Artikel nach *half:*

half an hour	eine halbe Stunde
half a bottle	eine halbe Flasche

Vergleichen Sie den unbestimmten Artikel nach *what.*

→ **G** Grammatik 10

2 Mengenangaben

Um eine Menge näher zu bezeichnen, verwendet man Begriffe wie *a piece/pound/glass/cup of …*

a piece of (cheese)	*a pound of (cheese)*		
a pint of (bitter)	*a glass of (wine)*	*a bottle of (beer)*	*a cup of (tea)*

Häufig werden in Großbritannien noch britische Maße und Gewichte verwendet, obwohl offiziell das metrische System eingeführt ist.

Gängige Speisen

fruit (Obst)

apple	Apfel	*orange*	Apfelsine
banana	Banane	*pear*	Birne
grapes	Trauben	*pineapple*	Ananas
melon	Melone		

breakfast (Frühstück)

bacon	Speck	*fruit juice*	Fruchtsaft
bread (a slice of)	Brot (eine Scheibe)	*honey*	Honig
butter	Butter	*jam*	Marmelade
cocoa	Kakao	*– marmalade*	– Orangenmarmelade
coffee	Kaffee	*milk*	Milch
croissant	Hörnchen	*omelette*	Omelette
egg	Ei	*roll*	Brötchen/Semmel
– boiled egg	– gekochtes Ei	*sausage*	Wurst
– fried eggs	– Spiegeleier	*sugar*	Zucker
– poached eggs	– pochierte Eier	*tea*	Tee
– scrambled eggs	– Rühreier	*toast*	Toast

meat (Fleisch)

beef	Rindfleisch	*pork*	Schweinefleisch
chicken	Hähnchen	*steak*	Steak
duck	Ente	*turkey*	Truthahn
lamb	Lamm	*veal*	Kalbfleisch

fish (Fisch)

cod	Kabeljau	*plaice*	Scholle
haddock	Schellfisch	*salmon*	Lachs
halibut	Heilbutt	*sole*	Seezunge
herring	Hering	*trout*	Forelle
mackerel	Makrele		

Zubereitung

baked	gebacken	*seasoned*	gewürzt
boiled	gekocht	*smoked*	geräuchert
braised/stewed	geschmort	*soft*	weich
cold	kalt	*steamed*	gedämpft/gedünstet
fresh	frisch	*tender*	zart
grilled	gegrillt	*toasted; roasted*	geröstet
hard	hart	*tough*	zäh
hot	heiß	*well done*	durchgebraten
juicy	saftig		
raw	roh		
roasted	gebraten		
– grilled	– vom Grill		
– fried	– in der Pfanne		

vegetables (Gemüse)

beans	Bohnen	*potatoes*	Kartoffeln
– French beans	– grüne Bohnen	*– baked potatoes*	– gebackene Kartoffeln
Brussels sprouts	Rosenkohl	*– boiled potatoes*	– Salzkartoffeln
cabbage	Kohl	*– chips/French fries*	– Pommes Frites
carrots	Karotten	*– fried potatoes*	– Bratkartoffeln
cauliflower	Blumenkohl	*– mashed potatoes*	– Kartoffelbrei
lettuce	Kopfsalat	*spinach*	Spinat
mushrooms	Pilze		
peas	Erbsen		

ÜBUNGEN

1 Complete the sentences with the following expressions.

075

a piece of • a cup of • a bottle of • a glass of • a pint of

a I would like _____ tea, please.

b Could you please bring me _____ water?

c That cake looks good. I would like _____ that cake, please.

d I would like _____ red wine and two glasses, please.

e Oh, Jack, _____ beer is about half a litre, isn't it?

2 Can you find the hidden *(versteckten)* words?

a C E I J U _____

b T E L T O B _____

c R A T T E R S _____

d L O U I S C E I D _____

e N E S T L E C O I _____

3 Complete the dialogue with words and phrases from the restaurant dialogue.

a Good evening. What _____ start _____?
– I would like the tomato soup, please.

b And _____ follow for the _____?

c What can you _____ for the main course?

d I can _____ an excellent T-bone steak with vegetables.

e That _____ good. I will _____ that.

f Would _____ your steak medium or rare?
– Medium, please.

4 Put the verbs in the *-ing* form to complete the sentences.

a We are _____ (to offer) a free *(kostenlos)* bottle of wine with all main courses.

b What are you _____ (to have)?

c We are _____ (to order) steak.

d He is _____ (to have) soup to start with.

e They are _____ (to eat) the dish of the day.
f I am _____ (to start) with fruit juice.

→ **G** Grammatik 30

▶ **5** What does he order? Tick (✔) the right answer.
076

a	1	a mixture of starters from the trolley	**c**	1	a steak
	2	tomato soup		2	the dish of the day
	3	melon		3	an omelette
	4	mixed salad		4	a hamburger
b	1	a bottle of red wine	**d**	1	chocolate cake
	2	a bottle of white wine		2	mousse au chocolat
	3	half a bottle of red wine		3	coffee
	4	half a bottle of white wine		4	four cups of hot chocolate

6 Read the dialogue in Unit 13 again and say if the sentences are True or False.

→ **D** Dialog 13

		True	False
a	Jack and Peter are in a pub.		
b	They eat steak.		
c	Peter drinks red wine.		
d	Jack eats cake for dessert.		
e	They don't have a starter.		

7 Match the German with the English expressions.

a	Jemanden fragen, ob er/sie jetzt Getränke bestellen möchte	**1**	If I may suggest something.
b	Jemanden fragen, was er/sie möchte	**2**	What have you got?
c	Sagen, dass Sie sich nicht sicher sind	**3**	What would you like?
d	Fragen, was angeboten wird	**4**	I am not sure.
e	Sagen, dass Sie etwas probieren möchten	**5**	I will take that.
f	Einen Vorschlag machen	**6**	I think I will try that.
g	Sagen, dass Sie davon nehmen	**7**	Would you like to order your drinks now?

14

Leisure activities

- *present continuous*
- Körperteile
- Possessivpronomen

1 *present continuous* (Verlaufsform des Präsens)

Man verwendet das *present continuous* auch, um über etwas für die Zukunft fest Geplantes oder Verabredetes zu sprechen:

What are you doing on Saturday?
I am joining some friends at my health club.

→ **G** Grammatik 30

▶ 2 Körperteile

3 Possessivpronomen in Verbindung mit Kleidung/Körperteilen

Körperteile und Kleidungsstücke stehen immer zusammen mit einem Possessiv-pronomen:

*He twisted **his** ankle badly and fell on **his** hand.*
*She took **her** coat and left the restaurant.*

→ **G** Grammatik 2

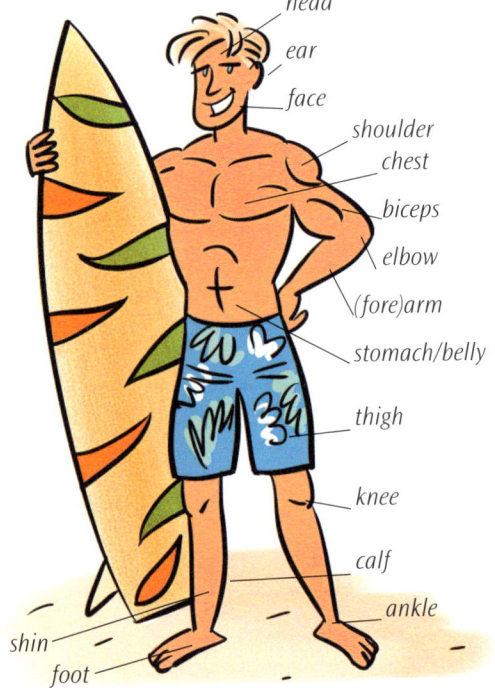

head
ear
face
shoulder
chest
biceps
elbow
(fore)arm
stomach/belly
thigh
knee
calf
ankle
shin
foot

ÜBUNGEN

1 Look at the information about the four hospital patients. Are the statements below True or False? Tick (✓) the right box.

Name: Peter Johnson
Address: 3 Beach Crescent, Liverpool
Age: 39
Height: 6'1"
Injuries*: left arm
Date of last X-ray: June 1995

Name: Michael Burke
Address: 38 Rose Lane, York
Age: 8
Height: 4'8"
Injuries*: left leg, right shoulder
Date of last X-ray: none

Name: Susan Miller
Address: 5 King Street, Manchester
Age: 22
Height: 5'6"
Injuries*: left foot, left knee
Date of last X-ray: 2000

Name: Sarah Beckett
Address: 125 Marlborough Avenue, Manchester
Age: 85
Height: 5'1"
Injuries*: ribs on right-hand side
Date of last X-ray: 1983

*Injuries = *Verletzungen*

		True	False
a	One person has hurt his/her left foot.		
b	Two of the people have hurt their left hand.		
c	Two of the people live in Manchester.		
d	Three of the people are taller than Michael Burke.		
e	One person is older than 70.		
f	Two of the people are men.		
g	One person has injured his/her left shoulder.		

2 Put the following dialogue into the right order (1–7).

a	I am joining my friend at the swimming pool.	
b	Yes, I'd love to.	
c	What are you doing on Sunday?	
d	What about you?	
e	Good. We are swimming from 10 until 12.	
f	Would you like to join us?	
g	I am going for a walk.	

3 Can you find the hidden *(versteckten)* words?

a N O R B E K _____
b D R O H E U L S _____
c T A C E R E N N _____
d L A H E T H B U L C _____
e P I H L A S T O _____
f D I W E T T S _____

4 Listen to the dialogue in Unit 14 again.
How many parts of the body do you
hear? Put the parts of the body you
hear in the right place.

080

→ **D** Dialog 14

5 Put the correct form of the following
words in the gaps.

break • fall • hurt • swell • twist

a She _____ off the chair
and _____ her hand.
b Ouch! I have _____ my
ankle.
c My shoulder is _____ .
I need to go to hospital.
d His foot is so _____ that he
can't wear his shoe.

1 _____
2 _____
3 _____
4 _____
5 _____
6 _____
7 _____
8 _____
hand
9 _____
10 _____
11 _____
12 _____
13 _____
14 _____ 15 _____

6 Please write the *-ing* form of the following verbs.

a come _____
b do _____
c fill in _____
d have _____
e interrupt _____
f look _____
g phone _____
h read _____
i sign _____
j write _____

7 Complete the sentences with the present continuous form of the verbs.

a Hello, Peter. What _____ you _____ on Saturday? (do)
b I _____ shopping for some shorts. (go)
c I _____ a party on Saturday. (have)
d I _____ all my sports friends. (invite) Would you like to come?
e Thanks for the invitation. _____ Jack _____ too? (come)
f Yes, he _____ (plan) to come with his wife Jane.
g They _____ (try) to find a baby-sitter for the evening.

→ **G** Grammatik 30

8 Listen to the dialogue and fill in the missing words.
081

a Well, what are we _____ today?
b First, we are _____ down to the reception to pick up the post.
c Then, we are _____ a video on how to operate the new machine.
d After that, we are _____ on the machine.
e When are we _____ lunch?
f Oh, we _____ lunch after the video so we can talk about the machine.

→ **G** Grammatik 29, → **G** Grammatik 30

9 Natalie is asking Peter what they are doing at the weekend. Look at the example. Then listen
082   to the recording and answer the questions before Peter does.

Example:
a What are we doing on Friday evening?
– *We are having dinner in Soho and watching a new James Bond film.*
b What are we doing on Saturday morning?

a	Friday	7.00 p.m.	have dinner in Soho
	Friday	8.30 p.m.	watch a new James Bond film
b	Saturday	10.00 a.m.	have a breakfast brunch
c	Saturday	3.00 p.m.	visit the Tate Gallery
d	Saturday	11.00 p.m.	go to a night club
e	Sunday	11.00 a.m.	meet Tom at the Film Museum
f	Sunday	2.00 p.m.	eat a pub lunch
	Sunday	4.00 p.m.	have afternoon tea
g	Sunday	7.30 p.m.	catch the train to Manchester

→ **G** Grammatik 30

10 Put the *–ing* form of the following verbs in the right places in this puzzle.

come • eat • go • help • meet • operate • phone • put • read • sign • wait • write

				I		
				N		
				T		
				E		
				R		
				R		
				U		
				P		
				T		
				I		
				N		
				G		

→ **G** Grammatik 42

11 Match the German with the English expressions.

a	Jemanden fragen, was er/sie (in naher Zukunft) vorhat		**1**	Maybe it is broken.
b	Jemanden einladen mitzugehen		**2**	Could you please …?
c	Eine Einladung annehmen		**3**	We/I don't know.
d	Sich für eine Unterbrechung entschuldigen		**4**	I am sorry to hear that.
e	Fragen, was passiert ist		**5**	What are you doing (on Saturday)?
f	Unwissen/Unkenntnis ausdrücken		**6**	Excuse me for interrupting…
g	Eine Vermutung ausdrücken		**7**	What has happened?
h	Bedauern ausdrücken		**8**	What does that mean?
i	Jemanden um einen Gefallen bitten		**9**	Yes, I'd love to.
j	Fragen, was etwas bedeutet		**10**	Would you like to come along?

15

In the department store

- unregelmäßiger Plural
- 's-Genitiv III
- Paarwörter
- *How much …? / How many …?*

- *you* = man
- *some* und *any*
- Zählbare und nicht zählbare Substantive

1 Das Substantiv: unregelmäßiger Plural

Im Plural haben einige Substantive eine unregelmäßige Form:
> *men – children – ladies*

→ **U** Unit 2.6

2 Das Substantiv: 's-Genitiv III (Plural)

An Substantive, die im Plural eine unregelmäßige Form haben (z. B. *man – men, child – children*), wird *'s* angehängt:
> *The men's toilet.   The children's department*

→ **G** Grammatik 15, → **U** Unit 3.1

3 Paarwörter

Paarwörter bezeichnen Dinge, die aus zwei gleichen Teilen bestehen. Dazu gehören:
> *glasses – dungarees – jeans – shorts – tights – trousers*

Im Englischen werden Paarwörter nur im Plural gebraucht. Sie dürfen nicht mit *a/an* oder Zahlwörtern verbunden werden. Will man eine genaue Anzahl nennen, stellt man *a pair of* oder *two/ three pairs of* voran:
> *A pair of shorts.*
> *Three pairs of trousers.*

4 *you* = man

You heißt auch ‚man‘:
> *You can't buy a car in a department store.*

5 *How much …? / How many …?*

> *How much is/are …?*   heißt: Wie viel kostet/kosten …?
> ***How much is** the skirt, please?*
> ***How much are** the skirts, please?*
> *How many …?*   heißt: Wie viele …?

Bei nicht zählbaren Sachen verwendet man immer *How much is …?*

> ***How much** is the* { cheese?
>   wine?

Bei zählbaren Sachen im Plural verwendet man *How many …?*

> ***How many** eggs would you like?*

→ **G** Grammatik 4, → **U** Unit 9.4

6 *some* und *any*

Some ist eine unbestimmte Mengenangabe, die bei zählbaren oder nicht zählbaren Substantiven in Aussagesätzen steht:

> *I'd like **some** apples.*   *I'd like **some** cheese.*

Im Deutschen bleibt dies häufig ungenannt:

> Ich möchte Äpfel/Käse.

In Fragesätzen oder negativen Aussagesätzen wird *any* gebraucht:

> *Are there **any** sports clothes here?*
> *I'm sorry, but there aren't **any** here.*

> **+** = some
>
> **–** und **?** = any

→ **G** Grammatik 5

7 Zählbare und nicht zählbare Substantive

Man unterscheidet zwischen zählbaren Substantiven:

> *friends, snacks, peanuts*

und nicht zählbaren Substantiven:

> *wine, cheese*

Nicht zählbare Substantive stehen gewöhnlich im Singular.
Abweichend vom Deutschen gehören auch Wörter wie *information* den nicht zählbaren Substantiven, die keinen Plural haben. Will man nicht zählbare Substantive zählbar machen, verwendet man *a / two / … piece(s) of:*

> *a piece of cheese*   *a piece of information*

ÜBUNGEN

1 Listen to Peter shopping.
How much …? or How many …? would he like?

085

Examples: I'd like some cheese, please.
   – Certainly. How much would you like?

   I'd like some eggs, please.
   – Certainly. How many would you like?

→ **G** Grammatik 4

2a Listen to the dialogue and circle the words you hear.

086

cheese   basement   men's department   T-shirt

   third   tea

               pullover   cafe

bananas   fourth   second

                         floor

2b Excuse me, can you tell me where I can find …?
   Where can you find the different things?

a	cheese		1	the music department is on the 3rd floor
b	jeans		2	the sports department is on the 4th floor
c	running shoes		3	the cafe is on the 4th floor
d	the best of Michael Jackson		4	the food hall is in the basement
e	have a snack		5	the men's department is on the 2nd floor

3a Can you find the missing words in this dialogue?

(At the information counter of a large department store on the ground floor.)

a Excuse _____ , can you tell me _____ I can find shoes?
b Yes, they are _____ the 2nd floor, _____ to the sport's department.
c And where can I _____ some bananas?
d You can get _____ in the food hall in the basement.
e Thank you. And, oh, one last _____ : where can I buy a newspaper?
f The newspapers are over _____ , next to the perfume department.

3b   Now re-read the mini dialogue above. Are the sentences True or False?

		True	False
a	The person is looking for jeans.		
b	The sports department is on the 2nd floor.		
c	The food hall is on the ground floor.		
d	The newspapers are on the ground floor.		
e	The person buys some perfume.		

4   Use the following words to fill in the gaps.

a • any • a pair of • men • men's • some • three • three pairs of

a   Excuse me, I'd like to buy _____ of running shorts.
b   Do you have _____ jeans here in the boutique?
c   I'm sorry, but the _____ department is on the 2nd floor, not the 1st floor.
d   I'm sorry, but _____ are not allowed in the ladies' changing rooms.
e   I will take _____ socks. One black, one blue and one brown pair, please.
f   Could I have _____ apples, please?
g   I'd like _____ coffee, please. About 250 grams.
h   Is there _____ children's department here?

5   Match the German with the English expressions.

a	Nach dem Weg innerhalb eines Gebäudes fragen		1	It is on the second floor, next to the children's department.
b	Sagen, wo sich etwas innerhalb eines Gebäudes befindet		2	You are welcome.
c	Etwas in einem Lebensmittel-geschäft bestellen		3	That is £3.20. And 80p change.
d	Bedauern ausdrücken		4	Can you tell me where the men's department is?
e	Englische Geldbeträge aussprechen		5	I would like [some of that Cheshire cheese], please.
f	Das (Nicht)Vorhandensein eines Artikels ausdrücken		6	I'm sorry, but [there aren't any here.]
g	Auf Dank reagieren		7	There aren't any here.

Shopping for clothes

- Konfektionsgrößen
- Preisangaben
- Steigerung von Adjektiven II

- *as … as*
- *do*, um Nachdruck zu verleihen

Konfektionsgrößen

Umrechnungstabelle für Konfektionsgrößen: amerikanische, britische und europäische Größen

Damengrößen / Women's Sizes				Herrengrößen / Men's Sizes		
Kleider / Dresses				Anzüge / Suits		
US	UK	EU		US	UK	EU
8	10	38		36	36	46
10	12	40		38	38	48
12	13	42		40	40	50
14	16	44		42	42	52
16	18	46		44	44	54
				Hemden / Shirts		
				14 1/2	14 1/2	37
				15	15	38
				15 1/2	15 1/2	39
				16	16	40
				16 1/2	16 1/2	41

| Damengrößen / Women's Sizes | | | Herrengrößen / Men's Sizes | | |
| Schuhe / Shoe Table | | | Schuhe / Shoe Table | | |
US	UK	EU	US	UK	EU
6 1/2	5	38	8	7	41
7	5 1/2	39	8 1/2	7 1/2	42
7 1/2	6	39	9 1/2	8 1/2	43
8	6 1/2	40	10 1/2	9 1/2	44
8 1/2	7	41	11 1/2	10 1/2	45
9	7 1/2	41	12	11	46

1 Preisangaben

fifty pounds (£ 50)   fifty p / fifty pence (50 p)
one pound twenty (£ 1.20)   six sixty (£ 6.60)

2 Die Steigerung von Adjektiven II

Formen

An alle einsilbig gesprochenen Adjektive hängt man *-er*, *-est*, um die beiden Steigerungsstufen (Komparativ und Superlativ) zu bilden:

dark   dark**er**   dark**est**
long   long**er**   long**est**
light   light**er**   light**est**

Das Gleiche gilt für alle zweisilbig gesprochenen Adjektive, die auf *-er*, *-le*, *-ow* und *-y* enden:

clever   clever**er**   clever**est**
simple   simpl**er**   simpl**est**
narrow (eng)   narrow**er**   narrow**est**
early   earli**er**   earli**est**

Sonst bildet man die Steigerungsstufen mit **more** und **(the) most**:

modern   **more** modern   **(the) most** modern
beautiful   **more** beautiful   **(the) most** beautiful
interesting   **more** interesting   **(the) most** interesting

Vergleiche kann man natürlich auch mit **less** (= weniger) machen:

The blue shorts are **more** expensive **than** the black ones.
The black shorts are **less** expensive **than** the blue ones.

Im Superlativ heißt es dann:

These are **the least expensive** shorts.

Einige zweisilbige Adjektive können sowohl mit *-er*, *-est* als auch mit ***more***, ***most*** gesteigert werden:

polite (höflich)	*politer* / ***more*** *polite*	*politest* / ***(the) most*** *polite*
pleasant (angenehm)	*pleasanter* / ***more*** *pleasant*	*pleasantest* / ***(the) most*** *pleasant*

Schreibregeln:

early	*earlier*	*earliest*
fine	*finer*	*finest*
big	*bigger*	*biggest*

Ausnahmen:

good	*better*	*best*
bad (schlecht)	*worse*	*worst*
far (weit)	*further*	*furthest*

→ **G** Grammatik 16, → **G** Grammatik 17

3 *as … as*

Mit *as … as* (so … wie) werden gleichwertige Dinge verglichen:
*This is **as** big **as** that.*
*They are not **as** nice **as** the navy blue ones.*

→ **G** Grammatik 17

4 Der Gebrauch von *do*, um Nachdruck zu verleihen

Will man eine Vorliebe unterstreichen oder einer Aussage Nachdruck verleihen, kann man eine Form von ***do*** vor das Hauptverb setzen:
*We **do** have some darker shorts in blue.*
*He **does** like Italian shoes.*

ÜBUNGEN

1 Listen to the dialogue and repeat.
089

– How may I help you?
– Do you have any jeans?
– Certainly. What size do you take?
– I take size 38.

– How about these?
– No, I am afraid they're too short.
– We have some longer ones in size 38 over there.
– I will try these. Thank you.

2 Read dialogue 16 again. Fill in the missing adjective. Then listen and check your answers.
090

→ **D** Dialog 16

a I'm afraid they are too _____. Do you have any shorter ones?
b I'm afraid those are the _____ we have. All the others are more expensive.
c These are too _____, or perhaps I am too big.
d These are less _____. They are only £ 13.

▶ 3 Circle the word that you hear.
091

   a there – here   **d** dark blue – dark black

   b shorter – smaller   **e** these – please

   c cheapest – cheaper

▶ 4 Listen and write down the objects you hear.
092

   a _____

   b _____

   c _____

   d _____

   e _____

▶ 5 Put the dialogue in the right order (1–10). Then listen to the recording to check your answer.
093

a	They are £35.	
b	I don't know. Can I try these?	
c	What size are you?	
d	Excuse me, I am looking for a pair of trousers.	
e	They are too big.	
f	Fine. I will take these, please.	
g	Yes, the changing rooms are over there.	
h	They are fine. How much are they?	
i	Yes, here try these.	
j	Do you have these in a smaller size?	

6 Use some of the words below to complete the sentences.

   bigger • expensive • cheaper • comfortable • small • smaller

   a I think I will try these on.

   b Oh, they look too _____ .

   c You are right. They do look _____ than my feet.

   d I will try a _____ size on.

   e They look very _____ .

   f Yes, they are and they fit perfectly, but they are too _____ .

   g Oh, what a pity. Well, how about these? They are _____ .

   → **G** Grammatik 16

7 *That* or *those*? Put the words in the correct list.

cheese • jeans • pullover • shorts • shoes • T-shirt

That: _____

Those: _____

→ **G** Grammatik 3

8 Crossword puzzle

a The … floor is after the 1st floor and before the 3rd floor.
b The opposite of right: … .
c When something costs a lot it is … .
d In boutiques you can buy the latest … .
e No, the men's department is on the fourth … .
f This and … , these and those.
g The changing … are over there.
h What … are these? 40 or 46?
i If you can't find something in a department store you can ask at the … counter for help.
j Can I … these on? Yes, the changing rooms are over here.
k A very big shop: a … store.

9 Read dialogues 15 and 16 again and say if the sentences are True or False.

→ **D** Dialog 15, → **D** Dialog 16

		True	False
a	Peter is in a supermarket.		
b	He buys bananas.		
c	The shorts are £25.		
d	The blue shorts are very cheap.		
e	He wants long shorts.		
f	The men's department is on the 2nd floor.		
g	Peter wants to try the shorts on.		
h	Peter buys a pair of tennis shoes.		

10 Match the products on the left with the places where you can buy them on the right.

a	cheese	**1**	department store
b	pullover	**2**	pharmacy
c	croissants	**3**	petrol station
d	petrol	**4**	bakery
e	medicine	**5**	supermarket

11 Match the German with the English expressions.

a	Sie möchten etwas kaufen	**1**	Do you have anything cheaper?
b	Ihre Kleidergröße angeben	**2**	They are not that bad either.
c	Sagen, dass Ihnen etwas zu teuer ist	**3**	Can I try them on?
d	Fragen, ob es etwas Billigeres gibt	**4**	I'm afraid that is too expensive.
e	Bitten, etwas anprobieren zu dürfen	**5**	I take size …
f	Dinge vergleichen	**6**	I would like to buy …
g	Sagen, dass jene auch nicht so schlecht sind	**7**	They are not as nice as …

17

You must come and visit me

- Verb (+Objekt) + Infinitiv mit *to*
- Adjektiv + Infinitiv mit *to*

1 Infinitiv mit *to* nach bestimmten Verben

Verb + *to*-Infinitiv

Peter **wants to try** the shorts on.

I **learn to speak** English.

I **would like to buy** a pair of running shorts

Verb + Objekt + *to*-Infinitiv

I don't **want you to go** to any trouble.

Im Deutschen ≈ „Ich möchte nicht, dass Sie sich Umstände machen."

Im Englischen ist *want that* … nicht möglich.

→ **G** Grammatik 41

2 Infinitiv mit *to* nach bestimmten Adjektiven

I am **sorry to hear** that.
Mr Jackson is **ready to see** you.
The question is too **difficult to answer**.

→ **G** Grammatik 41

ÜBUNGEN

1 What does the second speaker say?
Try to write down the sentences before you listen to the dialogue.

096

a Hello, Sam? This is Sue speaking.

– _____.

I'm fine, thank you. How are you?

b What are you doing now?

– _____.

What programme are you watching?

c   You must come and visit.

— _____ .

No, of course it is not too much trouble.

d   When do you arrive?

— _____ .

Good, then I'll pick you up from the 17.30 train.

2a   Listen to the dialogue and circle the words you hear.

097

arriving   call   Sunday   staying   check in

   listening   evening   visiting   me

come   sorry   speaking   excuse

2b   Tick (✔) the sentences you hear in the dialogue.

This is Tom calling.	How are you, Tom?
I'm visiting my friend.	I'd love to.
I'm busy on Saturday evening.	Can I call you later?

3   Now listen to the dialogue again and answer the questions.

a   Where is Tom at the moment?
b   Who is Tom calling?
c   Where is he staying at the moment?
d   When are they going to have a drink?
e   When is Tom going to call back?

4   *Want to…* or *want someone to…?*

Examples: Pierre: "I'd like to travel to America next year."
                              Pierre wants to travel to America next year.
              Mr Jackson: "Jack, will you pick Peter Hoffmann up from the airport?"
                              Mr Jackson wants Jack to pick Peter Hoffmann up from the airport.

Make similar (*ähnliche*) sentences:
a   Peter: "I must improve my English."
       Peter wants _____ .

b   Jack: "Can you tell Mr Jackson that Peter is here, Suzie?"
       Jack wants _____ .

c   Suzie: "Would you mind waiting a moment, Mr Hoffmann?"
       Suzie wants _____ .

d Peter: "Look, Natalie, I'd like to return some of your hospitality."
Peter wants _____ .

e Natalie: "Please ring me back tomorrow, Peter."
Natalie wants _____ .

▶ **5** Listen to the dialogue and say if the sentences below are True or False.
098

		True	False
a	Mike is from Ireland.		
b	Mike is in Berlin today.		
c	He will stay with Astrid.		
d	He is visiting his uncle in Berlin.		
e	Mike will meet Astrid on Tuesday evening.		
f	He will phone her at 7 o'clock on Tuesday evening.		

6 Match the German with the English expressions.

a	Sagen, dass Sie jemanden schon lange nicht mehr gesehen haben	**1**	I don't want you to go to any trouble.
b	Eine Einladung aussprechen	**2**	Super! / I'd be delighted (to have you here).
c	Jemandem einen Vorschlag machen	**3**	That sounds great.
d	Ausdrücken, dass Sie keine Mühe bereiten wollen	**4**	It's ages since we last met.
e	Ausdrücken, dass es Ihnen keine Mühe macht	**5**	You must come and visit me.
f	Freude ausdrücken	**6**	It's no trouble at all.
g	Auf eine Einladung / ein Angebot positiv reagieren	**7**	Would you like to stay at my place?

18

Asking the way

- Artikel und Straßennamen usw. II
- Wegbeschreibung

- Präpositionen
- *Don't mention it. / Not at all.*

1 Kein Artikel vor Namen von Straßen und Plätzen II

Vor Namen von Straßen und Plätzen steht normalerweise kein bestimmter Artikel:
> *I live in George Street.*
> *We are going to meet in Trafalgar Square.*

Ausnahme: *We are going to meet in **the** High Street*

→ **G** Grammatik 9, → **U** Unit 8.2

2 Wegbeschreibung

> *until …, then … and it's …*

> *You go along this street **until** you get to the crossing, **then** turn right **and it's** on your left.*

▶ 3 Präpositionen
101

turn right

straight ahead

turn left

4 *Don't mention it. / Not at all.*

Don't mention it und *Not at all* sind mögliche Erwiderungen auf *Thank you* oder *Thanks*. Im britischen Englisch reagiert man aber oft nur mit einem freundlichen Lächeln. Dagegen erwidern Amerikaner Dank fast immer mit *You're welcome*.

ÜBUNGEN

1 Match the questions with the right answers. Then listen to the recording and compare it with your answers.

102

a	Do you see the zebra crossing?	**1**	I'm sorry, but I'm a stranger here myself.
b	Excuse me, is this Bond Street?	**2**	No, Bond Street is the next street on the left.
c	Do I have to cross the road?	**3**	No, the post office is on this side of the road.
d	Excuse me. Can you tell me how to get to the station?	**4**	The one with the flashing lights?

2 Make sentences with these words.

a tell, are, where, you, toilets, can, me, the

_____?

b please, airport, where, the, is

_____?

c on, take, left, turning, your, second, the, and, is, it

_____.

d is, here, and, go, the, along, bus stop, George Street, in

_____.

e travel agency, yes, bank, the, next to, is, the

_____.

3 Ask questions about the answers on the right.

Example: Where is the post office (*Postamt*), please?
            The post office is on your right.

a _____?
2 Yes, the station is next to the airport.
b _____?
3 Well, yes, the bank is the second left turning, but it is on the right, not left.
c _____?
4 Go along the High Street to the crossing, then turn right and the shopping centre is opposite the Shell petrol station.

→ **G** Grammatik 50, → **G** Grammatik 52

4 Complete the sentences with the words below. Then listen and check your answers.

along • opposite • sports arena • stranger • take • traffic • turning • turn • your

a Excuse me, can you tell me how to get to the _____ _____ , please?
    – Yes, certainly. You go _____ here. Then _____ the first _____ on the left and you will see it in front of you.

b Excuse me, can you tell me how to get to the Royal Hotel, please?
    – Sorry, but I'm a _____ here myself.

c Excuse me, can you tell me how to get to the Royal Hotel, please?
    – Yes, of course. It is in King Street. Take the second turning on _____ right. That is Queen Street. Go straight along Queen Street and _____ right at the _____ lights. The Royal Hotel is on the _____ side, next to the travel agency.

5 Listen to the dialogue and look at the map (*Plan*). Where do the people want to go?

a Yes, certainly. You walk along Princess Street, turn left at the lights and it is next to the bank.

b Of course. Take the first turning on your left, go along that road for 30 metres and you will see it in front of you.

c Certainly. Go across Market Square. Then turn right into Mayfair Road and it is the second house on your left.

d Why, yes. You take bus number 8 to King Street. Get off the bus and turn left. Take the first turning into Ryde Avenue and it is opposite the swimming pool.

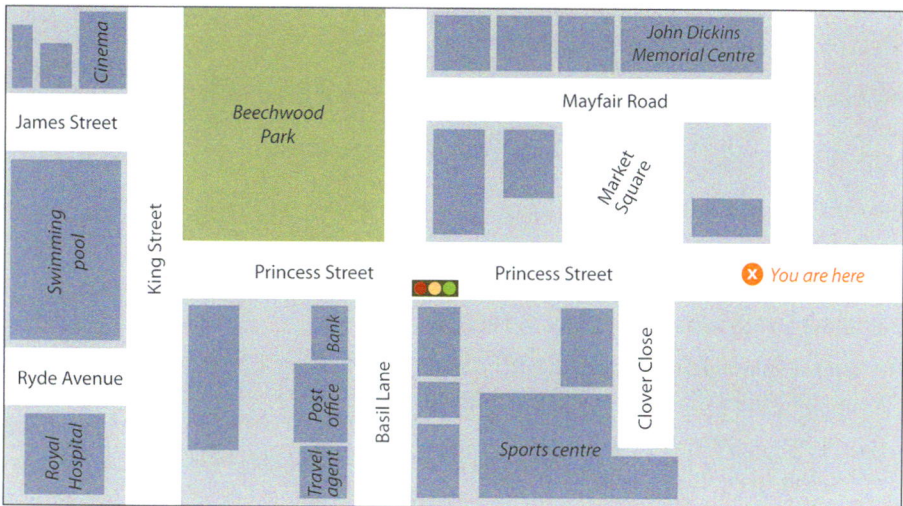

6 Match the German with the English expressions.

a	Nach dem Weg fragen		**1**	Turn left/right and go along … to …
b	Eine Wegbeschreibung geben		**2**	Yes, of course.
c	Sagen, in welcher Straße sich ein Ziel befindet		**3**	The one with the … ?
d	Auf eine Danksagung reagieren		**4**	Can you tell me how to get to …?
e	Positiv auf eine Bitte um Hilfe reagieren		**5**	Don't mention it.
f	Nachfrage, um etwas zu präzisieren		**6**	That's right.
g	Etwas bestätigen		**7**	It is the second street on the left/right.

19

At the travel agent's

- Artikel und Transportmittel
- Bus- und Bahnreisen
- *what* und *which*

1 Artikel und Transportmittel

Vor Transportmitteln steht kein bestimmter Artikel mit der Wendung *by*:
> *We are going to London by coach/bus/train.*

In anderen Fällen muss ein Artikel verwendet werden:
> *The bus is over there.*
> *A train is usually quicker than a bus.*

 → **G** Grammatik 9

🇬🇧 Bus- und Bahnreisen in Großbritannien

Seit 1995 wird das Netzwerk der Eisenbahn in Großbritannien von über 20 kommerziellen Gesellschaften bedient. Es ist aber Aufgabe der Regierung zu überwachen, dass sie miteinander in Hinblick auf Tarife, Fahrkartenausgabe sowie Informationen als National Rail zusammenarbeiten. Sie finden alle Informationen bzgl. Fahrplänen, Preisen etc. für alle Anbieter auf der Webseite http://www.nationalrail.co.uk.

Längere Strecken mit dem Reisebus zurückzulegen ist in Großbritannien gängig und eine kostengünstige Alternative zum Reisen mit der Bahn. Wie das Streckennetz der Eisenbahn werden Reisebuslinien von kommerziellen Firmen bedient. Die größte dieser Firmen ist **National Express**. Reisebusse und lokale Busse verfügen über ein größeres Netzwerk an Routen als die Bahn und sind daher ein gutes Mittel, um eher abgelegen Teile des Landes zu erreichen. Weitere Informationen erhalten Sie auf der Webseite http:www.nationalexpress.com/coacheslanding.aspx.

2 *what* und *which*

What und *which* sind beide sowohl Relativpronomen als auch Fragewörter. Manchmal sind sie als Fragewort fast gleichbedeutend.
> *Which/What is the best way to get there?*

Normalerweise jedoch verwendet man *what*, wenn eine Frage auf viele, fast unbegrenzte Möglichkeiten hinweist – wenn also die Auswahl üppig ist:

What would you like for breakfast?

Andererseits deutet *Which would you like to drink?* eher auf bestimmte, begrenzte Möglichkeiten – es gibt z. B. vielleicht nur die Wahl zwischen Tee oder Kaffee.

Als Relativpronomen werden *what* und *which* immer unterschiedlich verwendet. Wiederum deutet *what* auf unbegrenzte Möglichkeiten hin:

She wants to know what I want.

Dagegen ist *which* wiederum wesentlich spezifischer:

I don't know which train to take; the four o'clock or the five o'clock.

→ **G** Grammatik 52, → **G** Grammatik 59

ÜBUNGEN

1 Look at the timetables *(Fahrpläne)* for coaches and trains.
107 Ask and answer the questions. Then listen to the recording to check your answers.

NATIONAL EXPRESS COACHES					
Manchester – London London – Manchester					
Manchester	dep.	14.00	16.00	18.00	20.00
London	arr.	18.30	20.30	22.30	00.30
London	dep.	13.30	15.30	17.30	19.30
Manchester	arr.	18.00	20.00	22.00	24.00

NATIONAL RAIL					
Manchester – London London – Manchester (Direct)					
Manchester	dep.	16.00	17.30	19.00	20.30
London	arr.	18.34	20.04	21.34	23.04
London	dep.	15.30	17.00	18.30	20.00
Manchester	arr.	18.04	19.34	21.04	22.34

dep. = departure *(Abfahrt)*; arr. = arrival *(Ankunft)*

a Sie möchten wissen, wann Busse von London nach Manchester fahren.

– _____?

– _____ every two hours.

b Sie möchten wissen, wie lange der Zug von Manchester nach London braucht.

– _____?

– _____ two hours and 34 minutes.

c Sie möchten wissen, wie oft die Züge von London nach Manchester fahren.

– _____?

– _____ every _____.

d Sie möchten wissen, wann der 5-Uhr-Zug in Manchester ankommt.

– _____?

– _____.

e Sie möchten wissen, ob Sie mit dem 17.55-Uhr-Zug nach London umsteigen müssen.

– _____ on the 5.55 to London?

– _____

f Sie möchten wissen, ob der Bus schneller ist als der Zug.

– _____?

– _____

g Sie möchten wissen, wie viel eine Einzelfahrkarte mit dem Zug nach London kostet.

– _____?

– (£ 33.20) _____

▶ 2 Ask questions about the answers with the following question words.

108

How • How long • How often • What • When • Where

a _____

I want to travel to London by coach.

b _____

He is leaving for Manchester on Saturday.

c _____

Sam and Betty are flying to Paris.

d _____

We go to Edinburgh every summer.

e _____

It takes about 4 ½ hours by coach.

f _____

They want to see Big Ben.

3 Crossword puzzle

a A special ticket. It is cheaper. It is called a … ticket.

b The train from London to York … 4 ½ hours.

c Are you going by … or by coach?

d The trains … every two hours.

e What you must pay: …

f There is … at 16.00 and at 18.00.

g You can book a single or a … ticket.

4 Complete these sentences with the following words or their comparative forms.

cheap • fast • good • long

a Which is the _____ way to get to London ?
b How _____ does it take to get there?
c It takes 4 hours by car, but by train it is _____ .It takes 1½ hours.
d The coach takes _____ . It takes 4 ½ hours.
e Is there a _____ restaurant here in town?
f Yes, the "Bagpipes" is by far the _____ restaurant in town.
g No, it isn't. The "Bugle" is even _____ than the "Bagpipes" and it is _____ .
A good T-bone steak is only £ 12.99.

→ **G** Grammatik 16

5 Match the questions on the left with the answers on the right.

a	Is it any cheaper?		**1**	Yes, it is only 130 miles.
b	Is it any quicker?		**2**	Yes, it is much faster.
c	Is it any better?		**3**	Yes, it is (only) £ 35.
d	Is it any faster?		**4**	Yes, it only takes 2 hours.
e	Is it any shorter?		**5**	Yes, it is the best.

→ **G** Grammatik 16

6 Tick (✓) the right answers.

a	**How long does it take?**	**c**	**What time does the 8 o'clock train get to London?**
1	about 5 o'clock	**1**	four hours
2	about 5 hours	**2**	every 4 hours
3	every 5 hours	**3**	that is 4 p.m.
4	there is one at 5 p.m.	**4**	at 4 p.m.
b	**Do I have to change?**	**d**	**Is that any quicker?**
1	No, it's direct.	**1**	Yes, it can.
2	No, you change.	**2**	Yes, it takes more time.
3	Yes, you go direct.	**3**	No, it is faster.
4	Yes, it's direct.	**4**	Yes, it is.

e	Can I use a Saver ticket?	f	How often do the trains run from London to Dover?
1	Yes, you can save money.	1	every Friday
2	Yes, you can.	2	every 2 hours
3	Yes, it is quicker.	3	very direct
4	No, it is cheaper.	4	it takes 2 hours

7 Listen to the dialogue and say if the sentences below are True or False.

109

		True	False
a	He wants to buy a coach ticket.		
b	He wants to travel on the 5.30.		
c	There is no 5.30 on Friday.		
d	The next train is at 6.50 p.m.		
e	He cannot use the Saver ticket after 6 p.m.		
f	He wants to make a booking for the 5 p.m. train.		

8 *What* or *which*?

a _____ train are you taking to London, Peter – the 9 o'clock or the 10.30?
b _____ are you going to do at the weekend?
c _____ pair of shorts do you prefer – the blue ones or the black ones?
d _____ of your friends are coming to the party?
e She doesn't know _____ to take to London to wear.
f _____ do you want to do on holiday?
g _____ Winthrops' factory is bigger – the one in Manchester or the one in Scotland?

9 Match the German with the English expressions.

a	Nach dem besten Weg fragen	1	How long does it take?
b	Fragen, wie lange etwas (eine Reise) dauert	2	When do … from … to … run?
c	Fragen, wann Verkehrsmittel fahren	3	Do I have to change?
d	Fragen, ob man umsteigen muss	4	I'm afraid a … is not valid on …
e	Gültigkeit ausdrücken	5	I'd like to book a normal return, please.
f	Eine Buchung vornehmen	6	What/Which is the best way to get there?

A visit to London

- *simple past*
- Fragesätze / Kurzantworten *im simple past*

- *all day*

1 *simple past* (Präteritum)

Das *simple past* ist die Zeitform zur Beschreibung von Handlungen, die in der Vergangenheit abliefen und die man als beendet betrachtet.

> *We walked everywhere.*   *I visited an old friend.*

Unwichtig dabei ist es, wann die Handlung stattfand (vor einem Jahr, vor zwei Sekunden), nur abgeschlossen muss sie sein. Dies steht im Gegensatz zum Gebrauch des *present perfect,* wo die Handlung als unvollendet, nicht abgeschlossen betrachtet wird. Da im Deutschen keine strenge Unterscheidung zwischen dem Gebrauch des Präteritums und des Perfekts gemacht wird, führt dies oft zu Verwechslungen zwischen dem englischen *simple past* und *present perfect.*

→ **G** Grammatik 31, → **U** Unit 6.3

Formen

Einige Verben haben im *simple past* eine unregelmäßige Form (z. B. *go – went, buy – bought*). Eine Liste der Verben mit den unregelmäßigen Präteritum-Formen finden Sie im Lesebuch.

Zur Bildung des *simple past* mit regelmäßigen Verben wird *-ed* an den Infinitiv angehängt:

> *walk – walked, visit – visited, enjoy – enjoyed*

→ **G** Grammatik 31

Aussprache

112

| stayed
travelled
arrived
enjoyed | [d] | worked
watched
missed
helped | [t] nach [k], [tʃ], [s], und [p] | | visited
landed
wanted | [id] nach [t] und [d] |

Merke:
Nicht die Schreibweise, sondern die Aussprache des vorhergehenden Lautes entscheidet
über die Aussprache des Endlautes.

Schreibregeln

In den meisten Fällen wird **-ed** an den Infinitiv regelmäßiger Verben gehängt:
> *land**ed**, want**ed**, visit**ed***

Endet der Infinitiv auf **-e**, wird nur **-d** angehängt:
> *arrive – arriv**ed**, arrange – arrang**ed***

Endet der Infinitiv mit einem geschriebenen Konsonant + **-y**, wird **-y** zu **-ied** verwendet:
> *try – tr**ied***

Endet das Verb jedoch mit einem Vokal + **-y**, wird **-ed** angehängt:
> *enjoy – enjoy**ed***

Wenn der Infinitiv mit einem einfachen, kurzen, betonten Vokal + Konsonant endet, wird der
Konsonant verdoppelt:
> *stop – sto**pp**ed*

2 Fragesätze und Kurzantworten im *simple past*

Wie im Präsens bildet man Fragesätze, in denen kein anderes Hilfsverb vorhanden ist, mit einer
Form des Hilfsverb *do*, also im *simple past = did:*
> ***Did** you see Natalie in London?*

Kurzantwort: *Yes,* ***I did**.*

Fragen nach dem Subjekt werden auch mit einer Form von *do* beantwortet:
> *Who went to London? – Peter **did**.*

→ **G** Grammatik 49, → **G** Grammatik 50, → **G** Grammatik 56

3 *all day*

In der Kombination *all day* bedeutet *all* nicht ‚alle‘, sondern ‚den ganzen Tag‘.

→ **U** Unit 6.4

ÜBUNGEN

1 Write about Peter's trip to London.

a Peter _____ a good trip to London. (have)
b He _____ an old friend there. (meet)
c They _____ all the sights. (see)
d There _____ a lot of tourists in London. (be)
e Some tourists _____ flags along. (take)
f Natalie _____ some good places to visit. (know)
g They _____ some delicious food. (eat)
h Peter _____ some flowers to Natalie. (give)

→ **G** Grammatik 31

2 Complete the table.

ask	asked	
	was	been
change		changed
eat	ate	
	got	got
give		given
go	went	
	had	had
know		known
meet	met	
play		played
see	saw	
take		taken

3 Find the right answers to the questions. Then listen to the recording to check.

113

a	Did you see Tower Bridge?	**1**	No, I didn't. I don't really like military parades.
b	Did you have a good trip?	**2**	Yes, it was faster than the bus.
c	Did you like the changing of the guard?	**3**	No, we didn't. There are too many sights for one weekend.
d	Did you take the train?	**4**	Yes, I did, but now I'm tired.
e	Did you see everything in London?	**5**	Yes, we even walked across it.

▶ **4** Complete the questions and answers in the simple past.
114 Then listen to the recording and give the right answers.

a Did Peter go to Paris? No, he _____ .
He _____ to London.

b _____ Natalie _____ Jack No, she _____ .
the sights? (show) She _____ Peter the sights.

c _____ they _____ in a No, they _____ .
French restaurant? (eat) They _____ in a Chinese restaurant.

d _____ you _____ the Canadian? No, I _____ .
(see) I _____ Natalie.

e _____ we _____ squash on No, _____ .
Sunday? (play) We _____ on Saturday.

▶ **5** Here you can see part of Peter's diary *(Tagebuch)*. But you cannot read everything.
115 Ask him questions with *How, What, When, Where, Who, Why* in the simple past.

a left Manchester at [   ]

b took the train to [   ]

c ate [   ] on train

d met [   ] at railway station

e took a [   ] to restaurant because it rained

f brought flowers for Natalie to [   ] her for her hospitality

→ **G** Grammatik 52

6 Can you find the 15 hidden *(versteckten)* words?

A	B	A	N	A	H	M
U	R	R	U	T	A	E
W	O	R	K	E	D	T
E	U	I	N	O	T	N
R	G	V	E	A	T	O
E	H	E	W	E	N	T
I	T	D	A	S	K	I
G	O	T	S	A	W	C
P	L	A	Y	E	D	E
Z	P	I	C	K	E	D

7 Complete the sentences with the correct form of the verb.

a Last weekend Peter _____ (go) to London.

b He _____ (take) a train.

c Natalie _____ (meet) Peter at the station.

d They _____ (not see) everything, but they _____ (see) almost all the sights.

e They _____ (not eat) Japanese food, but they _____ (eat) Chinese food.

f He _____ (have) a fantastic trip.

→ **G** Grammatik 23, → **G** Grammatik 24, → **G** Grammatik 31

8 Listen to the dialogue in Unit 20 again. Tick (✓) the things he did.

→ **D** Dialog 20

a	He went to an Indian restaurant.	
b	He took the bus everywhere.	
c	He saw Tower Bridge.	
d	He waved a little flag.	
e	He went to the British Museum.	

9 Match the German with the English expressions.

a	Fragen, wie das Wochenende war		**1**	(Natalie) was a great hostess/host.
b	Sagen, dass Sie alle Sehenswürdig-keiten gesehen haben		**2**	We ate some delicious food.
c	Sagen, dass etwas sehr beeindruckend wahr		**3**	I saw all the sights.
d	Sagen, dass jemand eine gute Gastge-berin / ein guter Gastgeber war		**4**	It was quite impressive really.
e	Sagen, dass Sie etwas Leckeres gegessen haben		**5**	How was your weekend?

21

Developments at Winthrops

- Zusammensetzungen mit *some, any* und *no*
- Indirekte Rede

- Indirekte Fragen
- *say* und *tell*

1 Zusammensetzungen mit *some, any* und *no*

Some, any und *no* kommen in den folgenden Zusammensetzungen vor:

somebody	anybody	nobody
someone	anyone	no one
something [ŋ]	anything [ŋ]	nothing [ŋ]
somewhere	anywhere	nowhere

Die Verwendung der Zusammensetzungen in den beiden linken Spalten entspricht der von *some* und *any*.

→ **U** Unit 15.6, → **G** Grammatik 5

2 Indirekte Rede

Indirekte Rede vewendet man, um wiederzugeben, was ein anderer Sprecher oder Schreiber gesagt bzw. geschrieben hat:

> Guard: *"The drawers were closed when I began my rounds on Friday evening."*
> Jack to Peter: *The guard said the drawers had been closed when he began his rounds on Friday evening.*

Steht das einleitende Verb im *simple present*, ändert sich das Verb in der indirekten Rede nicht:

> Peter: *"I **am** not so fond of Chinese food."*
> Peter **says** he **is** not so fond of Chinese food.

Steht das einleitende Verb aber im *simple past* gibt es eine Verschiebung der Zeitform des Verbs in der indirekten Rede um eine Stufe zurück in die Vergangenheit, also von *present* zu *past*:

> Peter **said** he **was** not so fond of Chinese food.

Obwohl das einleitende Verb im *simple past* steht, verwendet man aber das *present*, wenn man meint, dass die Aussage zum Zeitpunkt des Berichtens noch Gültigkeit hat:

> Peter **said** he **is** not so fond of Chinese food.
> The radio **said** the Queen **is visiting** Balmoral all this week.

Einen Überblick über die Zeitformen in der indirekten Rede finden Sie in

→  Grammatik 60

3 Indirekte Fragen

Wenn das einleitende Verb im *simple past* steht, ändern sich die Zeitformen wie bei der indirekten Rede in Aussagesätzen:

> "Do you **walk** to work, Mr Brown?" → She **asked** Mr Brown if he **walked** to work.

Enthält die Frage in der direkten Rede ein Fragewort, so wird dies in der indirekten Rede wiederholt:

> **When** do you **leave** for work? → They wanted to know **when** I **left** for work.

Bei Ja/Nein-Fragen, in denen kein Fragewort vorhanden ist, steht am Anfang der indirekten Frage *if* oder *whether*:

> **Can** you speak Spanish, Peter? → He asked Peter **if**/**whether** he **could** speak Spanish.

Modale Hilfsverben ändern sich wie folgt in der indirekten Rede:

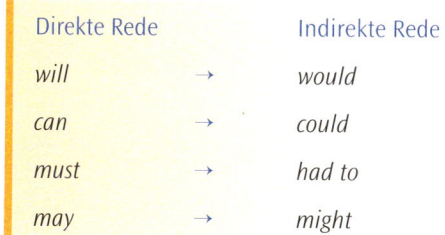

Direkte Rede		Indirekte Rede
will	→	would
can	→	could
must	→	had to
may	→	might

> **Will** you go back to Germany? → He **wanted to know** whether I **would** go back
> to Germany.

→  Grammatik 60

4 *say* und *tell*

Wenn man angibt, mit wem man gesprochen hat, verwendet man **tell**:

> The guard **told him** the drawers were closed.
> Didn't you **tell me** that you don't like Chinese cooking?

Im anderen Fall muss man **say** verwenden:

> The guard **said** the drawers were closed.
> Didn't you **say** that you don't like Chinese cooking?

Folgende Formen sind nicht möglich im Englischen:

> The guard ~~said him~~ they were closed.
> The guard ~~told they~~ were closed.

▶ Aussprache
118

Listen please and put a circle around the word you hear.
Then repeat the words after the speaker.

ate – at   *head – hat*   *met – mat*   *said – sad*

ÜBUNGEN

1 Put in the correct verb form.

a	**Oh, Jack I wanted to ask you how your weekend _____ .**	**d**	**You _____ to the crossing and turn left.**
	1 go		1 go
	2 goes		2 goes
	3 is going		3 went
	4 went		4 had gone
b	**Did you perhaps _____ to close the door?**	**e**	**Did you _____ your suitcase?**
	1 forget		1 find
	2 forgot		2 found
	3 forgotten		3 finds
	4 forgetting		4 founded
c	**The guard _____ his rounds at 8 p.m. every day.**	**f**	**Maybe the mysterious Canadian _____ exist.**
	1 begins		1 do
	2 began		2 doing
	3 begun		3 does
	4 is beginning		4 did

2 Complete the sentences with the words below.

anything • somebody • somehow • something • nobody • nothing

There was a break in at the local Crown Pub last night, but **(a)** _____ was seen and
(b) _____ was missing. **(c)** _____ , this seemed mysterious and the police
checked twice with the landlord to see if there was **(d)** _____ strange in the pub.
(e) _____ they did notice was that there was **(f)** _____ left in the big
glass container on the bar. Usually, the container is filled with peanuts. The police think that

(g) _____ ate them and, as the door was locked, they think that maybe an animal, perhaps a weasel, got in and had a big dinner.

→ **U** Unit 15.6, → **G** Grammatik 5

3 Fill the gaps in the text with *Anybody, Everybody, Somebody* and *Nobody*.

Whose (*Wessen*) job is it?
This story is about four people named *Everybody, Somebody, Anybody* and *Nobody*. There was an important job to be done and (a) _____ was asked to do it. *Everybody* was sure that (b) _____ would do it. (c) _____ could have done it, but *Nobody* did. *Somebody* got angry about that because it was (d) _____'s job. *Everybody* thought that (e) _____ could do it but *Nobody* realized that *Everybody* would not do it. It ended up that (f) _____ blamed *Somebody* when (g) _____ did what *Anybody* could have done. [Anon.]

→ **U** Unit 15.6, → **G** Grammatik 5

4 Say it is not true (present or past tense).

a Peter is from France.
No, he _____ . He's from Germany.

b Peter spent his last weekend in Paris.
No, he _____ . He spent his last weekend in London.

c Peter likes Chinese food.
No, he _____ . He likes Indian food.

d Peter was in London for one week.
No, he _____ . He was in London for a weekend.

e Peter's friend, Natalie, lives in Manchester.
No, she _____ . She lives in London.

→ **G** Grammatik 29, → **G** Grammatik 31, → **G** Grammatik 56

5 Complete the sentences with the correct form of the verb in the simple present or simple past.

a Peter usually _____ (get up) at 7.30.
b He always _____ (have) breakfast at 8 a.m.
c He often _____ (take) the bus at 8.15.
d Yesterday, he _____ (take) the train at 8.30 to London.
e He _____ (eat) breakfast on the train.
f He _____ (drink) tea and _____ (eat) a sandwich.
g He _____ (meet) a friend at the station.
h The friend _____ (work) in London, but she _____ (live) near Heathrow airport.
i She usually _____ (travel) to work by underground, but yesterday she _____ (take) the car because she _____ (pick) Peter up at the station.

→ **G** Grammatik 29, → **G** Grammatik 31, → **U** Unit 7.4, → **U** Unit 11.1

6 *Say* or *tell*? Complete the sentences with the correct form of *say* or *tell* in the simple present or simple past.

a Could you _____ me where the toilets are?

b Jack _____ Mr Baker that Natalie lives in London.

c Did you _____ that you like Indian cooking?

d He _____ me to ask you to look at the photograph.

e No, the guard _____ the drawers were closed.

7 Write what the people said.

a Jack: "Do you like your work at Winthrops, Peter?"
Jack asked Peter _____.

b Suzie: "Will you go to London again, Peter?"
Suzie wanted to know _____.

c Mrs Bambridge: "When will you return to Germany, Mr Hoffmann?"
Mrs Bambridge wanted to know _____
_____.

d Peter: "I'm going to Scotland next week, Jack."
Peter _____ Jack _____
_____.

e Mr Jackson: "Where do you come from in Germany, Peter?"
Mr Jackson asked _____.

f Jack: "I love a good, old English breakfast."
Jack said _____.

g Natalie: "How did you travel to Manchester, Peter?"
Natalie wanted to know _____.

→ **G** Grammatik 60

8 Match the German with the English expressions.

a	Eine Vermutung aussprechen		**1**	What do you mean?
b	Jemanden bitten oder auffordern, Ihnen zu folgen oder Sie zu begleiten		**2**	But there must be something interesting.
c	Fragen, was jemand meint		**3**	Perhaps you (forgot to close them).
d	Einem Vorschlag zustimmen		**4**	It doesn't make sense.
e	Einer Aussage Nachdruck verleihen		**5**	He told me he was going to Scotland
f	Berichten, was jemand gesagt hat		**6**	Yes, of course.
g	Sagen, dass etwas keinen Sinn macht		**7**	Follow me.
h	Einer Meinung/Vermutung widersprechen		**8**	No, not really.

22

The invitation

- *should/shouldn't – would/wouldn't*
- **Gradadverbien**
- **Einladungen**

1 should/shouldn't – would/wouldn't

Das modale Hilfsverb *should* wird verwendet, wenn es um Ratschläge oder Verpflichtungen geht:

> *You should join us.*
> *Should I wear a suit?*
> *You shouldn't wear green with blue.*
> *We should all save water.*

Should wird auch verwendet, um eine Erwartung oder Wahrscheinlichkeit auszudrücken:

> *These should be your size. Size 38.*
> *Peter shouldn't be long now. He left home an hour ago.*

Das modale Hilfsverb *would* wird ebenfalls verwendet, um Ratschläge oder Warnungen zu erteilen und bedeutet ‚würde‘:

> *I wouldn't drink so much. You won't be able to drive, if you do.*

2 Gradadverbien

Um ein Adjektiv, Verb oder Adverb zu verstärken oder abzuschwächen, verwendet man oft ein Adverb:

> *It was **quite** impressive, actually.*

Solche Adverbien geben Antwort auf die Frage ‚inwieweit?‘ oder ‚wie sehr?‘. Adverbien, die gern in diesem Zusammenhang im Englischen verwendet werden, sind:

> *extremely • fairly • hardly • just • nearly • not • particularly • pretty • quite • rather • really • too • very*

Diese Adverbien bilden eine Art Skala, von *hardly* (kaum) bis *extremely* (äußerst).

> *hardly* = kaum
> *fairly, quite, rather, pretty* ≈ ziemlich
> *very* = sehr
> *particularly* = besonders
> *extremely* = äusserst

hardly, fairly, quite, rather, pretty, very, particularly, extremely

3 Einladungen

Schriftliche Einladungen

Invitation

To: Peter Hoffmann
Place: 44 Gladstone Avenue
You are invited to: Bring a dish party
(we'll provide the rest!)
On: Saturday 24th April
At: 8 p.m.
From: Jack and Janet

The Chairman and Board of Directors of Winthrops' Ltd request the pleasure of your company at a reception in honour of the Honorary Consul of the Federal Republic of Germany, Dr. Max Grün, on 25th May at the Radisson Edwardian Manchester Hotel, Free Trade Hall, Peter Street, Manchester.

An aperitif will be served at 12.30 p.m. followed by luncheon.

Black tie

RSVP
The Company Secretary
Winthrops Ltd
Wigan Road
Manchester

Persönlich

Formell

Mündliche Einladungen

What about a drink at the pub?
Would you like to have lunch with me?
Would you like to go to the play at the Globe with me?
I wondered whether you would like to go to the theatre.
Formell: May I invite you for dinner?

+ That would be very nice, thank you.
Thank you, that's very kind of you.
Great!
OK. / Good idea!

– I'm sorry, I can't. I'm seeing X at …
I'd love to but I'm busy this evening.
Sorry, no time!
No, thanks.

ÜBUNGEN

1 Complete the sentences with *some* or *any*. Then listen to the recording to check your anwers.

122

a Do we need _____ drinks?

b Have you got _____ red wine?

c There are _____ delicious dishes on the buffet table.

d There is _____ beer in the bar.

e Are there _____ friends helping to organise the party?

f There won't be _____ food left if we are late.

g Waiter, I'd like _____ orange juice, please.

h – I'm sorry, we haven't got _____ orange juice.
    Would you like _____ tomato juice?

i Are there _____ good restaurants in town?
    – Yes, there are, but _____ are very expensive.

j Janet never drinks red wine. Do you have _____ white wine?

k Excuse me, can you give me _____ change for the phone?

→ **U** Unit 15.6, → **G** Grammatik 5

2 *Should* or *shouldn't*? Put in the correct form

a You really _____ clean your teeth regularly.

b Why _____ I watch the film? – Because you are not old enough!

c It is Mother's Day tomorrow. You _____ call your mum.

d What are you doing here? _____ you be in Manchester right now?

e Thank you for the food, but you really _____ have brought anything.

f When you go to the theatre you _____ leave your mobile phone at home.

3 *Should* or shouldn't?

a _____ I wear the blue T-shirt or the red one?

b _____ I better call Mr Jackson before I go to his office?

c You _____ really thank your mother for that present. She had a lot of trouble getting it.

d You _____ really speak in here. This is a quiet room.

e _____ you be at the airport now? Your flight leaves in 30 minutes.

→ **U** Unit 22.1

4 Complete the sentences with the following words.

should • shouldn't • will • won't • would • wouldn't

a I am sure it _____ be a nice day tomorrow.

b _____ you please pass me the wine?

c They _____ come to the party if they are invited.

d When _____ we go to London? What do you think?

e You really _____ drink so much beer and then drive the car.

f The coach is cheaper, but the train is faster. I think you _____ take the train.

g I _____ eat that old steak. You _____ be ill.

h He just _____ listen to me. He never does.

→ **G** Grammatik 27, → **G** Grammatik 35

5 Peter is at the Edinburgh Festival. Clare has told him to visit Madame Maxine so that he can find out about his future. What are his questions? And what are Madame Maxine's answers?

Peter would like to know:

a Wo er arbeiten wird, nachdem er sein Praktikum (*internship*) bei Winthrops beendet hat.

_____?

– _____ for a big international company.

b Wo er wohnen wird.

_____?

– _____ in Frankfurt.

c Ob er eine Frau finden wird.

_____?

– Yes, _____ a wonderful wife.

d Ob er Kinder haben wird.

_____?

– No, _____ any children.

e Ob er glücklich sein wird.

_____?

– Yes, _____ very happy.

f Ob er erfolgreich sein wird.

_____?

– Yes, _____ very successful.

→ **G** Grammatik 35

6 Listen to the dialogue and then decide who can, can't or doesn't know yet if he/she is going to come to the party.

123

	can come	can't come	doesn't know yet
Sue			
Jack			
Sam			

7 Now read your answers to exercise 5 again. Write what Peter asked Madame Maxine and what she said to him.

a Peter wanted to know _____

_____.

Madame Maxine said _____ for a big international company.

b Peter asked her _____ live.
She told _____live in Frankfurt.

c Peter wanted to know _____ find a wife?
Madame Maxine thought _____ a wonderful wife.

d He then asked Madame Maxine _____ have children?
She said that, unfortunately, _____ have any children.

e He also wanted to know _____ happy?
She was pleased to tell _____ very happy.

f He also asked _____ be successful.
She replied that, yes, _____ very successful.

→ **G** Grammatik 35, → **U** Unit 21

8 Match the German with the English expressions.

a	Höflich einen Vorschlag machen	**1**	Just watch and tell us (how you like it). Well, what do you think of …?
b	Sagen, dass Sie keine Ahnung haben	**2**	To be honest, I have no idea.
c	Jemanden bitten, seine Meinung zu äußern	**3**	Why don't we (ask Peter to watch us)? Shall we (go to the pub?) How do you feel about …
d	Jemandem einen Rat erteilen	**4**	I don't mind.
e	Ihre Meinung äußern	**5**	I've had enough (for one evening).
f	Sagen, dass es Ihnen reicht	**6**	I thought (the fight was very good).
g	Sagen, dass Sie es leid sind	**7**	I quite agree. I'll go along with that.
h	Jemandem zustimmen	**8**	I'm tired of (doing that scene again and again).
i	Sagen, dass Sie zufrieden sind	**9**	I'm quite satisfied with (things so far).
j	Fragen, ob jemand etwas dagegen hat	**10**	If I were you, I would (shorten …).
k	Sagen, dass Sie nichts dagegen haben	**11**	Do you object?

23

At the party

- **Bedingungssatz Typ 1**
- *past continuous*
- *simple past* und *past continous*

1 Bedingungssatz Typ 1 *(conditional sentence type 2)*

Dieser Typ Bedingungssatz (*if*-Satz Typ 1) enthält im *if*-Satz eine Voraussetzung bzw. Bedingung, die erfüllbar oder erfüllt ist, und im Hauptsatz die mögliche Folge (Was ist, wenn …?):

> If you **do not leave** Preston before 9.45, it **is** only £ 30 return.

Dieser Typ Bedingunggssatz kann sich auch auf bestehende Tatsachen beziehen:

> If Peter **is** German, he **can tell** you what a GmbH is.

Oder der Bedingungssatz Typ 1 sagt etwas über eine bestimmte Situation in der Zukunft:

> If there **are** no trains, we **will** travel by car.

Will steht im britischen Englisch nur im Hauptsatz, **nie** im *if*-Satz.

> if + simple present – will future oder modales Hilfsverb + Infinitiv

Bedingungssätze Typ 1 werden häufig verwendet, um Versprechungen zu machen:

> If I **come** to Germany, I'**ll** visit you.

→ **G** Grammatik 58

2 *past continuous* (Verlaufsform des Präteritums)

> Yesterday afternoon Peter Hoffmann **was working** in the factory.

Diese Zeitform kennt man im Deutschen nicht. Das *past continuous* beschreibt:

- eine Handlung, die zu einer bestimmten Zeit in der Vergangenheit gerade vor sich ging, d. h. noch nicht abgeschlossen war:
  > Where **were** you **working** yesterday afternoon when I was looking for you?
  > The machines **were operating** slowly all day yesterday.

- eine Handlung, die zu einem vergangenen Zeitpunkt gerade vor sich ging, als eine andere Handlung einsetzte:
  > I **was** just **telling** young Peter here about the trainee when you **came** in.

Im Deutschen wird die Verlaufsform des Präteritums häufig durch Zeitbestimmungen gekennzeichnet oder erklärt sich durch die Situation:

> Ich erzählte **gerade** dem jungen Peter hier, wie dein letzter Praktikant abhanden gekommen ist.
>
> Die Maschinen arbeiteten gestern **den ganzen Tag** zu langsam.

3 Unterschiede zwischen dem *simple past* und dem *past continuous*

Das *simple past* wird verwendet für Handlungen oder Vorgänge, die zu einem bestimmten Zeitpunkt in der Vergangenheit vor sich gingen. Die Handlung / Der Vorgang ist abgeschlossen:

> **On Saturday / Yesterday / This morning** Peter **went** for a run.

Das *past continuous* wird verwendet für Handlungen oder Vorgänge, die **zu einer bestimmten Zeit** in der Vergangenheit im Verlauf waren. Es drückt aus, dass die Handlung **noch nicht abgeschlossen** war.

> *Mr Jackson* **was playing** golf **when it started to rain.**

→ **G** Grammatik 32

ÜBUNGEN

1 Complete the type 1 *if*-sentences with the correct form of the verb.

a If he _____ (travel) by train, he _____ (to be) here in two hours.

b If we _____ (take) Peter's car, we _____ (get) there much quicker.

c If you _____ (call) me from the airport, I _____ (pick) you up.

d If I _____ (see) Jack, I _____ (ask) him to join us at the pub.

e If I _____ (visit) London, I _____ (buy) you a souvenir.

f If you _____ (not understand), I _____ help) you.

g If you _____ (not book) your holiday soon, there _____ (not be) any hotel rooms free.

h If I _____ (drink) alcohol at the party, I _____ (not drive) the car home.

i If you _____ (not stop) smoking, I _____ (leave) the room immediately.

j He _____ (be) late if he _____ (not go) now.

→ **U** Unit 23.1, → **G** Grammatik 58

▶ 2 Listen to the speakers, and then give them a piece of advice *(einen Rat)*.
126

Example: a I have a headache. (**take an aspirin**)
> – *If you have a headache, you should take an aspirin.*

b I can never find a parking space near my office. (**take the bus to work**)

c I want to improve my English. (**go to evening classes**)

d I can't find a babysitter for tonight. (**ask your mother to babysit**)

e I'm having a big party at the weekend. (**buy a lot of drinks**)

→ **U** Unit 23.1, → **G** Grammatik 58

3 Word order

a you, some, introduce, I, friends, to, will

_____ .

b London, in, doing, are, you, what

_____ ?

c name, just, I, did, hear, my

_____ ?

d strange, very, is, that

_____ .

e out, did, happened, you, what, find

_____ ?

4 Listen to the dialogue in Unit 23 again.

→ **D** Dialog 23

Are these sentences True or False?

		True	False
a	Peter brought Janet some flowers.		
b	Janet likes her present very much.		
c	Jack introduces Peter to some friends.		
d	Dennis likes joking.		
e	Peter is a trainee at Winthrops.		
f	Jack is Dennis' mentor.		
g	Jack lost his last trainee in France.		

5 **Listen to the example, and then make similar _(ähnliche)_ sentences.**

127

Example: He visited Manchester and met Kevin there.
– _Ah, I see, he was visiting Manchester when he met Kevin._

a He spoke to Janet. He saw an old friend.
b She told Peter about her boyfriend. Her boyfriend came into the room.
c He travelled to London. That was when he lost the present.
d She went to live in London. That was when her mother visited her.
e We lived in London then. That is when we had our first baby.
f They tried to contact his family but he disappeared.

→ **U** Unit 23.2, → **G** Grammatik 32

6 Complete the following *if*-sentences with the correct form of the verb.

a If you _____ (travel) by bus, it usually _____ (take) five hours.

b I _____ (pay) for the food if you _____ (pay) for the taxi.

c He _____ (not like) driving to London by car if there _____ (be) many cars on the road.

d She _____ (have to) book her ticket today if she _____ (want) to leave tomorrow.

→ **G** Grammatik 58

7 What was happening at the party when Peter arrived?

a Clare / talk / to Dennis and Susanne.

_____.

b Jack / have a drink / with Janet.

_____.

c Janet's mother / make sandwiches / and her father / read a newspaper.

_____.

d Harry / leave / to pick up / friends at the station.

_____.

→ **U** Unit 23.2, → **G** Grammatik 32

8 Can you find the hidden words?

a S P E N T E R _____

b G I L E N S _____

c E I N A T R E _____

d T E R M O N _____

e T I V A N I T I N O _____

9 Match the German with the English expressions.

a	Freude ausdrücken		**1**	You had better (take care).
b	Sagen, dass etwas nicht nötig gewesen wäre		**2**	That is very strange.
c	Ihre Freude darüber ausdrücken, dass jemandem etwas gefällt		**3**	I'm glad you like it.
d	Jemanden auffordern, Ihnen zu folgen		**4**	I'm glad you could come.
e	Einen Ratschlag erteilen		**5**	You shouldn't have.
f	Sagen, dass etwas sonderbar ist		**6**	Now, if you come this way …

24

A mystery solved

- Relativsätze und -pronomen
- Feiertage in Großbritannien

1 Relativsätze und Relativpronomen

Relativsätze (*relative clauses*) beziehen sich auf ein vorausgehendes Wort (Bezugswort). Die Relativpronomen (*relativ pronouns*) *who, whose, which, what, that* verbinden den Hauptsatz und den
Relativsatz miteinander. Für Personen verwendet man **who**, für Tiere und Dinge **which**. Das Pronomen **that** kann aber oft für beides verwendet werden. Das Pronomen **whose** (*wessen*) drückt
Besitz oder Zugehörigkeit aus.

> *I can't find the CV. He sent us the CV.* → *I can't find the CV **which**/**that** he sent us.*
> *That's Peter's friend. He lives in London.* → *That's Peter's friend **who** lives in London.*
> *That's my friend. His parents live in London.* → *That's my friend **whose** parents live in
> London.*

Das Pronomen kann weggelassen werden, wenn es Objekt ist.
> *I can't find the CV **which**/**that** he sent us.* → *I can't find the CV he sent us.*

→ **G** Grammatik 59

2 Bestimmende und nicht bestimmende Relativsätze

Wir unterscheiden zwischen bestimmenden (*defining*) und nicht bestimmenden (*non-defining*)
Relativsätzen (*relative clauses*).
Ein bestimmender Relativsatz ist für das Verständnis des Gesamtsatzes unentbehrlich:
> *Have you got a photo of the man who was your 'lost' trainee?*
Um zu wissen, um welchen Mann es sich handelt, brauchen wir die Information *who was your
last trainee*.

Dagegen ist in dem folgenden Satz die Information in dem nicht bestimmenden Relativsatz,
nämlich darüber, was der Mann getragen hat, nicht notwendig, um zu verstehen, welche Person
gemeint ist. Nicht bestimmende Relativsätze werden durch Kommas vom Hauptsatz getrennt.
> *The man you met in the factory, who was wearing a dark blue coat, is Mr Jackson's brother.*

→ **G** Grammatik 59

Feiertage in Großbritannien

Bank Holidays sind gesetzliche Feiertage in Großbritannien, an denen die Banken in der Vergangenheit keinen Handel treiben durften. Insgesamt gibt es im Jahr acht ständige gesetzliche Feiertage (*Bank Holidays* und *Public Holidays*) in England, Wales und Schottland und zehn in Nordirland. Früher hatten alle Geschäfte, Fabriken usw. an solchen Tagen geschlossen. Heutzutage findet man aber immer mehr Läden, die an diesen Tagen geöffnet haben.
Die Feiertage:

Christmas (Weihnachten): **Christmas Day:** *25th December;* **Boxing Day:** *26th December* (Wenn diese beiden Tage auf Samstag/Sonntag fallen, verschieben sich die arbeitsfreien Tage auf die darauf folgenden Wochentage.)
New Year's Day (Neujahrstag): *1st January*
Easter (Ostern): **Good Friday** (Karfreitag); **Easter Monday** (Ostermontag)
Early May Holiday: 1. Montag im Mai
Spring Holiday: Letzter Montag im Mai
Summer Bank Holiday: Letzter Montag im August

ÜBUNGEN

1 Complete the sentences with the words below. You may use some of the words several times.

who • which • what • that • whose

a They all went to visit Jack _____ was having a party.
b I don't know what to say. It is the nicest present _____ I have had so far.
c I never knew _____ found my passport. So I can't thank the person.
d Peter didn't remember _____ house Natalie lived in.
e A postman is a man _____ brings you your post.
f A zoo is kind of park in _____ you can see many wild animals.
g The hotel has 30 rooms _____ all have a bathroom and TV.
h He wanted to see the new science fiction film _____ everyone was talking about.
i No passenger _____ passport is not valid is allowed on the plane.

→ **G** Grammatik 59

 2 Listen to the example and then make similar sentences.

Example: That's a present. Peter sent it.
  – Oh, so that's the present that Peter sent.

a Do you see that woman over there. She came to help me.
b That's my friend over there. He lives in Berlin.
c Do you see that car? My father bought it.
d That man over there, he found my passport.
e That lady in the corner, she takes the children to school.

→ **G** Grammatik 59

3 Complete the sentences with the following question words.

how • what • when • where • who • whose • why

a _____ opened my suitcase? – The airport police, sir.
b _____ book is this? It is not mine.
c _____ are we going? – To London.
d _____ is the nearest pub, please?
e _____ pair of shorts do you like better? The blue ones or the red ones?
f _____ much do these jeans cost?
g _____ are you doing on Saturday afternoon?
h _____ didn't you call me? You know I am always pleased to help you.
i _____ film do you prefer? The detective film or the action film?
j _____ shoes are these? I found them in the changing room.
k _____ did you go to London and not to Paris?
l _____ is my car? I know it must be here somewhere.
m _____ about going for a drink after our game of tennis?
n _____ would you like to pick up your ticket?
o _____ is the new secretary's name?

→ **G** Grammatik 52

4 Ask questions to match the answers. Ask about the words which are <u>underlined</u>.

a _____?
I play <u>squash</u> and in summer I play <u>tennis</u>.

b _____?
Because these shorts are <u>too expensive</u>.

c _____?
I have to leave at <u>9 o'clock</u>.

d _____?
<u>Clare, Sam and Henry</u> are driving to Edinburgh with me.

e _____?
I'm going <u>to town</u> to buy some clothes.

f _____?
On Saturday <u>I am going to the cinema</u>.

g _____?
We are travelling to Paris <u>by car</u>.

h _____?
I bought them in London when I was there <u>last weekend</u>.

i _____?
I have been working for this company <u>for five years now</u>.

j _____?
I think it is <u>Jack's</u> coat.

k _____?

I was talking to <u>Suzie</u>, the receptionist, in the pub.

l _____?

I'm looking for <u>a pair of black jeans</u>.

m _____?

I will need the room <u>for five days</u>.

n _____?

I'm so happy <u>because I found such a good job</u>.

o _____?

My sister is <u>16 years old</u>.

5 Word order

a coming, many, party, how, the, people, to, are

_____?

b nearest, post office, is, please, where, the

_____?

c door, close, why, the, you, didn't

_____?

d name, the, man's, what, is

_____?

e theatre, did, the, last, who, you, at, night, see

_____?

6 Read the dialogue in Unit 24 again. Are the following sentences True or False?

› **D** Dialog 24

		True	False
a	Jack can't find the lost trainee's CV.		
b	The trainee was tall and about 30 years old.		
c	Janet's birthday is on the same day as Peter's.		
d	The trainee had a beard.		
e	The CV has been stolen.		
f	Mrs Kilbride is Jack's wife.		

132

7 Who is it? Listen to the woman describing a man to a police officer.
Compare the three descriptions below and decide which man she means.

	ID 1	ID 2	ID 3
Age	27	26	28
Colour of eyes	blue	green	green
Colour of hair	brown	brown	blond
Height	6'5"	6'5"	6'3"
Special features	handsome	beard	handsome with a beard

8 Add the missing relative pronoun. Then add the missing commas in the non-defining relative clauses.

a Have you seen the girl … found my keys?
b The man standing over there … is looking at the photos is my husband.
c We want to buy a new computer … we can use to make short films with.
d There are three shops … employees are very knowledgable that I can recommend.

9 Match the German with the English expressions.

a	Sagen, dass etwas unwahrscheinlich ist	**1**	Funnily enough …
b	Sagen, dass etwas merkwürdig ist	**2**	(He/She) It is a kind of (person) programme, etc. that …
c	Fragen, was los ist	**3**	What's wrong?
d	Sagen, dass es (er/sie) eine Art von (Person) Programm etc. ist, der/die/das …	**4**	That's hardly likely.
e	Sagen: Komischerweise …	**5**	That's strange.
f	Ein Gespräch einleiten	**6**	That's not very likely.
g	Zweifel ausdrücken	**7**	What does/did he look like?
h	Nach jemandes Aussehen fragen	**8**	I was wondering …

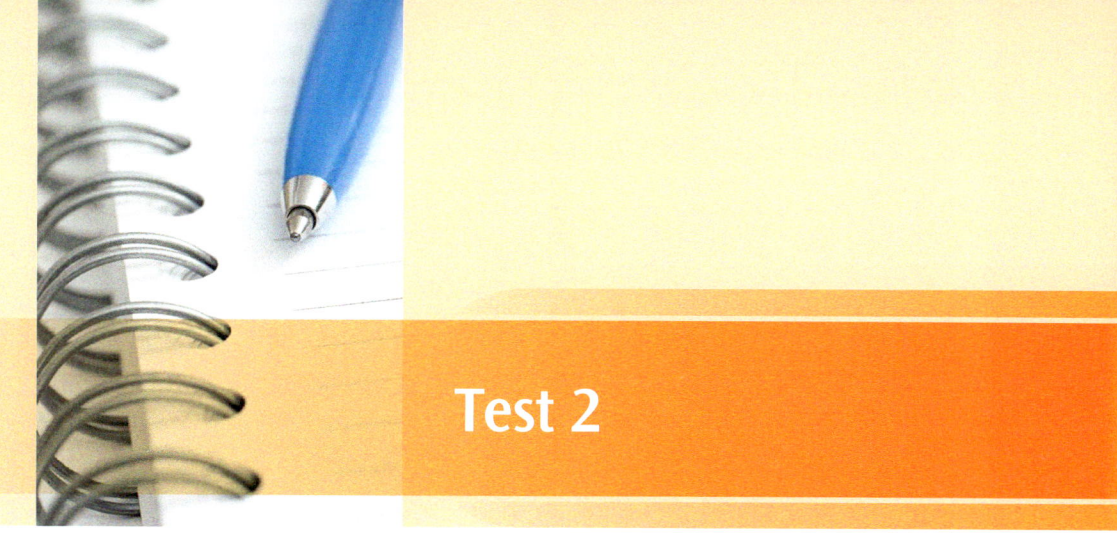

Test 2

Here you can check how much you have learnt from Units 13 to 24.

1 Match the measurements to the items.

a	a cup of		**1**	milk
b	a slice of		**2**	cheese
c	a glass of		**3**	beer
d	a pound of		**4**	tea
e	a pint of		**5**	bread
f	a piece of		**6**	cake

2 Write the correct prepositions in the lines below.

Richtung:

h _____   i _____   j _____

3 Complete the missing forms of the words below.

a early   _____   earliest
b late   later   _____
c _____   better   best
d fat   _____   fattest
e bad   worse   _____

4 You are spending a holiday in London. A friend has given you a list of restaurants near your hotel. Your partner wants to know what is best. Compare the restaurants and answer his/her questions.

	Food	Wine	Atmosphere	Prices
The Swan	Plain, but good	Good	Cosy	Fair
Chez Maxime	Portions too small	Excellent choice	Cold	Expensive
San José	Exotic dishes	Wide choice of Spanish wines	Lively	Moderate
The Malborough	Super	Average	Nice	Good value for money

a Is the food good at the San José?
– Well, it is _____ but not _____ at the Malborough.

b Is the atmosphere at Chez Maxime nice?
– No, it's rather _____ . The atmosphere at the other restaurants is much

_____ .

c Is the food expensive at the Swan?
– No, Chez Maxime is the _____ _____ restaurant near the hotel.

d What about wines? Which restaurant has the best wine?
– Well, I think Chez Maxime has the _____ choice, but the San José also has a wide choice, a much _____ choice than the Malborough, anyway.

5 Underline the mistakes in the text and write the correct words on the lines.

Deer Susan,   _____
I realy enjoyed my visited at your house.   _____
I walkt in the beach every day.   _____
I mised you very much, but fine wether helpped me.   _____
I watcht the sun go down every night.   _____
I cann't wait for you to arive and   _____
I have arrangged everyting for you.   _____
See you soon,
Yours,
Tom

6 Complete the sentences with the correct form of the verbs.

Peter I _____ (**a** try) to phone you last night, Jack, but you _____ not
(**b** be) at home.

Jack What time _____ you _____ (**c** call)?

Peter Oh, it _____ (**d** be) about eight o'clock.

Jack I _____ (**e** babysit) for my sister all evening. _____ you
_____ (**f** want) anything in particular?

Peter Well, I _____ just _____ (**g** wonder) if you _____
(**h** like) to play squash this evening?

Jack I'm sorry, but I can't. I _____ (**i** play) with Jim this evening. What about Paul?
_____ you _____ (**j** see) him in the office yet this morning?

Peter No, because he _____ (**k** work) in Liverpool all day to day.

Jack But do you know what time he _____ (**l** be back) in Manchester?

Peter I think he said he _____ (**m** go) to the theatre in Liverpool this evening.

Jack I know what. I _____ (**n** ring) my friend George, if you _____
(**o** like). He _____ (**p** play) squash very well.

Peter That's very kind of you, Jack. But if you _____ (**q** give) me his telephone
number, I _____ (**r** phone) him myself.

7 Complete the sentences with the words below. You may use some of the words several times.

any (2x) • are (2x) • as nice as • a pair of • some (3x)

Shop assistant: Good morning. How may I help you?

Customer: I am looking for _____ (**a**) jeans. Have you got _____ (**b**) blue
jeans?

S: Yes, we have _____ (**c**) over here.

C: Ah, yes, they are nice. How much _____ (**d**) these?

S: They _____ (**e**) £ 50.

C: I see. And what about these? Do you have _____ (**f**) of these in size 12?

S: No, I'm sorry. We don't have _____ (**g**) of those in size 12. But we have
_____ (**h**) in black.

C: Oh, I see. I don't think that the black ones are _____ (**i**) as the blue ones.
I think I'll take the ones for £ 50.

8 Match the German with the English expressions.

a	Fragen, was jemand möchte		**1**	When do … from … to … run?
b	Einen Vorschlag machen		**2**	You had better (take care).
c	Fragen, was jemand (in naher Zukunft) vorhat		**3**	We would like to invite you to our party on Saturday.
d	Bedauern ausdrücken		**4**	What do you mean?
e	Fragen, wo sich etwas befindet		**5**	It's no trouble at all.
f	Ausdrücken, dass es Ihnen keine Mühe macht		**6**	Can you tell me where (the men's department) is?
g	Nach dem Weg fragen		**7**	How long does it take?
h	Fragen, wie lange etwas (eine Reise) dauert		**8**	Can you tell me how to get to…?
i	Fragen, wann Verkehrsmittel fahren		**9**	What would you like?
j	Fragen, was jemand meint		**10**	I am sorry to hear that.
k	Eine Einladung aussprechen		**11**	What are you doing (on Saturday)?
l	einen Ratschlag erteilen		**12**	If I may suggest something …

Getting to know people

- *because (of)*
- *used to*
- *anyway*
- Englisches Schulsystem

1 *because*

because = weil, denn

Because ist eine Konjunktion und wird eher in nachgestellen Sätzen verwendet:

> *That's interesting **because** in Germany teachers are civil servants and earn quite a good salary.*
> *Well, in Germany I don't often eat breakfast **because** I usually leave home at ten past seven.*

because of = wegen

Because of ist eine Präposition und steht vor dem Substantiv:

> ***Because of** the problem with the apartment in Castle Heights, Peter had to take a room in a B&B.*

2 *used to*

Used to beschreibt eine Situation oder einen Zustand, die bzw. der nicht mehr aktuell ist (jetzt arbeitet sie als Lehrerin; jetzt spielt er aber Tennis).

> *I used to work in a tax office.*
> *I didn't use to play tennis.*

Used to kann auch etwas über eine ehemalige Gewohnheit aussagen:

> *I used to play football when I was at school.*

Used to verwendet man nur im *simple past*.

Aussage

I, You, He, She, It, We, They	used to	work in London.
		play golf.
		visit English friends every weekend.

Verneinung

I, You, He, She, It, We, They	didn't use to never used to	drink so much.
		play golf.
		wear glasses (Brille).

Frageform & verneinte Frage

Did(n't)	he, she, they I, you, we it	use to	wear glasses? look so puzzled? be easier?

> **Merke:**
> Es gibt einen Unterschied zwischen *used to* + Infinitiv (*do*) und *to be used to* + *-ing*-Form (*doing*).
> **Used to** + Infinitiv wird verwendet, wenn man über frühere Zustände und Gewohnheiten und über regelmäßige Handlungen in der Vergangenheit spricht. *Used to* ist eine Verbform der Vergangenheit.
>   *I **used to** only **speak** German.* = Früher habe ich nur Deutsch gesprochen.
>
> **To be used** to ist eine Präposition und darauf folgt die *-ing*-Form
>   *I **am used to** speak**ing** English now because I have practised so much with Lextra Sprachkurs Premium Englisch.* =
>   Ich bin es jetzt gewohnt, Englisch zu sprechen, weil ich so viel mit *Lextra Sprachkurs Premium Englisch* geübt habe.

3 anyway

Das Wort *anyway* kann vielfältig verwendet werden. Es ist beispielsweise ein sehr nützliches Wort, um das, was man sagt, zu betonen. In Unit 4 heißt es:
   Well, I am grateful that you are here to pick me up, anyway.

Hier betont *anyway,* dass der Sprecher dankbar ist, egal mit was für einem Auto er abgeholt wird.

In Unit 25 hören/lesen wir:
   Anyway, everyone is so nice in the group.

Hier verwendet die Sprecherin *anyway,* um das Gespräch auf ein neues Thema zu bringen. Dies ist eine sehr gebräuchliche und nützliche Art, um ein Gesprächsthema zu beenden bzw. zu wechseln. Der Gebrauch von *anyway* kann ein allzu abruptes Wechseln des Gesprächsthemas vermeiden. Aber Vorsicht: Je nach Intonation kann es auch ziemlich ruppig ein neues Thema einleiten. Hören Sie sich mehrere Muttersprachler genau an, bevor Sie sich den Ausdruck zu eigen machen!

Das englische Schulsystem

Das englische Schulsystem ist anders strukturiert als das deutsche. Kinder werden bereits im Alter von fünf Jahren eingeschult. Die allgemeine Schulpflicht in Großbritannien beträgt insgesamt elf Jahre.

Den ersten Abschluss erreichen Schüler/innen mit dem *GCSE (General Certificate of Secondary Education)*. Danach können sie zwei weitere Jahre in der *Sixth Form* absolvieren, um dann mit dem *A-Level* abzuschließen, eine Qualifikation, die mit dem deutschen Abitur vergleichbar ist. Innerhalb der Schulformen *Primary Education* und *Secondary Education* werden insgesamt vier Stufen (*Key Stages*) unterschieden.

Schulart	Key Stages	Klasse	Alter
Primary	1	1	5
		2	6
	2	3	7
		4	8
		5	9
		6	10
Secondary (Comprehensive School, Grammar School)	3	7	11
		8	12
	4	9	13
		10	14
		11	15
Further Education / Sixth Form College		lower 6th	16
		upper 6th	17

ÜBUNGEN

1 Complete the sentences with *must, mustn't* or *have to*.

a I can't meet you at the pub. I _____ babysit tonight because my wife is going out.

b I _____ remember to take my passport to the airport.

c Peter _____ change trains twice to go to Liverpool.

d You _____ use a mobile phone here in the hospital.

e You _____ go to see your mother. It is Mother's Day today.

f You _____ do that because it will break.

g He _____ go to the doctor's because he has hurt his hand.

h They really _____ leave at 5.30 p.m. because their plane leaves at 8.30 p.m.

i Do you really _____ go now?

j You _____ drink alcohol and drive.

→ **G** Grammatik 22

2 Listen to these people and encourage them to do what they suggest.

135

a I need to improve my English. Perhaps I should join an evening class.
– Yes, why don't you join an evening class?

b I need more money. Perhaps I should get a second job.

c I need to make more friends. Perhaps I should join a club.

d I need a rest. Perhaps I should take a holiday.

e I need to learn French. Perhaps I should go to France.

→ **G** Grammatik 44

3 Complete the sentences with *everyone, everything* or *everywhere.*

a _____ knows that the Queen of England likes to drink tea.

b _____ he goes, the President of the USA has to have bodyguards.

c I want _____ in this room to listen for a moment.

d _____ he says is true.

e When we have finished with _____, the house will look quite nice.

f _____ we went we saw tourists: in the bars, in the museums, in the parks.

g Where have you been? I have looked _____ for you!

h Why does _____ want to see this film?

i _____ who has been to the top of the Mount Everest, says it is great!

j He put _____ in one suitcase and then left.

→ **G** Grammatik 7

4 Listen to some people and then make similar sentences.

136

a I saw a lot of Peter then. It was when we played football.
– Oh, I see. You used to play football, but you don't any more.

b I worked with Mary then. It was when I taught French.

c It took two hours to get to work. That was when I worked in London.

d I went to a restaurant every day. That was when I earned a good salary.

5 Read the dialogue in Unit 25 again. Are the following statements True or False?

→ **D** Dialog 25

		True	False
a	Clare works in a tax office.		
b	Clare's pay is very good.		
c	Peter wants to improve his English.		
d	Clare recommends evening classes.		
e	Peter will have to perform on stage.		
f	Peter must do a lot of paperwork.		
g	The people in the theatre group are nice.		

6 *Used to (do)* or *used to (doing)?*

Michael has lived in Germany for more than ten years. He is talking to his German friend, Marc, about how things have changed for him.

Michael: When I first came to Germany, it was difficult to drive on the right, but not any more.
Marc: I see. In England, *you used to drive* on the left, but now you *are used to driving* on the right.

a *Michael:* Beer was my favourite drink in England, but now it's wine.
   Marc: So you _____ beer in England, but now you _____ wine.

b *Michael:* I never spoke foreign languages before, but I'm quite happy with German now.
   Marc: Really? So you _____ foreign languages, but now you _____ German.

c *Michael:* Back home I started work at 9 o'clock. Here we start at 7.30, but it's no longer a problem for me.
   Marc: I see, in England you _____ late, but now you _____ early.

d *Michael:* In York, I lived in a house and never wanted to live in a flat, but the one I've got here is very nice.
   Marc: So you _____ in a house, but you _____ in a flat here in Munich.

e *Michael:* I never watched football at home, but here I watch Bayern Munich every week
   Marc: Really? So you _____ football in England, but you _____ Bayern Munich regularly.

→ Ⓤ Unit 25.2

7 Complete the sentences with *used to, use to* or *didn't use to*.

a When I was a child I _____ like playing cards but not any more.
b Didn't he _____ work in HR?
c I started going to the gym recently. I _____ do any exercise.
d We haven't been to the theatre for ages. We _____ go nearly every month.
e Has she stopped making so many mistakes? She _____ have lots of problems with the computer.
f I thought you drove a red car. – That's true, I _____ .
g Didn't they _____ live near the post office? I'm sure I _____ see them there.
h I'm so fed up with my job. I _____ look forward to retirement but now I can't wait till I'm 65.

› Ⓤ Unit 25.2

8 Match the two halves of the sentences. Sometimes the first half of the sentence is on the left and sometimes it is on the right.

a	Peter took a room in a B&B.		**1**	There is a slight problem with them.
b	Mr Brown leaves for work at 7.45.		**2**	It is quicker to travel by train than by bus.

c Look, we have to inspect the machines.	**3** The apartment in Castle Heights wasn't ready.
d He is travelling to London at the weekend.	**4** Peter phoned Natalie.
e Peter travelled to London by train.	**5** Jack wants to invite Peter to his home.
f They are having a party at the weekend.	**6** He doesn't start work until nine o'clock.

→ **U** Unit 25.1

9 Solve the crossword puzzle

a Someone who works in a school is a …
b When people work together for something they are a …
c A word similar in meaning to 'suggest': …
d When you become a member of a club or group you … them.
e When you get money for work you … the money.

10 Match the German with the English expressions.

a Jemanden nach seinem Beruf fragen		**1** I used to work in a tax office.
b Fragen, ob etwas Spass macht		**2** Do you have to …?
c Fragen, ob jemand etwas machen muss		**3** What do you do for a living?
d Eine Situation / einen Zustand beschreiben, die bzw. der nicht mehr aktuell ist		**5** Anyway, perhaps we could …
e Einen Themenwechsel einleiten		**6** Do you enjoy …?

Joining a theatre group

- Bedingungssatz Typ 2
- Britisches Amateurtheater
- Edinburgh Festival

1 Bedingungssatz Typ 2 *(conditional sentence type 2)*

Diese Art von Bedingungssatz (*if*-Satz Typ 2) enthält im *if*-Satz eine Voraussetzung, von der der Sprecher annimmt, dass sie nicht erfüllt wird.
Im Alltagsgebrauch wird diese Art von *if*-Satz oft verwendet, um einen Wunsch zu äußern:

> *If I had a lot of money, I would stop working.*

oder um einen Rat zu erteilen:

> *If I were you, I would shorten it a little.*

Im *if*-Satz steht das **past** und im Hauptsatz *would, could* oder *might* + Infinitiv:

> *if* + past – *would/could/might* + Infinitiv

Would, could, might verwendet man im britischen Englisch **nie** im *if*-Teil des Satzes.

→ **G** Grammatik 58

 ## Amateurtheater in Großbritannien

Das Amateurtheater erfreut sich in Großbritannien großer Beliebtheit. Die Schauspieler/innen, die Helfer/innen (Beleuchtung usw.) und die Zuschauer/innen sind Menschen aus den unterschiedlichsten sozialen Schichten. Viele Kinder erleben hier ihre erste live Theatervorführung bei den jährlichen örtlichen Weihnachtspantomimen. (Diese ‚Pantomime' ist eine musikalische Komödie, die zu Weihnachten aufgeführt wird.). Manchmal ist das Amateurtheater sogar ein Sprungbrett für junge Schauspieler/innen, aber für die meisten zählt der Spaß, in der Freizeit gemeinsam an einer Theaterproduktion mitzuwirken. Es wird geschätzt, dass ca. 437.800 Personen aktiv in solchen Theaterproduktionen mitwirken, davon sind ungefähr 29 % unter 21 Jahren. Die Zahl der Theaterbesucher beläuft sich in etwa auf 7.315.840 pro Jahr.

Sie finden dazu weitere Informationen auf der Webseite:
http://en.wikipedia.org/wiki/Amateur_Dramatics#Amateur_Theatre_in_the_United_Kingdom

Edinburgh Festival

Das Edinburgh Festival setzt sich aus verschiedenen Einzelfestivals zusammen, die jedes Jahr im August und September in Edinburgh, Schottland, stattfinden. Es zählt jährlich mehr als zwei Millionen Besucher. Die wohl wichtigste Einzelveranstaltung der darstellenden Künste ist das *Edinburgh Fringe Festival*, für das jährlich mehr als eine Millionen Karten verkauft werden. Das Angebot reicht von Shakespeare bis hin zu Experimentellem und wird von sowohl professionellen als auch von Amateurgruppen dargeboten.
Siehe: *http://de.wikipedia.org/wiki/Edinburgh_Fringe*

ÜBUNGEN

1 Use the following words to fill in the gaps.

about • enough • honest • mind • object • quite • will

a To be _____ , I have no idea.
b I _____ agree.
c I've had _____ .
d How do you feel _____ …?
e Anything _____ do.
f Can we go now or do you _____ ?
g You decide where to go. I don't _____ .

2 Read the dialogue in Unit 26 again. Are these statements True or False?

→ **D** Dialog 26

		True	False
a	Peter hasn't seen the play yet.		
b	Peter doesn't like the fight.		
c	Clare wants to go for a drink.		
d	Peter wants to go to the festival.		
e	Peter has been to Edinburgh before.		

3 Listen to the mini-dialogues. Are the second speakers positive, negative or indifferent (*gleich-gültig*) about the suggestions made by the first speakers? Tick (✔) the correct answer.

139

		positive	negative	indifferent
a	Why don't we ask Peter to watch us?			
b	He is an outsider and hasn't seen the play yet.			
c	Just watch and tell us how you like it.			
d	Do you want to watch us perform our play at the festival?			

4 Use the verbs in brackets to complete the conditional Type 2 sentences.

a If the new technology _____ (be) available now, we _____ (be able) to expand the business.

b If we knew what the weather _____ (be like) tomorrow, we _____ (have) a garden party.

c If the Odeon _____ (close) down, there _____ (be) no cinema in town.

d I _____ (go) on holiday tomorrow, if I _____ (have) the money.

e We _____ (buy) the house immediately, if the owner _____ (want) to sell it, but he doesn't.

f I _____ (be) very excited, if I _____ (win) a million Euros.

g If Peter _____ (be) offered a job, he _____ (not have to worry) about money any longer.

h Clare _____ (to fly) to Australia tomorrow to visit her parents, if it _____ (not to be) so far away from the UK.

→ **U** Unit 26.1, → **G** Grammatik 58

5 Conditional 1 or Conditional 2?
Use the verbs in brackets to complete the sentences.

a If Peter _____ (live) in London, all his friends _____ (visit) him. They don't think Manchester is very interesting.

b If you _____ (come) over to my house now, I _____ (help) you with that German letter.

c If he _____ (have) enough money, he _____ fly home to Germany at the weekend, but his trip to London last week was too expensive.

d The next time you _____ (be) in Germany, I _____ (invite) you to come and meet some of my friends.

e If they _____ (practise) a little more, the play _____ (be) perfect, but there is not enough time before the Festival.

f Look, you're tired. If I _____ (be) you, I _____ (stop) now and go home. You can finish that tomorrow morning.

→ **U** Unit 23.1, → **U** Unit 26.1, → **G** Grammatik 58

6 Match the German with the English expressions.

a	Erhebliches Missfallen ausdrücken		**1**	It's not good enough. In fact, it is terrible.
b	Jemanden um seine Meinung/seinen Rat bitten		**2**	I'm quite satisfied with …
c	Uneingeschränkte Zustimmung ausdrücken		**3**	I quite agree.
d	Unzufriedenheit ausdrücken		**4**	What do you think of …
e	Sagen, dass man etwas nicht länger machen möchte		**5**	I'm tired of (do)ing …
f	Zufriedenheit ausdrücken		**6**	I've had enough!

27

Booking a hotel room

- Am Telefon II (beruflich)
- Indirekte Aufforderungen/Bitten
- Indirekte Fragen II

Am Telefon II (beruflich)

Before the call

1 Plan what you are going to say.

> Make a note of what you want to say and you will remember to look for all the words you need before you make the call. Then you can listen carefully to what the other person has to say and react in an appropriate way, without stopping to look for words.

2 Think about what the other person might ask.

> 'Can I get back to on this?'
> 'Have you got any more information about …?'
> 'Could you send me some sales literature?'
> 'Could you put all this in writing?'

During the call

1 Introduce yourself.

> 'Hello, this is …'   'My name is ….   I'm calling from [Winthrops].'

2 Say why you are calling.

> 'I'd like to speak to …'
> 'I'm calling to ask / find out / invite you …'
> 'I'm calling about [our meeting on …].'

3 Say who you are again if the operator puts you through.

> Remember that English speakers often do not give their name when they answer the phone.

4 Remember to be polite. Don't forget to say 'please' and 'thank you'.

> 'Could you take a message for me, please?'
> 'Could you put me through to the [human resources manager], please?'

5 If you have a lot to say, warn your listener.

> 'Have you got a couple of minutes?'
> 'I'd like to ask you a few questions about […].'

6 Finish politely.

> 'Thank you for your help / time.'   'Is this a good time to call?'

Telefonalphabet

Das folgende Alphabet hilft Ihnen, Ihrem Gesprächspartner die Schreibweise von Wörtern oder Namen unmissverständlich zu vermitteln.
Sagen sie beispielsweise *A for Alpha*.

Alpha • Bravo • Charlie • Delta • Echo • Foxtrot • Golf • Hotel • India • Juliet • Kilo • Lima •
Mike • November • Oscar • Papa • Romeo • Sierra • Tango • Uniform • Victor • Whiskey •
X-ray • Yankee • Zulu

1 Aufforderungen/Bitten in indirekter Rede

Aufforderungen und Bitten drückt man in indirekter Rede mit dem *to*-Infinitiv aus. Als einleitende Verben werden z. B. *tell* (für Aufforderungen), *ask* (für Bitten), und *invite* (für Angebote) verwendet:

"Please call me Jack"   He invited him **to call** him Jack.
"Please put your helmet on now."   He told him **to put** his helmet on *(immediately)*.
"Come to the front of the plane, please."   She asked Mr Hoffman **to come** to the front of the plane.

→ **G** Grammatik 60

2 Indirekte Fragen II

Briten ziehen es meistens vor, indirekte Fragen zu stellen.
Dies gilt als ausgesprochen höflich. Beachten Sie dabei die Wortstellung:

What is the time? Can/Could you tell me what the time is?
Can you help me? – I wonder if you could help me.
When are you coming tomorrow? – I wanted to know when you are coming tomorrow.

→ **U** Unit 21.3

ÜBUNGEN

1 Complete the dialogue.

142

Reservations. Jo speaking. How may I help you?

a My name is Jackson. _____? (14 July)
Yes, Mr Jackson, we have rooms available. Would you like a single or a double room?

b _____. (👫👫)
Do you prefer a bath or a shower?

c _____. (shower)
So that is one double room for the 14th July with a shower. How would you like to pay?

d _____. (Eurocard?)
Yes, we accept Eurocard. What is the number, please?

e _____. (593 876 4218)
Thank you.

2 Listen to the dialogue. Are the following statements True or False?

143

		True	False
a	The man wants a room for 30th May.		
b	He asks for a double room.		
c	He would prefer a room with shower.		
d	He wants to pay by cheque.		
e	His credit card number is 593 876 4218.		

3 Match the questions and answers.

a	Can you recommend anywhere to eat?		1	Yes, I do. It's just along here.
b	Do you know where I can find the art gallery?		2	Yes, here it is. 596732.
c	Do you think all the hotels are full at this time of the year?		3	Yes, why don't you try the new French restaurant. It is really good.
d	Can I book a single room for the 24th August, please?		4	I'm not sure, but why don't you try the Tourist Board. They should know.
e	I can't understand this letter. What shall I do?		5	Why don't you ask Peter for help? He speaks German.
f	Do you have their telephone number by any chance?		6	Yes, that is no problem.

4 Complete the sentences with the following words.

booking • calling • minute • might • official • speaking

a Just a _____ , please.
b Reception. Betty _____ .
c Who are you _____ ?
d Excuse me, I have a _____ for tonight.
e They _____ be able to help you.
f Are you here on an _____ visit or a private one?

5 Can you rewrite this dialogue to make it more polite?

Winthrops Ltd.
How can I help you?

– Give me Mr Black.
a _____ .

Just one moment, I'll put you through.

– What?
b _____ .

I'm connecting you with Mr Black.

– Huh?
c _____ .

Hold the line, please. I'm sorry, but he's on another line. Will you wait or call back?

– Mr Black ring me back.
d _____ ?

I'll put you through to his secretary. She'll take a message.

– All right.
e _____ .

→ **Ⓤ** Unit Unit 27.2

6 Make suggestions in the form of questions in response to the answers.

a _____ ?
Yes, you are right. I should try a Scottish dish when I am in Edinburgh.

b _____ ?
No, I don't think you will need a coat. It is quite warm today.

c _____ .
Yes, you are right, we had better make a reservation for a table because that restaurant is always very busy.

d _____ .
Yes, let's visit all the sights while we are here.

e _____ ?
No, I don't think we will need our passports in Scotland.

7 Complete the sentences with the correct word.

a They might be able to _____ you the best way to the station.
   help   tell   say   speak

b That is _____ the festival and all hotels are fully booked.
   during   at   in   on

c Can you _____ any other hotels?
   say me   tell me   recommend   make

d One moment, please, I will _____ you through.
   put   connect   direct   pass

e I am sorry, but we are completely _____ out during the festival.
   full   reserved   booked   busy

8 Say what they want to know or what they want people to do.

a Paula: "Are you coming tomorrow, Peter?"
Paula wants to know _____.

b John: "When do you arrive?"
John asked Peter _____.

c Angela: "Would you get me a cup of coffee, please, Peter."
Angela asked Peter _____.

d Policeman: "What's your name?"
The policeman wanted to know _____.

e Receptionist: "Could you please repeat your name."
The receptionist asked the guest _____.

f Secretary: "Who is calling?"
The secretary wanted to know _____.

g Teacher: "Put the books on the desk, Anne."
The teacher told Anne _____.

→ **U** Unit 21.3, → **U** Unit 27.2, → **G** Grammatik 60

9 Match the German with the English expressions.

a	Jemanden am Telefon verbinden		**1**	How may I help you?
b	Eine Hotelreservierung machen		**2**	Do you think that would be possible?
c	Sagen, dass Sie eine Unterkunft suchen		**3**	Could I ask you a favour?
d	Fragen, ob etwas möglich ist		**4**	I would like to make a booking for the …, please.
e	Jemandem höflich Ihre Hilfe/Dienste anbieten		**5**	What shall I do?
f	Jemanden um einen Gefallen bitten		**6**	I am looking for accommodation.
g	Jemanden um eine Empfehlung bitten		**7**	Can you recommend …?
h	Jemanden um einen Rat bitten		**8**	Just a moment, I will put you through.
i	Sich am Telefon melden		**9**	854 386. Peter Berg speaking.

28

Hiring a car

- *future continuous*
- Autofahren in Großbritannien

1 *future continuous* (Verlaufsform des Futurs)

Das *future continuous* verwendet man, um sich höflich nach jemandes Absichten oder Plänen zu erkündigen:

> *Will you be paying by credit card or in cash?*

Diese Form wird auch für Handlungen oder Vorgänge verwendet, die zu einem bestimmten Zeitpunkt in der Zukunft im Verlauf sein werden:

> *We will be talking to Mr Jackson tomorrow.*
> *I will be visiting Natalie all next weekend.*

Diese Form kann auch verwendet werden, um über Handlungen und Vorgänge zu sprechen, die zwangsläufig passieren werden:

> *I will be seeing Jack tomorrow at work.*

Das *future continuous* wird gebildet mit *will* + *be* + *-ing*-Form.

→ **G** Grammatik 38

 Autofahren in Großbritannien

Autofahren in Großbritannien gilt bei den meisten Besuchern aus dem kontinentalen Europa als interessant und die Umstellung auf Linksverkehr fällt den meisten nicht (so) schwer. Trotzdem möchten wir hier einige Ratschläge geben.

Linksverkehr
In Großbritannien wird links gefahren, nicht rechts wie sonst in Europa. Achtung bei Kreisverkehr und Weiterfahrt nach einer kurzen Parkpause! Man gewöhnt sich aber erstaunlich schnell an den Linksverkehr.

Geschwindigkeitsbegrenzungen
Die Geschwindigkeitsbegrenzungen liegen in Städten bei 30 Meilen pro Stunde (mph) (= 48 km/h), auf Landstraßen bei 60 mph (= 97 km/h) und auf Autobahnen darf man höchstens 70 mph (= 113 km/h) fahren. Übrigens: Entfernungen und Geschwindigkeit werden noch in Meilen bzw. Meilen pro Stunde gemessen.

Zebrastreifen

Auf gekennzeichneten Überwegen haben die Fußgänger absoluten Vorrang. Sie werden also feststellen, dass britische Fußgänger einfach draufloslaufen.

Kreisverkehr

In Großbritannien gibt es sehr viel Kreisverkehr. Fast jede Kreuzung ist ein Kreisverkehr, der in England als *roundabout* bezeichnet wird. Auch bei kleineren Kreuzungen ist der Verkehr oft durch einen Kreisverkehr geregelt, der meist nur aus einem Punkt mit einem halben Meter Durchmesser besteht, der einfach auf die Straße gemalt wurde. Im Kreisverkehr hat immer der von rechts Kommende Vorfahrt, also der, der sich im Kreisverkehr befindet.

Hecken

Besonders in ländlichen Gebieten findet man entlang der Straße viele Hecken. Die Hecken befinden sich direkt neben der Straße und sind zwischen einem und drei Meter hoch.
Für diejenigen, die mit einem Auto fahren, in dem sich das Lenkrad auf der linken Seite befindet, ergibt sich oft ein Problem. Der Fahrer sitzt auf der linken Seite und das Auto fährt auf der linken Straßenseite; der Fahrer befindet sich also ganz außen auf der Straße. Wenn kurz hinter einer Kurve ein Auto steht oder ein Kreisverkehr kommt, dann sieht der Fahrer dies erst ganz spät, weil seine Sicht durch die Hecken eingeschränkt ist. Hier ist man oft auf die Hilfe eines Beifahrers angewiesen.

Infos zur britischen Straßenverkehrsordnung liefert *http://www.dft.gov.uk/pgr/roadsafety/drs/highwaycode*.
Allgemeine Informationen zu Großbritannien finden Sie unter *http://ukingermany.fco.gov.uk/de/about-uk/visitinguk/uk-facts-figures*

ÜBUNGEN

1 Put the sentences of this dialogue in the right order.

a	What can you recommend?	
b	It is £64.80 per day.	
c	What is the charge?	
d	I would like to hire a car.	
e	Fine. I will take that.	
f	I would recommend type C.	
g	What type of car would you like?	

2 Which words are hiding here?

a M O C E R E M D N _____
b G I L A M E E _____
c P A C E C T _____
d R E H G A C _____
e R I N E S A U N C _____

3 Put in the correct words.

a I would like to _____ a bike for the weekend, please.

1 hire
2 take
3 buy
4 sell

b Normally it _____ £64.80 per day.

1 rates
2 charges
3 costs
4 prices

c If you could just _____ here, please.

1 sign
2 write
3 underwrite
4 read

d We have a special weekend _____.

1 prices
2 rate
3 cost
4 money

e Does that _____ mileage?

1 have
2 count
3 take
4 include

f Would you like to pay _____ cash?

1 by
2 with
3 in
4 through

4 Listen please and tick (✓) the correct box to say if the the following statements are True or False.

146

		True	False
a	He wants to change his reservation.		
b	His name is Jack Porter.		
c	He cannot find his reservation number.		
d	He wants a smaller car.		
e	There will be six people with Mr Porter.		
f	He takes an estate car.		
g	The charge for a big car is £95 per day.		
h	He calls more than 48 hours before hiring the car.		

5 Ask questions matching the given answers.

147

a _____?

Well, I recommend type C, because it is a more comfortable car.

b _____?

Yes, that is right. I need to see your driving licence.

c _____?

Yes, that does include mileage.

d _____?

No, I'm sorry we don't accept cheques.

e _____?

The car will be ready on Friday at 5 p.m.

f _____?

Yes, of course you can. Just sign here, please.

→ **G** Grammatik 49, → **G** Grammatik 50, → **G** Grammatik 52

6 Hans wants to visit Peter but Peter has lots of excuses (*Ausreden*) when Hans calls him so that he won't have to see him. Complete the sentences using the excuses Peter has written down with the verbs in the future continuous.

Monday:	Write some letters in German for Mr Jackson.
Tuesday:	Help Jim home from hospital and cook him dinner.
Wednesday:	Read and check a report for headquarters.
Thursday:	Help paint the props for the play.
Friday:	Take part in the dress rehearsal (*Generalprobe*) for the play.
Saturday:	Do my washing at the launderette.
Sunday:	Have dinner at Jack's house.

Hans: Hi, Peter. It's me, Hans. Did you get my e-mail?
Peter: Yes, I did, but I'm afraid I'll be very busy that week.
Hans: Oh, really? What are you doing on Monday?
Peter: On Monday I **(a)** _____ some letters in German for Mr Jackson.
Hans: I see. And what are your plans for Tuesday?
Peter: On Tuesday I **(b)** _____ Jim home from hospital and cooking him dinner.
Hans: Aha. And what about Wednesday?
Peter: On Wednesday I **(c)** _____ a report for headquarters.
Hans: You really work too much. And are you busy on Thursday?
Peter: I'm afraid so. On Thursday I **(d)** _____ paint the props for the play.
Hans: Oh, I didn't know you were doing anything in theatre. But on Friday you must be able to see me …

Peter: Not really. You see, on Friday I (**e**) _____ part in the dress rehearsal *(Generalprobe)* for the play and then on Saturday I finally (**f**) _____ my washing at the launderette.

Hans: Don't tell me you are not free on Sunday either?

Peter: Well, 'No', actually, Hans, but I am not free because Jack and his wife have invited me over and I (**g**) _____ dinner at Jack's house. I am awfully sorry, but I won't have time for you during the week you plan to visit Manchester.

Hans: Oh, alright then. Maybe I can go and visit Martin. He's staying in London, which is probably more exciting than Manchester anyway.

→ **G** Grammatik 38

7 Match the German with the English expressions.

a	Jemanden bitten, seinen Führerschein zu zeigen		**1**	Do you accept (Eurocards)?
b	Sagen, dass Sie etwas mieten möchten		**2**	What can you recommend?
c	Fragen, was genau jemand haben möchte		**3**	May I see your driving licence, please?
d	Um eine Empfehlung bitten		**4**	I would like to hire a … for …
e	Etwas empfehlen		**5**	What type of (car) would you like?
f	Fragen, welches Zahlungsmittel akzeptiert wird		**6**	I would recommend …
g	Fragen, was die Gebühr für etwas ist		**7**	What is the charge for …?
h	Einem Vorschlag zustimmen		**8**	OK, that sounds fine.

29

The breakdown

- *let*
- Frageanhängsel
- Autoteile/Autopanne

1 *let*

Let bedeutet ‚lassen' im Sinne von ‚zulassen':

> *Let me have a look.*
> *Let me see.*

Let us (Lasst uns) wird häufig verwendet, um Vorschläge zu machen. Die Kurzform *let's* ist gebräuchlicher als die Langform *let us*:

> *Let's go to the cinema.*

2 Frageanhängsel

In der Umgangssprache werden Feststellungen häufig kurze Fragen angehängt, die inhaltlich dem deutschen **nicht wahr?** oder **oder?** ähnlich sind. Zur Bildung eines solchen Frageanhängsels *(question tag)* werden das erste Hilfsverb des Aussagesatzes + Personalpronomen verwendet. Enthält der Satz kein Hilfsverb, wird *do*, *does* oder *did* verwendet. Es handelt sich hier aber nicht um eine Frage, sondern um eine Aufforderung zur Zustimmung oder wenn man aus Unsicherheit nachfragen will.

Wenn der Aussagesatz positiv ist, ist das Frageanhängsel negativ.
Das Frageabhängsel für *I am* ist *aren't I.*

> *I'm right,* **aren't I?**
> *It's a nice room,* **isn't it?**
> *Peter and Jack are playing squash,* **aren't they?**
> *You had better pay attention,* **hadn't you?**
> *It looks as though the fan belt has broken,* **doesn't it?**

Wenn der Aussagesatz negativ ist, ist das Frageanhängsel positiv.

> *You haven't seen Jack,* **have you?**
> *Peter isn't coming,* **is he?**
> *Suzie can't play squash,* **can she?**
> *Peter and Jack didn't play squash yesterday,* **did they?**

In den obigen Fällen erwartet der Sprecher Zustimmung. Deshalb ist es keine echte Frage und die Satzmelodie fällt am Ende des Frageanhängsels:

> Peter and Jack didn't play squash yesterday, **did they?**

Nach *let's* + Infinitiv (ohne *to*), um einen Vorschlag zu machen, kann als Frageanhängsel *shall we* angefügt werden.

> Let's go and see Suzie, **shall we?**

Im letzten Fall dient das Frageanhängsel einem anderen Zweck. Hier geht es um einen Vorschlag, daher steigt die Satzmelodie:

> Let's go and see Suzie, **shall we?**

→ **G** Grammatik 48

3 Autoteile und Autopanne

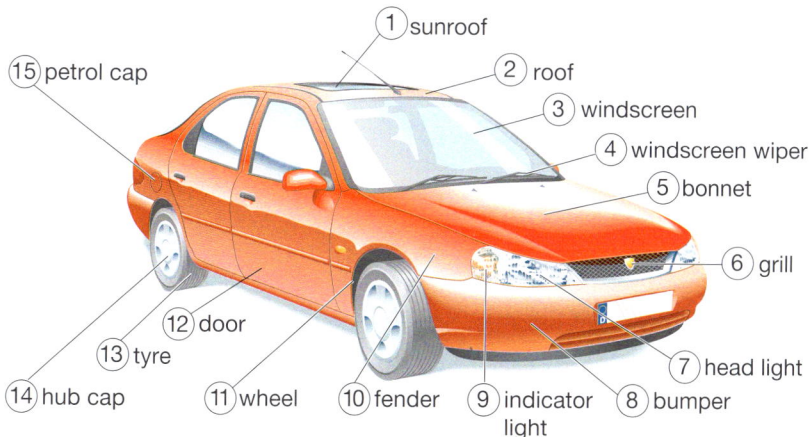

1 sunroof
2 roof
3 windscreen
4 windscreen wiper
5 bonnet
6 grill
7 head light
8 bumper
9 indicator light
10 fender
11 wheel
12 door
13 tyre
14 hub cap
15 petrol cap

Wenn Sie in Großbritannien eine Autopanne haben, könnten Ihnen folgende Ausdrücke helfen, wenn Sie Hilfe brauchen:

There seems to be a problem with the …

starter	Anlasser	*turbocharger*	Turbolader
battery	Batterieprobleme	*anti-theft device*	Wegfahrsperre
dynamo / alternator	Generator	*spark plugs*	Zündkerzen
clutch	Kupplung	*spark coil*	Zündspule
filter	Partikelfilter		

ÜBUNGEN

1 Complete the sentences with the correct words.

a I can _____ a strange noise coming from the engine.
see   listen   hear   notice

b Look there is a _____ for the next service station.
sign   poster   information   crossing

c I will _____ her up while we are waiting.
put   charge   fill   make

d Could you please _____ the tyres?
look   see   fill   check

e Don't forget to _____ your lights on.
put   see   make   take

2 Complete the sentences with the correct form of the verb *to have*.

a I _____ an idea.
b We _____ better stop and ask for directions.
c Oh, dear! The glass _____ broken.
d Let me _____ a look.
e I _____ filled her up, but I _____ better check the oil before we leave.
f I'm not sure, but I think I _____ some in my bag.

→ **G** Grammatik 24, → **G** Grammatik 31, → **G** Grammatik 39

3 Word order

a reserve, had, a, I, better, room _____ .

b oil, better, we, some, buy, had _____ .

c idea, has, a, he, good _____ .

d opportunity, use, fill up, will, car, I, the, and, the _____ .

e service, better, next, had, stop, we, station, at, the _____ .

4 Complete the sentences with the right word.

a I could _____ your radio if you want.		**c** We'd better _____ the AA.
1 see		**1** speak
2 fix		**2** talk
3 fill up		**3** call
4 mechanic		**4** phoning

b Put your bag in the _____ of the car.

1 case

2 door

3 suitcase room

4 boot

d Look, the warning light _____ come on.

1 have

2 has

3 had

4 haven't

5 Ask questions about the <u>underlined</u> words.

150

a _____ ? Yes, I am wearing <u>blue jeans</u>.

b _____ ? Yes, please <u>fill her</u> up.

c _____ ? No, thanks, the <u>tyres</u> don't need <u>checking</u>.

d _____ ? It takes unleaded <u>petrol</u>.

e _____ ? The <u>toilets</u> are over there.

f _____ ? Yes, I think you <u>had better stop</u>.

→ **G** Grammatik 50, → **G** Grammatik 52

6 Read the dialogue in Unit 29 again. Are these statements are True or False?

→ **D** Dialog 29

		True	False
a	Peter stops the car because there is a strange noise coming from the engine.		
b	They decide to call the AA.		
c	Clare is wearing stockings which she takes off to fix the fan belt.		
d	A mechanic at the service station fills the car up with petrol.		
e	Sam buys some oil for the car.		
f	Clare goes to the toilet.		
g	Henry checks the tyres.		

7 Listen to the dialogue and circle the words you hear.

151

broken   motorway   engine fan belt

       call   street   warning

member   noise   smoke   petrol station

139

8   Match the sentences with the correct question tags.

a	The police arrested him,		1	will you?
b	Let's go to the Edinburgh Festival,		2	doesn't she?
c	Don't drive on the right side of the road,		3	did they?
d	There wasn't a free hotel room left,		4	didn't they?
e	We've seen Edinburgh Castle,		5	didn't it?
f	Clare hates haggis,		6	was there?
g	The car broke down,		7	haven't we?
h	They didn't have a pub lunch,		8	shall we?

9   Offer to help or suggest what you could do using *Let* or *Let's*.

a   You want to go to the theatre with your friends. _____ .
b   You tell your friend that you want to finish the job. _____ .
c   You suggest having lunch in town. _____ .
d   You want to buy Natalie a drink. _____ .
e   You think you and Peter should go to London by coach. _____ .
f   Offer to help an old lady across the street. _____ .

→ **U** Unit 29.1

10   Complete the sentences with the correct question tag.

a   There is a strange noise coming from the engine, _____?
b   The warning light has come on, _____?
c   You had better let me have a look at the engine, _____?
d   I had better put on the warning lights, _____?
e   Clare, you haven't got a pair of stockings, _____?
f   OK, I'll see if there is a mechanic around, _____?

→ **U** Unit 29.2, → **G** Grammatik 48

11   Match the German with the English expressions.

a	Jemandem einen Rat geben		1	That was a great idea of yours.
b	Sagen, dass jemand wohl recht hat		2	Oh, don't mention it.
c	Jemanden loben		3	You had better …
d	Sagen, dass etwas nicht der Rede Wert ist		4	I could fix the fan belt. We could drive to the next garage. You could check the tyres.
e	Etwas vorschlagen		5	I think you are right.
f	Einen Grund angeben		6	… because the warning light has come on.

30

At Winthrops' subsidiary

- Passiv
- Maße und Gewichte
- *also, too; so; neither, not either; neither… nor*

1 Das Passiv

Das Passiv verwendet man am häufigsten, um das Objekt des Aktivverbs zu betonen:

> They built **the machine** in Manchester.
>
> **The machine** was built in Manchester

Das Passiv wird auch verwendet, wenn es als unwichtig erachtet wird, wer etwas gemacht hat:

> We made it here. → It was made here

Im ersten Aktivsatz stehen die handelnden Personen im Vordergrund, im zweiten Passivsatz der Gegenstand, der produziert wird.

Formen des Passivs

Das Passiv wird gebildet aus einer Form von **be** + Partizip Perfekt (**-ed**-Form des Verbs).
Für die Verwendung der Zeitformen gelten die gleichen Regeln wie im Aktiv.

Infinitiv:	Nothing **is to be seen**.
simple present:	600 people **are employed** here.
present continuous:	The machines **are being built** in Manchester.
simple past:	The plans **were drawn up** by an engineer here in Scotland.
past continuous:	The number of staff **was being cut back**.
present perfekt:	The engineers **have been asked** to draw up new plans.
Mit modalen Hilfsverben:	More people **should be employed** at the Manchester plant.
(*could, should, must, can* etc.)	

→ **G** Grammatik 61

 Maße und Gewichte

Die angloamerikanischen Maßsysteme werden nach wie vor in vielen Länder verwendet: z. B. im Vereinigten Königreich, in den USA, in Irland, Kanada, Indien, Malaysia, Australien und Neuseeland. Großbritannien hatte sich zwar 1973 verpflichtet, das Imperiale Maßsystem zugunsten des metrischen Systems aufzugeben, aber die Umstellung auf das metrische System stieß in Großbritannien auf großen Widerstand. So sind die Maßeinheiten des Imperialen Systems nach wie vor weit verbreitet, vor allem im normalen Umgang unter den Bürgern.

Beispiele für wichtige und häufig verwendete Maßeinheiten der angloamerikanischen Maßsysteme sind Zoll: (*inch*), Fuß (*foot*), Schritt (*yard*), Meile (*mile*), Seemeile (*nautical mile*), Unze (*ounce*), Pfund (*pound*), Stein (*stone*), Flüssigunze (*fluid ounce*), Pint (*pint*), Quart (*quart*), Gallone (*gallon*). Benzin wird in den USA als *gas* in *gallons* verkauft, in Großbritannien als *petrol* offiziell in Liter, umgangssprachlich aber noch in *gallons* und die Briten kaufen ihr Bier immer noch in *(half) pints*. Entfernungen werden noch in *miles* angegeben.

Längenmaße

		1 inch (in.)	= 2,54 cm
12 inches	=	1 foot (ft.)	= 30,48 cm
3 feet	=	1 yard (yd.)	= 0,914 m
1,760 yards	=	1 mile	= 1,609 km

Flächenmaße

		1 square inch	= 6,452 cm²
144 square inches	=	1 square foot	= 929,03 cm²
9 square feet	=	1 square yard	= 0,836 m²
4,840 square yards	=	1 acre	= 0,405 ha
640 acres	=	1 square mile	= 2,59 km² / 259 ha

Raummaße

	1 cubic inch	= 16,4 cm³	
1,728 cubic inches	= 1 cubic foot	= 0,028 m³
27 cubic feet	= 1 cubic yard	= 0,764 m³

Hohlmaße

4 gills	= 1 pint (pt.) (1.201 US pints)	= 0,568 l
2 pints	= 1 quart (qt.) (1.201 US quarts)	= 1,136 l
4 quarts	= 1 gallon (gal.) (1.201 US gallons)	= 4,546 l

> **Merke:**
> Dezimalzahlen in Englisch werden mit einem Punkt und nicht mit einem Komma versehen!
> Kommas setzt man bei Tausendern, z.B. 10,000 = (deutsch) 10.000.

Einen ausführlichen Überblick über die gängigen Maßeinheiten liefert Wikipedia:
http://de.wikipedia.org/wiki/Angloamerikanisches_Maßsystem

2 also, too; so; neither, not either; neither … nor

In der Regel steht **also** (auch) vor dem Verb:

The cheapest way is by coach,	→	Der billigste Möglichkeit ist mit dem Reisebus,
*but it **also** takes longest.*		aber das dauert **auch** am längsten.

Das deutsche ‚ebenfalls' in einer Kurzantwort entspricht dem englischen **so**:

*I like Indian food. – **So** do I.*	→	Ich ebenfalls.

Im Gegensatz zum deutschen ‚auch' steht **too** immer am Satzende:

Jack is nice and Suzie is		
*very nice, **too**.*	→	… und Suzie ist **auch** sehr nett.

Die Verneinung von *too* lautet **neither** oder **not either** (auch nicht):

I don't like Chinese food. –		
***Neither** do I. / I don't **either**.*	→	Ich auch nicht.

Zwei Verneinungen lassen sich wie im Deutschen mit **neither … nor** (weder … noch) zusammenfassen:

*We had **neither** the building*	→	Wir hatten **weder … noch …**
*materials **nor** the capacity.*		
***Neither** I **nor** Jack like Chinese food.*	→	**Weder** ich **noch** Jack …

ÜBUNGEN

1 Read the dialogue in Unit 30 again. Are the statements True or False?

› **D** Dialog 30

		True	False
a	Mr Black is the Regional Manager for Great Britain.		
b	The plant has about 1600 workers.		
c	It is bigger than Peter had expected.		
d	The company used to make the Super 8 machine.		
e	The company used to be a lot smaller.		
f	One of the engineers went to Germany.		

2 Word order

a managed, idea, come, we, to, up, an, with

_____.

b situation, companies, same, many, are, in, the

_____.

c showing, giving, around, you, me, time, me, thank, for, up, your, me, and, for

_____.

d expected, had, I, bigger, it, than, is

_____.

e should, a, been, ago, you, have, here, few, years

_____.

f because of, rationalise, costs, we, had, to

_____.

3 Crossword Puzzle

a The past tense of _draw_.
b The farm … more than ten acres.
c Mr Black is … Peter the plant.
d Another word for _great_.
e When you have to produce less and/or lose staff.
f He / She tells people what to do in a company.
g A lot.
h If a country exports a lot, it usually has a healthy …

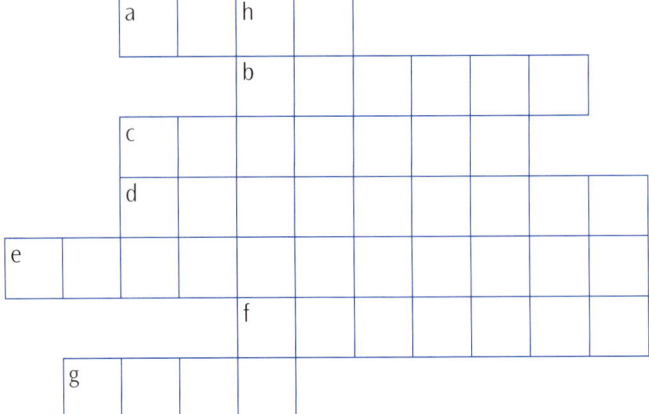

4 Listen to the dialogue. <u>Underline</u> the words that are wrong.
Write the correct word on the line.

154

Duncan: I should really show you the plant first. _____
Peter: That would be very kind of you. _____
Duncan: We used to have a subsidiary in Newcastle with 700 workers. _____
Peter: Wow! That is very big. _____
Duncan: Well, it was, but we had to rationalise and so we closed Newcastle. _____
Peter: Ah, I see. _____

Now listen to the dialogue between Duncan and Peter again.
Check your answers and then take Peter's role.

5 Complete the sentences below with the Imperial measurements. Then match the Imperial measurements with the metric measurements.

20 US gallons • 172 acres • 6 US quarts • 115 yds x 75 yds / 8,625 square yards •
29,029 ft • 1.7 miles • 40 pints

a Mount Everest is _____ high
b The Golden Gate Bridge is _____ long.
c My car takes about _____ .
d The average American adult drinks about _____ of milk a week,
e I think the average Englishman drinks about _____ of beer a month.
f By the mid-1970s the average *(durchschnittlich)* farm in England and Wales was _____ .
g Fifa recommends the following size for international football fields: _____ long and
_____ wide. That makes _____ .

1 ≈ 75.70 litres = _____
2 8,848 m = _____
3 2.7 km = _____
4 ≈ 19 litres = _____
5 ≈ 696,059 m^2 = _____
6 ≈ 105 m x 68,5 m = _____
7 7,212 m^2 = _____
8 ≈ 6.8 litres = _____

Auf dieser Webseite finden Sie mehr zu metrischen und imperialen Maßeinheiten:
http://www.metric-conversions.org/length/yards-to-meters.htm

6 Change the following active sentences into passive sentences.

a They finished the plans six months ago.

_____ .

b The engineers were designing plans for a new machine.

_____ .

c They send the building materials from Manchester to the plant in Scotland.

_____ .

d Management have told the engineers they must cut costs.

_____ .

e   Winthrops will open the new factory next year.

_____ .

f   They cannot do anything about the problem.

_____ .

g   We are telling everyone to be careful.

_____ .

→ **U** Unit 30.1, → **G** Grammatik 61

7   Make one sentence out of the two sentences using *also, too, so, neither, not … either* or *neither … nor*.

a   Peter doesn't like Chinese food. Natalie doesn't like Chinese food.
Peter doesn't like Chinese food and _____ .
Peter doesn't like Chinese food and _____ .
_____ .

b   Peter likes squash. Jack likes squash.
Peter likes squash and _____ .
Peter likes squash and _____ .
Peter likes squash and _____ .

c   I don't speak Spanish. Jack doesn't speak Spanish.
I don't speak Spanish and _____ .
I don't speak Spanish and _____ .
_____ .

d   Mr Jackson likes Indian food. Mrs Jackson likes Indian food.
Mr Jackson likes Indian food and _____ .
Mr Jackson likes Indian food and _____ .
Mr Jackson likes Indian food and _____ .

→ **U** Unit 30.2

8   Match the German with the English expressions.

a	Sich bei jemandem bedanken, der sich für Sie Zeit genommen hat		**1**	I didn't realise …
b	Sagen, dass es Ihnen ein Vergnügen war		**2**	Thanks for giving up your time.
c	Ihr Verständnis ausdrücken		**3**	We had neither the (building materials) nor the (capacity).
d	Sagen, dass Ihnen etwas nicht bewusst war		**4**	It's a pleasure.
e	Sagen, dass Sie weder das eine noch das hatten		**5**	I understand.

31

The spy is spotted

- E-Mails (beruflich)
- Telefon
- Twitter
- Videokonferenz
- Instant Messaging
- SMS

1 E-Mails (beruflich)

- **Betreff** (*Subject*)**:** Geben Sie immer genau an, worum es in Ihrer E-Mail geht.
- **Länge:** Lieber längere E-Mails mit sämtlichen Informationen, als mehrere kürzere E-Mails, die die Informationen stückweise übermitteln.
- **Format:** Aufzählungszeichen und ausreichender Platz dazwischen, um das Lesen zu erleichtern.
- **Anlage** (*Attachment*)**:** Nicht vergessen anzuhängen, wenn sie in der E-Mail erwähnt ist!
- Warten Sie ein paar Tage, bevor Sie ein Erinnerungsschreiben schicken – lassen Sie Ihrem Geschäftspartner Zeit, eine (angemessene) Antwort zu geben.

2 Twitter

Ein hervorragendes Marketing-Mittel, sowohl um Ihre Produkte und Dienstleistungen bekannt zu machen als auch um Kontakt aufrechtzuerhalten. Achten Sie aber darauf, dass das, was Sie *tweeten*, wirklich nützlich ist und vergessen Sie dabei nicht, dass Sie an einem informellen Gespräch teilnehmen. Bitte kein marktschreierisches Getue!

Ihre *Tweets* sollen nicht nur Ihre Produkte vermarkten, Sie sollen auch Fragen beantworten, nützliche Tipps und Informationen usw. enthalten.
- *Tweeten* Sie keine banalen oder uninteressanten Inhalte.
- Begrenzen Sie die Anzahl Ihrer Tweets. Zu viele tägliche Mitteilungen können dazu führen, dass Ihre wichtigen Bekanntmachungen oder Informationen verlorengehen.
- Lernen Sie *txt language* sowie gängige Abkürzungen für häufig verwendete Wörter.
- Falls Sie Text weiterleiten, machen Sie den Empfänger darauf aufmerksam.
- Heben Sie Informationen von anderen hervor und leiten Sie sie weiter, um die Kommunikation in Gang zu halten.

3 Instant Messaging (IM)

IM ist das schnellste Kommunikationsmittel überhaupt (abgesehen vom Telefon oder direkten Gespräch).

- Beim IM nicht vergessen, dass Ihr Partner womöglich gleichzeitig über andere Medien *(multitasking)* kommuniziert – Telefon, Skype, – oder aber zzt. gar nicht am Arbeitsplatz ist und nicht sofort antworten kann.
- Vergessen Sie nicht, sich zu verabschieden, bevor Sie sich abmelden oder abschalten. Ausdrücke, die Ihre Absicht kundtun, sind z. B. *Nice chatting, will catch up later* oder *Need to go – will speak later.*

4 Telefon

Telefonieren ist oft effektiver als hunderte von E-Mails. Sie haben die volle Aufmerksamkeit Ihres Gesprächspartners und ein Telefongespräch ist ideal für Problemlösungen. Hilfe bei Verständigungsschwierigkeiten finden Sie in → **U** Unit 27.

5 Videokonferenz (Skype)

Noch besser als ein Telefongespräch ist natürlich ein Videogespräch oder eine Videokonferenz. Hier können Sie auch Ihren Gesprächspartner sehen und andere Mittel als nur das gesprochene Wort zur Verständigung einsetzen.

6 SMS

Falls Sie mit Englisch sprechenden Kollegen/Kolleginnen zusammenarbeiten, verschicken Sie sicherlich auch SMS-Nachrichten *(text messages)*. Solche Nachrichten können schwer verständlich sein, wenn sie sowohl Symbole als auch Abkürzungen beinhalten. Hier geben wir Ihnen einige Tipps, um solche Mitteilungen verständlicher zu machen:
RU wrkng in biz 2day & txtng? Read this b4 U start. Its 4 NE1 & every1.

Merkmale des *texting* im Englischen

- Anfangsbuchstaben ergeben Abkürzungen
  FYI *(for your information)*
  lol *(laugh out loud / lots of love)*
  brb *(be right back)*
- „Lautmalerei“: Buchstaben oder Zahlen, die wie die Wörter klingen, die sie ersetzen: 4 NE1 *(for anyone)*   2 *(to)* b *(be)*

  Eine Kombinationen der o. a. Merkmale:
  2day *(today)*

- Vokale werden ausgelassen:
  wrkng *(working)*

- Unkonventionelle Rechtschreibung:
  biz *(business)*   coz *(because)*
  wot *(what)*   av *(have)*

Aufpassen bei der Schreibweise

Nicht standardisierte Rechtschreibung ist zwar gang und gäbe beim *texting*, aber Neuschöpfungen müssen leicht erkennbar sein. Zum Beispiel klingt *wot* wie *what*. Andere wie *biz* werden seit langem im Englischen verwendet und sind daher leicht verständlich. Wenn Sie unsicher sind, verwenden Sie lieber die Standardform, besonders dann wenn Sie Personen anschreiben, für die *texting* noch ungewohnt ist.

Gängige Abkürzungen beim *texting*, die auch kleingeschrieben sein können:

AFAIK = as far as I know
ASAP = as soon as possible
B = be
I may b l8 2nite = I may be late tonight
BTW = by the way
B4 = before
C = see
C U 2moro = see you tomorrow
C U L8R = see you later
CID = consider it done
EZ = easy
FWIW = for what it's worth (when you're not sure if the other person is interested in your idea)
FYI = for you information (when you want to say something important)
GR8 = great
IMO = in my opinion (when you give your opinion)
IMHO = in my humble opinion
L8 = late
L8R = later
LOL = laughing out loud (when you want to show that you think something is funny)
LOL = lots of love (used to sign off a text to a friend or family member)
M8 = mate (friend)
msg = message
NE = any

NE1 = anyone
NO1 = no one
OTOH = on the other hand
PLS = please
R = are
where r u? = Where are you?
RUOK? = Are you OK?
RGDS = regards
SPK = speak
SRY = sorry
THNQ = thank you
THX/TX = thanks
U = you
UR = your, you're
U2 = you too
W8 = wait
WAN2 = want to
WRK = work
XLNT = excellent
Y = why
YR = your
1 = one
2 = to, two, too
2day = today
2moro = tomorrow
2nite = tonight
4 = for
4 now = for now
8 (replaces the sound ate)

ÜBUNGEN

1 Mr Black asked Peter a lot of questions about Christian Fauré. Can you report his questions to Jack?

a "Do you know Christian Fauré?"
He wanted to know _____.

b "How long have you known him?"
He asked him _____.

c "Where did you first meet him?"
He wanted to know _____.

d "Have you seen him since you met him on the plane?"
He asked him _____.

e "What was he doing when you last saw him?"
He wanted to know _____.

f "Will you be able to report everything to the police?"
He asked him _____.

2 Listen to the mini-dialogues and take the role of speaker B. Then fill in the missing words.

157

a A: Is this the way to the post office?
B: I'm not _____. Why don't you ask that police officer over there?

b A: So, if you look at these plans, you will see how to construct this machine.
B: I'm not quite sure I _____.

c A: I would like to thank you by presenting you with this computer.
B: I _____ what to say.

3 Word order

a understand, not, I, quite, sure, I'm

_____.

b matter, is, what, the, so

_____?

c I, him, at, Manchester, headquarters, in, Winthrops', saw

_____.

d to say, what, know, I, don't

_____.

e Jack, back, call, the, news, with, let's

_____.

4 Txtng: Please write these texts out in full.

a if U cn read this short msg U av made a gd start.

b AFAIK all my m8s R usng txt msgs in biz.

c NE1 cn learn txtng v quickly. If U WAN2 save time & costs txtng is gr8.

d OTOH U av 2 B careful IMO coz NO1 wants 2 B rude. FWIW I blv more & more PPL wl Uz this in future

e Hi, P where RU? RU OK? WAN2 invite U 2 lunch 2moro. Cn U txt me ASAP if OK?

f Hi J. TX 4 invite. SRY cnt make it 2moro. Cn we spk 2nite? CU L8R P.

5 Match the German with the English expressions.

a	Sagen, dass Sie sprachlos sind		**1**	I'm not quite sure.
b	Eine Folgerung einleiten		**2**	I suspect …
c	Jemanden auffordern, Ihnen etwas zu erzählen		**3**	I don't quite understand.
d	Unsicherheit ausdrücken		**4**	I don't know what to say.
e	Sagen, dass Sie etwas vermuten		**5**	If you are right, then …
f	Sagen, dass Sie etwas nicht ganz verstanden haben		**6**	Tell me, …
g	Sagen, dass etwas möglich wäre		**7**	Let's …
h	Einen Vorschlag machen		**8**	It would/could be possible …

32

Buying a kilt

- **Adverbien der Art und Weise**
- **Adjektiv statt Adverb**
- **Steigerungsformen der Adverbien**
- **Adverbien der Häufigkeit**

1 Adverbien der Art und Weise

Adverbien der Art und Weise werden gebildet, indem man **-ly** an das Adjektiv hängt:

     *usual – usual**ly**   slow – slow**ly**   bad – bad**ly**   serious – serious**ly***

Endet ein Adjektiv auf **-y**, so wird daraus im Adverb **-i**; endet ein Adjektiv auf **-ll**, wird das Adverb ebenfalls mit **-ll** geschrieben:

     *necessary – necessar**ily**   funny – funn**ily**   full – fu**lly***

Wenn das Adjektiv auf **-le** endet, wird **-le** zu **-ly**:

     *terrible – terrib**ly***   **ABER**   *whole – who**lly***

Einige Adverbien haben die gleiche Form und Bedeutung wie das Adjektiv:

     fast – fast   hard – hard

Weitere Wörter dieser Art sind:

     deep (tief), fair, high (hoch), late, right, wide, wrong

> **Merke:**
> Hängt man diesen Adverbien **-ly** an, dann ändert sich ihre Bedeutung:
> Das Wort *hardly* (*That's hardly likely* – → **U** Unit 24) bedeutet nicht ‚hart' sondern ‚kaum':
>   *He works hard.* = Er arbeitet hart.
>   *He hardly works.* = Er arbeitet kaum.

Adjektive, die auf **-ly** enden, z. B. *friendly* (*The landlady is very friendly.* → **G** Grammatik 20, → **U** Unit 8) und *lovely* brauchen eine Umschreibung, wenn sie als Adverb verwendet werden:

     *She spoke **in a friendly way**.*

Für gewöhnlich stehen Adverbien der Art und Weise am Ende des Satzes:

     *He twisted his ankle **badly**.*

Im Gegensatz zum Deutschen stehen sie nie zwischen Verb und Objekt:

     He speaks English perfectly. ⟷ *He ~~speaks perfectly~~ English.*

2 Adjektiv statt Adverb

Nach einigen Ausdrücken verwendet man ein Adjektiv statt Adverb:

That **seems** good. (→ Unit 10)
Yours **looks** safe. (→ Unit 34)
The engine is **getting** hot. (→ Unit 29)
I **feel** good.

3 Steigerungsformen der Adverbien

Adverb	Komparativ	Superlativ
slowly	more slowly (than)	the most slowly
	less slowly (than)	the least slowly
	as slowly as	
funnily	more funnily (than)	the most funnily
	less funnily (than)	the least funnily
	as funnily as	
terribly	more terribly (than)	the most terribly
	less terribly (than)	the least terribly
	as terribly as	

Unregelmäßige Steigerungsformen

Adverb	Komparativ	Superlativ
a little	less	the least
well	better	the best
badly	worse	the worst
much / a lot	more	the most
far	further	furthest

→ **G** Grammatik 19

4 Adverbien der Häufigkeit

Adverbien der Häufigkeit besagen, wie oft etwas geschieht.

He **always** goes to work at 7.45.
I have **never** seen anything like that before.

Diese Adverbien bilden eine Art Skala,
von **nie** bis **immer**: → **G** Grammatik 21

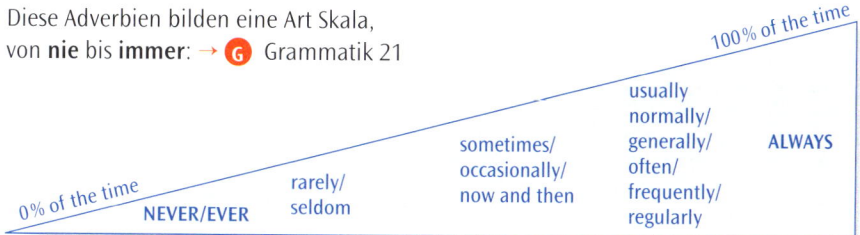

Übungen

160

1 Ask what these things cost and then answer the questions.

Example: How much is that hat? (hat, £30)
– It is £30.

a _____? (coat, £95)
_____.

b _____? (pullover, £69)
_____.

c _____? (blanket, £55)
_____.

d _____? (skirt, £35.90)
_____.

e _____? (blazer, £183.50)
_____.

→ **G** Grammatik 4, → **G** Grammatik 52

2 Match the questions on the left with the answers on the right.

a	So, what would you like to do?	1	Yes, there is one on the corner.
b	Have you any other colours?	2	I take size 38 in Germany.
c	What size do you take?	3	No, sorry only in sizes 14 and 16.
d	Do you have those blue jeans in size 12?	4	Why don't we go to the pub?
e	Would you like to try it on?	5	Yes, we have some in orange.
f	Are there any shops here that sell traditional Scottish products?	6	Yes, please. Where are the changing rooms?

3 Underline the expressions that do not go with the others

a	I thought of …	You could …	That will be …	Perhaps we …
b	size	colour	length	height
c	about	just	almost	quite
d	buy	shop	customer	waiter
e	speak	listen	go	write

4 Read the dialogue in Unit 32 again. Are the statements True or False?

> **D** Dialog 32

		True	False
a	Clare wants to buy a kilt.		
b	It is Peter's birthday soon.		
c	The shop assistant tries the kilt on.		
d	Peter buys a kilt.		
e	There are many different colours and patterns for kilts.		
f	Clare is as tall as Peter's mother.		

5 Listen to the dialogue. Are the statements True or False?

161

		True	False
a	The present is for a man.		
b	The man wants to spend no more than £75.		
c	He thinks a sweater is a good idea.		
d	The man doesn't try the sweater on.		
e	The shop assistant recommends a bigger size.		
f	The second sweater fits perfectly.		
g	He doesn't buy the sweater. It is too expensive.		
h	The sweater costs £80.		

6 Adjective or adverb? Are the underlined words in the sentence right or wrong? If they are wrong, write the correct form of the word on the line.

a Jack plays tennis very good. _____

b The last scene of the play was terribly. _____

c It does not necessary mean it is important. _____

d He doesn't usual come at this time. _____

e That is not wholly true. _____

f Funnily enough, Jack also knows Martina Glass. _____

g Mr Jackson works hardly. He is in the office every day from 8 a.m.–6 p.m. _____

h He spoke to Peter friendly. _____

i The business with the thief at Winthrops looks very seriously. _____

j Peter found his way to Winthrops very easily. _____

k Peter speaks very well English. _____

→ **U** Unit 32.1, → **G** Grammatik 20

7 Compare Adrian, Gavin and Stephen.

Adrian	Gavin	Stephen
Earns £4,200 a month	Earns £3,600 a month	Earns £5,500 a month
Works 10 hours a day	Works 8 hours a day	Works 6 hours a day
Speaks French quite well	Speaks French very well	Does not speak French
Usually drives 40 mph	Usually drives 50 mph	Usually drives 60 mph
Lives 20 minutes from his workplace	Lives 40 minutes from his workplace	Lives 10 minutes from his workplace

a Adrian earns _____ money than Gavin, but Stephen earns the _____.
b Adrian works _____ than Gavin. (hard)
c Stephen works _____ hours than Adrian. In fact, he works _____ number of hours of the three of them.
d When Gavin and Adrian compare the number of hours they work, they say that Stephen _____ works at all.
e Stephen drives _____ than Adrian and Gavin. He's the _____ driver and Adrian is the _____.
f Adrian's French is not _____, in fact it's quite _____, but he doesn't speak French _____ Gavin.
g Stephen doesn't feel _____ if he has to listen to French. (comfortable)
h Adrian lives _____ from his workplace than Stephen, but Gavin lives _____.

→ 🔵U Unit 16.2, → 🔴G Grammatik 16

8 Match the German with the English expressions.

a	Sagen, dass etwas nicht für Sie selber ist		1	I thought of buying…
b	Sagen, dass Sie etwas Bestimmtes suchen		2	Gavin works harder than Stephen.
c	Fragen, welche Größe jemand hat		3	He drives carefully.
d	Fragen, ob etwas in derselben Farbe, aber in einer anderen Größe verfügbar ist		4	I am looking for (kilts).
e	Sagen, dass Sie etwas Bestimmtes für den Kauf im Sinn haben		5	Do you have that blue one in a size 14?
f	Einen Vergleich anstellen		6	What size are you?
g	Beschreiben, wie jemand etwas macht		7	It's not for me.

33

At the post office

- Geschäftsbriefe
- Private Briefe

1 Geschäftsbriefe

Am häufigsten rechts, kann aber links stehen

Adresse des Absenders

Untermainkai 17
60329 Frankfurt
Germany

26 March 2010

Datum
26 March, 2010
26th March, 2010
26.03.2010
AE: 03/06/2010

Adresse des Empfängers immer links

Director of Human Resources
Winthrops Lrd.
102 Peter Street,
Manchester M2 5GP
England

Anrede
Wenn Sie weder den Namen wissen, noch ob der Empfänger männlich oder weiblich ist.

Dear Sir/Madam

Sonst
Dear Mr. **oder** (= Titel) **Nicht beides!** (Name des Empfängers) Oder *Dear Ms* (Name), wenn eine Frau angeschrieben wird.

Application for an internship

I am writing to you on the recommendation of Mr Axel Schmidt, one of your distributors in Germany.

Betreff kann hier stehen. In den USA oberhalb der Anrede

Wie Sie den Empfänger kennengelernt haben

I am an engineer, recently graduated from the Technical University of Darmstadt, Germany, and am at present employed as a development engineer with Hartmann & Braun in Frankfurt, specialists in measurement and control systems.

Wer Sie sind

As our business is becoming more and more global, I am anxious to improve my written and spoken English with particular reference to its use in business and technical contexts. I would also like to spend some time in a British engineering company to experience a different working environment.

Was Sie möchten, allgemein gehalten

Ihre spezielle Bitte/Anliegen

For these reasons, I would like to apply for an internship at Winthrops from 1st to 31st of July. I do not expect any remuneration for the internship, but would welcome a contribution to my board and keep while in Manchester. By way of compensation, I would be pleased to offer my skills and know-how in the field of measurement and control engineering. Please find attached my CV for further information.

Führen Sie die Anlagen auf

Schreiben Sie, dass Sie auf den guten Willen des Empfängers hoffen (wo es angebracht ist)

Hoping that my application is of interest to you, I remain,

Yours faithfully,

Denken Sie immer daran, den Brief korrekt zu beenden:
Dear Sir/Madam = Yours faithfully
Dear Mr Smith = Yours sinccerely

Peter Hoffmann

Unterschrift

Peter Hoffmann

Falls Sie eine bestimmte Position in der Firma innehaben, in deren Namen Sie schreiben, erwähnen Sie ihre Stellung unter Ihrer Unterschrift

Anlagen: führen Sie eine Liste der Anlagen auf.

Enc. CV

Schreibkonvention: Kurzformen wie *I'm, I'll* verwendet man nicht in Geschäftsbriefen.

2 Private Briefe

Private Briefe entsprechen weitgehend dem obigen Muster des Geschäftsbriefes. Folgende Formulierungen werden Ihnen helfen, Briefe zu verfassen:

Grüße am Ende des Briefes für:

Bekannte	Freunde	Gute Freunde & Verwandte
Best wishes,	Yours ever,	Love,
Kind regards,	All the best,	Lots of love,

Merke:
Im Englischen beginnt der Brief nach der Anrede immer mit einem Großbuchstaben, obwohl hinter der Anrede ein Komma steht!

ÜBUNGEN

164

1 Put these sentences in the right order to make a dialogue.
Then listen to the recording and compare it with your answers.
Practise the dialogue with the speakers.

a	How much would that be?	
b	I would like to send this parcel to France.	
c	Yes, you can pay by credit card.	
d	Can I pay by credit card?	
e	That weighs 2 kilos. That will be £23.60.	
f	Yes, please?	
g	Please place it on the scales here. Thank you.	

165

2 Listen and complete the mini-dialogues by replying to the speaker.

a How much will that be?
(£5.22) _____ .

b How long will that take?
(2 days) _____ .

c Then I need you to fill in this document.
(borrow/pen?) _____ ?

d I would like five 50p stamps.
(£2.50) _____ .

e How much do postcards to Italy cost?
(50p) _____ .

3 Listen to the dialogue and write down the missing words.

a How much is a _____ to Germany?

b _____ pence.

c And _____ ?

d The _____ – 50 pence.

e In that _____ I would like four _____ stamps, please.

f That will be _____, please. – Thank you.

g You are _____. Next, please.

4 Can you find the words?

a L S E S A C _____

b C A L P E R _____

c M O T E D U C N _____

d C H A T T A _____

5 Complete the sentences with the following words.

place • will • would • weighs

a How much _____ that be?

b Please _____ it on the scales here. Thank you.

c That _____ 2 kilos. That will be £23.60.

d How long _____ that take?

6 Can you put this letter in the right order?

a	Drop me a line if you find time.	
b	Vanessa	
c	Colin asks if you want any of the video downloads he has made.	
d	We're all looking forward to seeing you all again soon.	
e	I'm just writing to say that we will be able to come over to visit you at the weekend, as promised.	
f	50 Beech Close	1
g	You'll be pleased to hear that Timmy is doing very well at school.	
h	He said you particularly liked the Westerns he recorded last time.	
i	Biddulph Moor	
j	Dear Philip,	
k	Love,	
l	Stoke-on-Trent, ST8 7NT	
m	He is so good in German that he has won a trip to Germany!	
n	21st October, 2010	

7 Please write a letter of application for a placement like the one written by Peter Hoffmann to Winthrops for the following person.

Name: Svenja Grünhage
Age: 25
Profession: systems engineer
Present position: assistant to development manager
Employer: Westerhagen GmbH, Essen
Reason for letter: Application for a placement / internship of three months,
    if possible in the marketing department
Dates available: 01.09.20XX – 30.11.20XX.
No salary necessary, but board & lodgings, if possible
Can offer: skills and know-how in systems engineering
Name of company applying to: NSI, Unit 14A, Chorley Industrial Estate, Southport Road,
    Chorley, PR7 2NB, Lancashire, England
Enclosures: CV, Letter of Recommendation

8 Match the German with the English expressions

a	Fragen, wie lange (die Post) braucht		1	I would like to send this parcel.
b	Fragen, wie viel Postkarten nach Deutschland kosten		2	How much would that be?
c	Fragen, wie viel das kostet		3	Best wishes
d	Sagen, dass Sie ein Paket verschicken möchten		4	Isn't there a quicker way?
e	Jemanden bitten, ein Formular/Dokument auszufüllen		5	Dear …
f	Fragen, ob es nicht einen schnelleren (Postweg) gibt		6	How much are postcards to Germany?
g	Schlussformel eines Geschäftsbriefs an jemanden, dessen Name Ihnen unbekannt ist		7	Yours sincerely, …
h	Schlussformel eines Geschäftsbriefs an jemanden, dessen Name Ihnen bekannt ist		8	Yours faithfully, …
i	Schlussformel eines Briefes an einen Freund oder Bekannten		9	How long will that take?
j	Allgemeine Anrede in einem Brief		10	I need you to fill in this document.

A pub lunch

- *present perfect continuous*
- *past perfect continuous*

1 *present perfect continuous* (Verlaufsform des Perfekts)

Das *present perfect continuous* wird für Handlungen oder Vorgänge verwendet, die zu einem vergangenen Zeitpunkt begonnen haben. Durch die Verwendung dieser Zeitform wird hervorgehoben, dass die Handlung oder der Vorgang noch andauert:

> Peter **has been** work**ing** at Winthrops for several weeks now.
> The Canadian **has been** look**ing** for the plans since he arrived in England.

Das *present perfect continuous* unterscheidet sich im Gebrauch vom *present perfect,* weil durch das *present perfect continuous* mehr Gewicht auf die noch andauernde Handlung oder den noch andauernden Vorgang gelegt wird, als auf dessen Ergebnis.

> We **have been** decorat**ing** the bathroom.
> (Tätigkeit bis zur Gegenwart = *present perfect continuous*)
> We **have** decorat**ed** the bathroom.
> (Ergebnis einer vergangenen Handlung = *present perfect*)

→ **G** Grammatik 40

2 *past perfect continuous* (Verlaufsform des Plusquamperfekts)

Das *past perfect continuous* wird verwendet, wenn man ausdrücken will, dass eine Handlung oder ein Vorgang vor einem bestimmten Zeitpunkt in der Vergangenheit begonnen hatte und bis (oder fast bis) zu diesem Zeitpunkt andauerte:

> Peter **had been** work**ing** at Winthrops for several weeks
> before he visited the factory in Edinburgh.

→ **G** Grammatik 34

ÜBUNGEN

1 Translate the following sentences into English.

a Wie wäre es mit Mittagessen?

_____

b Das klingt interessant.

_____

c Wollen wir hineingehen?

_____

d Was haben Sie zu Essen?

_____

e Ich würde das gerne probieren.

_____

f Es schmeckt ekelhaft.

_____

2 Complete the sentences with the correct word.

a It is _____ a good dish, actually.
quite   quiet   very   surely

b It is a _____ Scottish dish.
typically   very   extra   normal

c It tastes disgusting! I will _____ something else.
ask   order   say   serving

d What have you _____ to eat?
offer   give   like   got

e Oh, I _____ like to try that.
could   had   would   will

3 Read the dialogue in Unit 34 again. Are the following sentences True or False?

→ **D** Dialog 34

		True	False
a	Peter is hungry.		
b	They eat lunch at the 'Red Lion'.		
c	Clare gets the drinks.		
d	The pub only serves haggis.		
e	Clare doesn't like haggis.		

4 What do the people order? Tick (✓) what you hear.

169

tomato soup		chicken Kiev	
potato soup		fresh salmon	
steak & kidney pie		boiled potatoes	
hamburgers		chips	
roast lamb		vegetables	
roast pork			

5 Listen to the dialogue and write down the missing words.

170

Anne: I'm _____ (**a**) hungry.
Jim: _____ (**b**) am I.
Anne: How _____ (**c**) a pub lunch?
Jim: Yes, that _____ (**d**) like a good idea.
Anne: Look. There's The Red Lion pub. _____ (**e**) we go in?
Jim: Yes, _____ (**f**) try it.
Anne: What _____ (**g**) you like to drink?
Jim: No, _____ (**h**) me get the drinks.

6 Complete the crossword puzzle with words from Unit 34.

a In a restaurant they … lunch.
b When you have a wide selection you can make a …
c A Scottish dish made from sheep offal: …
d If you tell somebody that it is better not to do something or to be careful, you … them.
e Something that tastes awful is …
f If you haven't eaten you may feel …
g A drink which is a mixture of beer and lemonade: …

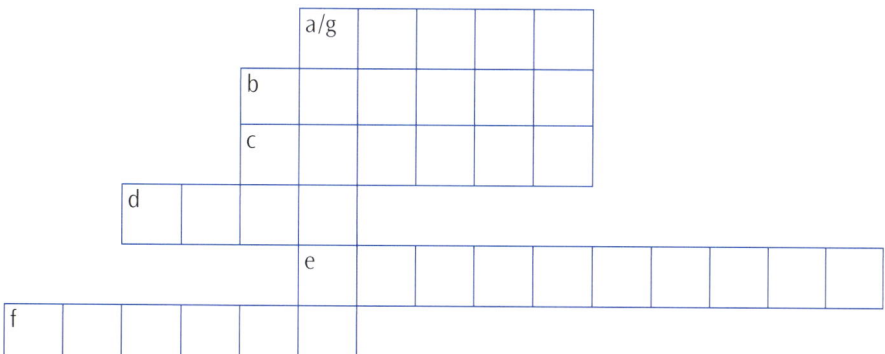

7 Answer with *So am I, So do I, So have I* or *Neither am I, Neither do I* or *Neither have I.*

a I am hungry. _____.
b Kim does her shopping in the evenings. _____.
c Jack has a company car. _____.
d I'm not going to the cinema tonight. _____.
e I haven't got any idea where the station is. _____.
f Jim doesn't like the haggis. _____.

→ **U** Unit 30

8 Complete the sentences with the correct form of the verb.

a Jack wants to get fit, so this week he is walking to work every day. On Friday Peter asks him: "Where is your car? I haven't seen it this week."
Jack replies: "I _____ to work this week because I want to get fit."

b Peter _____ (work) on a problem for one hour now, but he still can't find the answer.

c She _____ (go) to the hospital three times a month for four months now, but she is still no better.

d Do come in! We _____ (paint) the kitchen all morning, and we need a cup of coffee.

e For years now, they _____ (come) to this little hotel on holiday, so I'm sure they'll be here next year, too.

f Suzie thinks she should learn some German. She started last month, so she
_____ (learn) German for four weeks now.

→ **U** Unit 34, → **G** Grammatik 34

9 Can you complete the sentences?

a Alison and Barbara had lunch in the restaurant of the department store.
(shop / all morning) They were tired because they _____
_____.

b Alex and John took a taxi home after the party.
(drink / all evening) They decided not to drive home because they _____
_____.

c Janet opened all the windows in the living room when her friends left.
(smoke / all evening) She opened the windows because they _____
_____.

d Harry has just taken his grandchildren (*Enkelkinder*) to the cinema.
(rain / all afternoon) He has just taken the grandchildren to the cinema because it _____
_____.

e George has just decided to stop for a cup of coffee.
(drive / all morning) George stopped for a cup of coffee because he _____
_____.

f Katie sent the children out to play.
(watch TV / all morning) Katie insisted that the children should go out to play immediately because they _____

_____ .

→ **U** Unit 34, → **G** Grammatik 34

10 Write what they had been doing when/before something happened.

Example: He / wait for half an hour when the bus finally came.
He had been waiting for half an hour when the bus finally came.

a They / drive / for three hours when they had the accident (Unfall).

_____ .

b She / work / for an hour on the computer when it broke down.

_____ .

c They / play tennis / for only ten minutes when it started to rain.

_____ .

d He / cook / for an hour when the electricity went off.

_____ .

e They / walk / for miles before they found a pub.

_____ .

f She / wait / at the hospital for four hours before she saw a doctor.

_____ .

→ **U** Unit 34, → **G** Grammatik 34

11 Match the German with the English expressions.

a	Jemandem einen guten Appetit wünschen		**1**	I'm quite hungry
b	Sagen, dass etwas fürchterlich schmeckt		**2**	The choice isn't as wide as in a restaurant, though.
c	Sagen, dass Sie Hunger haben		**3**	So do I.
d	(in einer Gaststätte) Fragen, was es zu essen gibt		**4**	It tastes disgusting.
e	Jemanden auf eine beschränkte Auswahl aufmerksam machen		**5**	Neither have I.
f	„Ich auch nicht" sagen		**6**	I hope you will enjoy it.
g	„Ich auch" sagen		**7**	What have you got to eat?

35

The trap

- **Bedingungssatz Typ 3**
- **Postkarten schreiben**

1 Bedingungssatz Typ 3 *(conditional sentence type 3)*

Bedingungssätze Typ 3 beschreiben eine Bedingung in der Vergangenheit, von der der Sprecher weiß, dass sie nicht erfüllt wurde.

> *If he had already made copies of the plan, he would have disappeared quickly.*
> *(But he did not, so he is still around.)*
> *If only I had realised what he was up to, I could have reacted sooner.*
> *(But I did not realise, so I did nothing.)*

Im *if*-Satz steht das ***past perfect*** und im Hauptsatz *would, could* oder *might + have* + Partizip Perfekt:

> *if + past perfect – would/could/might + have* + Partizip Perfekt

→ **G** Grammatik 58

2 Postkarten schreiben

Beim Schreiben von Postkarten gibt es keinen großen Unterschied zum Schreiben von persönlichen Briefen. Anrede, Redewendungen und Schluss sind weitgehend identisch. Oft aber werden Sätze gekürzt:

> *Having a wonderful time.*
> *Weather perfect.*
> *Wish you were here.*

Costa del Sol, 10ᵗʰ July

Dear Jim,

Having a wonderful time.
Weather perfect. Hotel
excellent. Food fantastic.
Wish you were here.

Love Emma

Mr J Shackleton
65 Ings Lane
Dunswell HU6 1FB
England

ÜBUNGEN

173 **1** Match the sentences on the left with those on the right. Then listen to the recording for the right answers and repeat.

a	If I were you,		1	I would help you.
b	If I knew the answer,		2	I would go to the doctor's.
c	If I had a lot of money,		3	I'd lose weight.
d	If I didn't eat chocolate and sweets,		4	I wouldn't work any more.
e	If I didn't smoke so much,		5	I wouldn't keep it.
f	If I found someone's cheque book,		6	I'd feel better.

→ **U** Unit 26.1, → **G** Grammatik 58

174 **2** Listen and circle the wrong words. Then write down the correct words.

a If I were rich, I'd buy a big cat. _____

b If I went to London, I'd see Tower Bridge. _____

c If I go shopping, I will buy some cheese. _____

d If I speak to Ted, I will tell him you called. _____

e If I were you, I wouldn't have any more beer. _____

→ **U** Unit 23.1 + 26.1, → **G** Grammatik 58

175 **3** Listen and circle the words you hear.

bank   stealing   vase   department   store   take away   sailing

Spain   call   jeans   lunch   police   dinner   pullover

4 You are on holiday in London. Write a postcard to an English friend.

Begin your postcard with the normal greeting and then write:

a Where you are just now. (spend / London / holiday)

b What you are doing. (visit / Buckingham Palace / all other well-known sights)

c What you usually do when you are in London. (eat / Indian restaurant)

d What you want to do on Monday. (visit / Tate Art Gallery)

e What you like/don't like about your holiday. (people ☺ / food ☹)

Don't forget to send best wishes to your friend!

5 Match the sentence beginnings with the sentence endings.

a	If Peter had not fixed the fan belt on the car,
b	If Duncan Black had not given Christian Fauré a job,
c	If Peter had not found out about the industrial spy,
d	If Jack Baker had not picked up Peter from the airport,
e	If Jim had been more careful,
f	If Peter had not found a room in the guest house,

1	he would not have had any trouble with industrial espionage.
2	the company would have lost its plans for the machine.
3	he would not have broken his arm.
4	they would not have made it to the service station.
5	he would not have gone to Edinburgh.
6	he would have taken a taxi.

→ **U** Unit 35.1, → **G** Grammatik 58

6 Match the German with the English expressions.

a	Etwas bestätigen
b	Sagen, dass sich jemand keine Sorgen machen soll
c	Sagen, dass Sie nur noch warten brauchen
d	Fragen, ob sich jemand seiner Sache sicher ist
e	Sagen, unter welchen Bedingungen Sie anders reagiert hätten
f	Gründe auflisten
g	Einer Aussage/Argumentation zustimmen
h	Etwas folgern

1	Don't worry.
2	Are you sure this is going to work?
3	Yes, that is true.
4	All we have to do is wait.
5	For (three) reasons: first …, second …, … third …
6	So, when (he comes out), (he) will be (trapped).
7	That makes sense.
8	If only I had realised what he was up to, I could have reacted sooner.

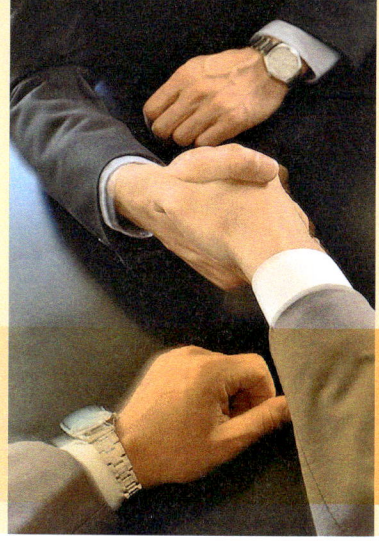

Goodbye

- *-ing*-Form
- *to*-Infinitiv

1 Die *-ing*-Form

Sie haben sicherlich bemerkt, dass die *-ing*-Form sehr häufig im Englischen vorkommt. Sie wird vielfältig eingesetzt und wir möchten hier einige Beispiele aus den Units aufgreifen und kommentieren.

Die *-ing*-Form …
- wird als Substantiv verwendet:

    The **changing** of the guard.

- folgt auf gewisse Verben:

to avoid	(es) vermeiden
to mind	etwas dagegen haben
to suggest	vorschlagen

    He **avoided** look**ing** at her.
    Would you **mind** wait**ing** a moment?
    Jack **suggested** go**ing** to the cinema.

- folgt auf gewisse Adjektive, Verben und Substantive + Präposition:

be interested in	interessiert sein an, sich interessiern für
be tired of	genug haben von, es leid sein zu
to complain of	sich beschweren über
to insist on	bestehen auf
to look forward to	sich freuen auf
to succeed in	Erfolg haben bei/mit
to talk about	sprechen über
to worry about	sich Sorgen machen wegen/um
chance of	Chance/Gelegenheit (zu)
way of	Art und Weise

    I'm **tired of** do**ing** that scene again and again.
    I **look forward to** meeting you.
    I **thought of** buy**ing** her something
    I like **his way of** think**ing**.

- nach gewissen Ausdrücken:
  How about …?   Wie wäre es …?
      ***How about** going there for lunch?*

- statt eines Nebensatzes:
  *You can check my story **by calling** Jack. (= You can check my story if you call Jack.)*

→ **G** Grammatik 42

2 Infinitiv mit *to*

Der Infinitiv mit *to* steht …
- nach gewissen Adjektiven:
  be ready to   bereit sein zu
  important to   wichtig zu
      *Mr Jackson is **ready to see** you.*
      *It is **important to practise** every day.*

- nach gewissen Verben:
  to agree   zustimmen
  to choose   sich entscheiden
  to decide   sich entscheiden, beschließen
  would like/love   möchte(n) gern, gern (tun)
      *Peter **agrees to go** to Edinburgh.*
      *I **would like to buy** a pair of running shorts.*

Verb + Objekt + Infinitiv mit *to*

Nach bestimmten Verben kann ein Objekt mit einem *to*-Infinitiv stehen:
      *Jack **asked*** <u>Peter</u> **to be quiet**.*
      *Why don't we **ask*** <u>Peter</u> **to watch** us?*
      *I **would like**** <u>you</u> **to come** to dinner.*
      *I **want**** <u>him</u> **to help** me.*

* Im Deutschen folgt meistens ein Infinitiv mit ‚zu': Jack bat Peter, leise zu sein.
** Deutsche Entsprechung: Ich möchte, dass …
  Im Englischen ist *would like / want that* nicht möglich.

3 *-ing*-Form und *to*-Infinitiv

Einige Verben können sowohl mit der *-ing*-Form als auch mit dem *to*-Infinitiv verwendet werden.
Dann allerdings haben sie eine andere Bedeutung. Hier sind einige Beispiele:

*Did you **remember to invite** Peter?*	daran denken, (in der Zukunft) etwas zu tun
*Do you **remember inviting** Peter?*	sich daran erinnern, dass man (in der Vergangenheit) etwas getan hat
*He **stopped to ask** the way.*	anhalten, um etwas anderes zu tun
*If I had a lot of money, I would **stop working**.*	aufhören, etwas zu tun
*Please **try to remember**.*	sich bemühen
*You could **try calling** the Scottish Tourist Board.*	ausprobieren, es probieren mit

→ **G** Grammatik 43

ÜBUNGEN

1 Listen to the dialogue and put the sentences in the correct order.

178

a	Yes, thank you, very much.	
b	It's no trouble at all.	
c	And thank you for making my stay so interesting.	
d	Thank you for bringing me to the station.	
e	It was a pleasure having you and we hope you found your time here useful and worthwhile.	
f	Yes, I'd love to come back.	
g	We hope to see you here again soon.	

2 Listen and <u>underline</u> the wrong words. Then write down the correct words.

179

a We are very thankful to you. _____

b You saved the programme for the machine. _____

c Our lawyers are dealing with the suitcase at the moment. _____

d I'd like to thank you with this book. _____

e I can't possibly take that. _____

f We are giving you a post in our company. _____

3 Complete the sentences below with the following words.

accept • enjoyed • grateful • gratitude • pleasure • thank you

a We are _____ to you for helping us with our work.

b It was a _____.

c I would like to show my _____ by paying for you to travel first class.

d I can't _____ that, it is too much.

e I have _____ my stay here very much.

f I can't _____ enough for all your help.

4 Match the beginning of the sentences on the left with the endings on the right.

a	Thank you for bringing me	1	what to say.
b	Thank you for making my stay	2	very much.
c	I don't know	3	here again soon.
d	I have enjoyed my stay	4	to the airport.
e	We hope to see you	5	so interesting.

5 Complete the sentences with the correct prepositions.

at • by • for • to • with

a We hope you found your time _____ us useful .
b No, I don't mind waiting _____ all.
c We hope _____ see you again soon.
d The plans _____ the weekend have changed.
e They thanked me _____ presenting me with a present.

→ **G** Grammatik 22

6 Word order. Write complete sentences.

a possibly, that, I, accept, can't

_____ .

b your, useful, hope, time, we, us, worthwhile, found, you, with, and

_____ .

c bringing, airport, much, to, me, thank, very, for, the, you

_____ .

d come, will, Germany, visit, you, won't, me, you, and, in

_____ ?

e enjoyed, much, stay, I, very, have, my

_____ .

7 Complete these sentences with the correct *-ing*-form of the verbs.

a The Canadian was afraid Peter would recognize him, so he _____ (avoid / meet) him.
b The police finally _____ (succeed in / arrest) the Canadian.
c Winthrops _____ (insist on / offer) Peter a job after his studies.
d Mr Brown _____ (complain of / have) a bad day on Friday the 13th.
e I am looking _____ (forward to / hear) from you.
f Clare had the _____ (chance of / go) to Australia this summer, but she didn't go.
g We were _____ (talk about / ski) in Austria this year. We used to go to Switzerland, but it's so expensive now.
h Because Winthrops is so _____ (worried about / spy) they employ a lot of security guards and a night watchman.
i Albert Einstein's _____ (way of / think) was brilliant.
j Jack is _____ (interested in / meet) Peter's family.
k Would you _____ (mind / not smoke) in here, please?
l Jim _____ (suggested / eat) a pub lunch on Sunday.
m I'm _____ (tired of / write) all these business reports.

→ **U** Unit 36.1, → **G** Grammatik 42 + 43

8 Complete these sentences with the correct form of the verbs.

a I must remember _____ (close) the door when I leave.
b They stopped _____ (eat) lunch on their way to Edinburgh
c Would you like _____ (eat) now or later?
d Can you try _____ (open) this for me, please?
e If the door won't open, try _____ (kick) it.
f He stopped _____ (ask) Clare about the play because he could see
   that she was tired.
g Do you remember _____ (visit) that beautiful house in Italy?
h Would you like _____ (work) at Winthrops next year?

→ **U** Unit 36, → **G** Grammatik 42 + 43

9 Match the German with the English expressions.

a	Ein Geschenk/Angebot höflich ablehnen		**1**	What happens now?
b	Jemandem für ihre/seine Freundlichkeit danken		**2**	I'm glad to hear that.
c	Fragen, was jetzt passieren wird		**3**	I can't possibly accept that.
d	Einem Gastgeber für einen angenehmen Aufenthalt danken		**4**	I insist.
e	Freude über etwas Gesagtes ausdrücken		**5**	I have enjoyed my stay very much.
f	Auf etwas bestehen		**6**	You are very kind.

Test 3

1 Match the sentences a–f with 1–6

a	Where did you get that kilt?		**1**	I can't get this one to work, either.
b	Did you get here very early?		**2**	That is because I always get here very early.
c	I just can't get this pen to write.		**3**	I got it at the Scottish shop.
d	Is the engine temperature getting higher?		**4**	Oh, I got it a few months ago.
e	You are lucky. You always get the best seats.		**5**	Yes, I got here hours ago.
f	When did you get that new car?		**6**	Yes, it is. The warning lamp has been on for a while now.

2 Choose the correct form of the verb to complete the sentence.

a Peter _____ in the Bed & Breakfast since May.
is living   lived   has been living

b The play _____ ten minutes ago.
began   has begun   had begun

c Everyone _____ for ten minutes by the time Peter got to the squash centre.
had already been playing   already played   was already playing

d We'd better hurry because the train _____ in two minutes.
was leaving   leaves   has left

e This time next week Peter _____ in Manchester.
works   will be working   is working

3 Complete the gaps with the correct form of *must, mustn't* or *have to*.

a She rang me this morning to say she didn't know if she would be at the station in time for her train. The train has arrived here in London; she isn't on the train, so she _____ (to miss) it.

b Why didn't you apply for the job at Winthrops? It's too late now. You _____ (to apply) for another job.

c Jack can't do the job alone (*allein*), you _____ (to help) him tomorrow when you come.

d Jack couldn't do the job alone, someone _____ (to help) him.

e Jack and Janet _____ (to promise) Peter they would visit him in Germany.

f You really _____ (to come) to visit us in Germany.

4 Complete the letter below using the correct tense – simple present or simple past, past continuous, present perfect, past perfect or the present perfect progressive.

I'm sorry I **(a)** _____ (not / to write) to you before today, but I
(b) _____ (to move) to Manchester last week, and I
(c) _____ (to work) hard for the last two months.
How **(d)** _____ (to be)? Well, I hope.

At the beginning of my internship I **(e)** _____ (to stay) at a boarding house, but
then I **(f)** _____ (to move) in with some colleagues from work and I
(g) _____ (to live) there ever since.
Last weekend we **(h)** _____ (to travel) to Edinburgh, in Scotland, and I
(i) _____ (to fall) in love with the place.
By the way, **(j)** _____ (you / ever / to visit) Scotland? The Edinburgh Fringe Festival
(k) _____ (to take place = *stattfinden*) while we
(l) _____ (to be) there, and we
(m) _____ (to see) a lot of interesting plays and shows.
Well, I **(n)** _____ (to finish) now because I
(o) _____ (to go) to the pub with some friends and with Clare. It's her birthday today.

Just imagine! In one week's time I **(p)** _____ (to travel) back to Germany!

I look forward to **(q)** _____ (to hear) from you soon.

Take care.

Yours,

Peter

5 Complete the *if*-sentences with the correct form of the words in brackets.

a If the plans _____ (to be) available last year, we _____
(to be able to) expand the business this year.

b If they _____ (to know) what kind of person he was, Winthrops
_____ (never / to employ) the Canadian.

c We _____ (to go) to Germany next year, if Peter _____
(to invite) us, but we know he won't.

d If you _____ (to need) my help, just _____ (to phone) me.

e If Peter _____ (not / to remember) the Canadian, they
_____ (not / to catch) him.

6 Complete these sentences.

a When Peter first came to England he didn't like English beer, but now he drinks it almost every evening. – I see, now he _____ (used to / drink) English beer.

b I never _____ (used to / watch) quiz shows on television, but now I watch 'Who wants to be a millionaire?' every week.

c They are not coming to the party _____ (because OR because of?) Janet is not very well.

d They had to work every weekend in November _____ (because OR because of?) the problems they had with the new machine.

e John: "When do you leave for Germany, Peter?"
John asked Peter _____.

f "Would you help me with this business letter please, Jack?"
Peter wanted Jack _____.

7 Complete these sentences with question tags.

a You're going back to German, Peter, _____?
b You've been here three months, _____?
c You had better let me help you with that, _____?
d Janet, you have got a friend in Germany, _____?
e That is a very interesting machine, _____?
f OK, I'll see if I can find Mr Jackson, _____?
g You were here last week, _____?
h You can speak Spanish, _____?
i That isn't yours, _____?

8 Change these sentences into passive sentences.

a They finished the factory one year ago.
_____.

b The engineers were developing a new design for the XR23.
_____.

c They are building a new plant in Scotland.
_____.

d They told management to cut costs.
_____.

e Winthrops will employ a new trainee next year.
_____.

f They have given all the staff more pay this year.
_____.

g They can do a lot to solve the problem.
_____.

9 Make single sentences out of the following pairs using *also, too, so, neither, not… either* or *neither… nor*. (There are several ways to join them.)

a Peter doesn't like Henry. Natalie doesn't like Henry.
Peter doesn't like Henry and _____.

b Peter likes learning languages. Jack likes learning languages.
Peter likes learning languages and _____.

c Suzie comes from Australia. I come from Australia.
Suzie comes from Australia and _____.

d My friend doesn't like working on Saturdays. My friend doesn't like working on Sundays.
_____.

10 Adjective or adverb? Are the <u>underlined</u> words in the sentence right or wrong? Write the correct words on the line.

a Peter speaks English very <u>good</u>. _____

b He doesn't <u>usual</u> speak English at home. _____

c Mr Jackson works very <u>hardly</u>. He works ten hours a day. _____

d It is not <u>necessary</u> to phone him. He'll be here in a few minutes. _____

e We have a <u>terrible</u> problem with the new factory. _____

f She said "You're welcome" very <u>friendly</u>. _____

g We are thinking about your idea very <u>seriously</u>. _____

h Peter found the internship at Winthrops very interesting and quite <u>easily</u>. _____

11 Complete the sentences using the comparative and superlative forms of the adjectives.

a Jim: 170 words per minute   Henry: 185 words per minute   Roger: 200 words per minute
Jim speaks _____ (normal), Henry speaks _____ (quick) than Jim, but of the three Roger speaks _____ (fast).

b After his car accident last year, Jack drives _____ (careful).

c Could you speak _____ (clear), please? There is so much noise in here.

d Peter worked _____ (hard) at Winthrops than he had in his German company.

e When you are driving, anyone going _____ (slow) than you is an idiot and everyone driving _____ (fast) than you is a maniac.

12 *To*-infinitive or *-ing*-form? Complete the sentences with the correct form of the verb.

a Would you like _____ (to see) the new James Bond film?

b Jack and his wife had an accident in Germany because they couldn't get used to _____ (to drive) on the right.

c Do you like winter holidays? Do you like _____ (to ski)?

d She's not good at _____ (to speak) in front of a lot of people. She gets very nervous.

e Suzie is looking forward to _____ (to see) her parents when they come to visit her for Christmas.

f Please try to remember _____ (to buy) some milk when you go to the shops.

g You ought to stop _____ (to smoke) – it's not good for you.

h My husband wants me _____ (to be) ready at 8 p.m. to go out for dinner.

i Do you remember _____ (to see) 'The London Eye'? I thought it was great.

j It's important _____ (to get) enough sleep in order to stay healthy.

k And it's important _____ (practise) your English if you want to be perfect!

LÖSUNGSSCHLÜSSEL / KEY

Unit 1

1 a Are **b** am **c** Are
d am not **e** is **f** is **g** is

2 a 5 **b** 4 **c** 1 **d** 7 **e** 3 **f** 6 **g** 2

3 a Is this row 10?
b I am German.
c Are you here on holiday?
d That is very kind of you.
e I am here to improve my English.

4 Waagerecht: am – you – thanks – holiday – he –
very – are

Unit 2

1 a 5 **b** 1 **c** 3 **d** 4 **e** 2

2 a Can I help you?
b Thank you. Can I have a newspaper, please?
c Can Ms (Mrs) Johnson come to the front of the
plane, please?
d Is this your book?
e Yes, it is. Thank you very much.

3 a Good morning, I am Sue Johnson.
b Is your name Ms Johnson?
c Is this your seat?
d Sorry, this seat is for business class travellers.
e Would you like this book?

4 Waagerecht: very – have – like – to
Senkrecht: traveller – would

5 a Can **b** is **c** are **d** Would

6 a an **b** a **c** an **d** an **e** a, a **f** an, a

Unit 3

1 b No, I am not.
d That is all right
f I am.
h How do you do?

2 a Excuse me, are you Mr Hoffmann?
b Nice to meet you.
c How do you do?
d There are lots over there.
e Please call me Sue.
f Can I help you with your luggage?

3 a 1 **b** 1 **c** 4

4 a Are you – *am*
b Is – *is*
c Are – *are*
d Is – *is not*
e Are – *are*

5 a 4 **b** 6 **c** 5 **d** 3 **e** 1 **f** 2

Unit 4

1 a newspaper **b** magazine **c** hand luggage
d car **e** trolley

2 a car **b** there **c** programme **d** British
e German **f** Frankfurt **g** friend, name
h sister

3 a What a great car!
b That is very kind of you to say so.
c There is a letter for you.
d There is a problem.
e First we meet the director.

4 a 4 **b** 4 **c** 1/4 **d** 1/3

5 a False **b** False **c** True **d** False **e** False

6 a mine **b** Her **c** She **d** father's

Unit 5

1 b Good afternoon.
d My name is Bond.
f How do you do?
h Yes, please do.
j Not at all.
l Thank you.

2 a 4 **b** 3 **c** 1 **d** 2

3 a This is Peter Hoffmann.
b He is from Germany.
c Mr Hoffmann is here to see Mr Baker.
d Would you mind waiting for a moment?
e No problem at all.
f Would you like a drink? Tea? Coffee?
g No, thank you.
h Mr Baker is ready to see you now.

4 a Can I tell Peter you are here?
b Would you mind waiting a moment?
c It is no problem at all.
d Could you tell me where the toilets are?
e The line is engaged.

5 a 4 **b** 2 **c** 4 **d** 4

6 a True   **b** True   **c** False
d False   **e** False   **f** True

Unit 6

1 a Is there a lift here in the building?
b What is the matter?
c I hope you enjoy your stay here.
d Have you been to London before?
e Please call me if you need help.

2 a 5   **b** 3   **c** 2   **d** 6   **e** 4   **f** 1

3 a 3   **b** 3   **c** 2   **d** 4   **e** 2

4 a What is the matter (with you)?
b It is nothing really.
c Call me if you need my help.
d That is very kind of you.
e Goodbye.

5 a Pleased to meet you.
b Nice to meet you.
c Have you been to Manchester before?
d Are you here on business?
e Would you like a drink?

6 a been   **b** Has   **c** matter   **d** there   **e** has

7 a Have, been   **b** has shown   **c** has, gone
d has lost   **e** have picked, up
f have not seen

Unit 7

1 a He is going to read a book.
b He is going to put his luggage / it under his seat.
c He is going to help Peter with his luggage.
d They are going (to go) to the production line.
e No, we are going (to go) to Ireland on holiday.
f He is going (to go) to Liverpool in the morning.

2 a A plane is bigger than a car.
b Your thumb is thicker than your / a finger.
c Canada is bigger than Germany.
d Peter is taller than Jack.
e Peter's English is better than Jack's German.
f A single room is smaller than a double room.
g Italian clothes are nicer than English clothes.

3 a wear   **b** use   **c** measures
d feeds   **e** operates

4 a reads   **b** meets   **c** knows   **d** hope
e live   **f** come   **g** puts   **h** see   **i** picks
j Has   **k** help   **l** has   **m** thinks   **n** says
o improve   **p** looks

5 a Do you like London?
b Do you have any sisters?
c Do they operate flights to Liverpool?
d Do I have to wear a helmet (here)?
e Do we leave for Edinburgh in an hour?
f Do you know Peter Berg?
g Do they live in Manchester?

6 a We are now going to the production line.
b We have to wear protective overalls because it is company policy.
c How tall are you?
d Here is your protective overall.
e Here we are.
f Please put your helmet on now.

7 a We are going to the production line.
b I am 5'6" (5 foot 6 inches).
c Yes, she is standing next to the trolley.
d The computer operates the machine.

Unit 8

1 a 1   **b** 4   **c** 2   **d** 3

2 a Good morning.
b My name is Mr Brown.
c I have a reservation for an apartment in Castle Heights.
d I am afraid there is a problem.
e Oh, really?
f Can you recommend a hotel?
g Thank you. Can you give me the telephone number, please?
h I will (I'll) phone.

3 a Good afternoon.
b My name is Samson. I believe you have a reservation for me.
c Oh, really? That is very unfortunate.
e How much is the double room?
f No problem. I will take the double room.
g Yes, please do.

4 a reservation   **b** Excuse me.   **c** two rooms
d much   **e** unfortunate   **f** room

Unit 9

1 a 3   **b** 5   **c** 1   **d** 2   **e** 4

2 a There are   **b** There is   **c** there is
d there is, there is   **e** Is there
f Are there   **g** There are

3 a I, my   **b** your   **c** His, he   **d** they
e Their, they   **f** you   **g** our   **h** your   **i** we

4 forty-five = 45
eight = 8
ninety-nine = 99
sixteen = 16
fifty = 50
six = 6
three = 3
eighty-seven = 87

fifteen = 15
thirteen = 13
eighty = 80
five = 5
thirty = 30
sixty = 60
one hundred = 100

5 a speak
b Just a moment
c speaking, calling
d any
e Just a moment, have
f How much
g bed & breakfast
h will

6 a True **b** True **c** False **d** True **e** True

7 b the twelfth of January
c the eighteenth of October
d the first of May
e the thirty-first of July
f the thirteen of February

8 a How much are the rooms, please?
b Can I speak to Mrs Thompson?
c Who is calling?
d Do you want a single or double room?
e I think I would prefer the double room, please.
f Can you spell that, please?

Unit 10

1 a BOARDING
b BREAKFAST
c CONTINENTAL
d USUALLY
e GUEST

2 Transcript:
Patricia Jenkins usually starts her day very early.
She usually gets up at about 7 o'clock and then
she often reads the morning newspapers in bed.
Sometimes she has a Continental breakfast, but
she usually only has coffee. She often walks to
work, but sometimes she takes the bus at 8.30.
She always starts work at 9 a.m.

always: h **ususally:** a, b, e
often: c, f **sometimes:** d, g

3 a gets up **b** eats (has) **c** takes **d** flies
e picks Peter up **f** has (eats) **g** walks **h** play
i jog (walk) **j** read, read **k** go **l** take

4 a Do you want breakfast at 7.30?
b Do you want tea or coffee for breakfast?
c Do you want an English or Continental breakfast?
d Do you speak English?
e Do you want to see your room, Mr Hoffmann?

5 a Do you speak English?
b Do you have any rooms free for tonight?
c Do your single rooms have baths?
d Do you offer (English/Continental) breakfast?
e Do you get German newspapers?

6 a When **b** How **c** Where
d What **e** Why (How) **f** Who

7 a Where do you work in Germany?
b How do you travel to work there?
c When do you usually start work in Gemany?
d What do you do for lunch?
e When do you usually get home?
f How many foreign languages do you speak?
g What do you think of your job in Germany?
h Why do you like Winthrops?

8 a any **b** one **c** unfortunate
d Continental **e** walk

9 a 4 **b** 6 **c** 5 **d** 3 **e** 1 **f** 7 **g** 2

10

 a c  e 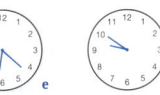 g

 b  d  f

11 (at) ten past seven
(at) a quarter to eight
7.57
Three minutes to eight
9 o'clock
7.45

12 a When do the restaurants open?
b When do you usually have breakfast?
c When does Peter leave the house?
d When does work at Winthrops start?
e When can Peter see Mr Jackson?

Unit 11

1 a 25th
  b 20 minutes
  c 9 p.m.
  d Monday
  e November
  f weekend

2 a a pity **b** September **c** breakfast
  d eat **e** of

3 a Do, work – *Yes, they do.*
  b Does, work – *No, she doesn't.*
  c Do, work – *No, they don't (work on Sundays).*
  d Does, speak –*Yes, he does.*
  e Does, speak – *No, she doesn't.*
  f Does, come – *Yes, she does.*
  g Do, like – *Yes, they do.*
  h Do, like – *Yes, they do.*
  i Does, like – *No, she doesn't.*

4 a When would you like to have breakfast?
    At 7.30.
  b When do you go to work?
    At 8.30.
  c When does the bus leave?
    At 8.32.
  d When does my working day at Winthrops start?
    At 9 a.m.
  e When does the plane leave?
    At 11.53.

5 a 3 **b** 4 **c** 4 **d** 1

6 a gets up **b** plays **c** use **d** drink
  e see **f** makes **g** works

Unit 12

1 a am walking **b** are learning **c** are having
  d is travelling **e** is picking, up **f** Are, living

2 a Jack is operating the machine today.
  b Peter is settling in well.
  c We are working in London at the moment.
  d They are eating Chinese food.

3 a Do you like Chinese food?
  b Would you like a dessert?
  c Do you like jazz music?
  d Do you like computer games?
  e Would you like a drink?
  f Would you like to visit the British Museum?

4 a False **b** True **c** True **d** False **e** True

5 1 love **2** like **3** dislike **4** hate

6 a (Yes, I) do. I love jazz.
  b (No, I) don't. I dislike Indian food.
  c (Tea, please.) I hate coffee.
  d (Yes, I) would. (I really) like (bacon and eggs).

7 a True **b** False **c** True **d** True **e** False

8 wear a protective overall wear a tie write a report

Test 1

1 a Is, Are, am **b** Can **c** are
  d can **e** are **f** are

2 a My **b** His **c** your **d** Their
  e your **f** Our **g** Her

3 a learn **b** help **c** near **d** some
  e about **f** kind / nice **g** mine

4 a What is your name?
  b Is Jean-François French?
  c Can I ask you to come to the front of the plane?
  d Where can I get a German newspaper?
  e Is there an Irish pub in Park Road?
  f No, there is not/isn't.
  g When do you arrive in London?
  h Where do you live in Germany, Peter?
  i Does Jack speak Spanish?
  j Where do Jack and Peter work?

5 a 4 **b** 6 **c** 5 (11) **d** 1 **e** 3 (9) **f** 2
  g 7 **h** 11 **i** 9 **j** 12 **k** 8 **l** 10

Unit 13

1 a a cup of **b** a glass of **c** a piece of
  d a bottle of **e** a pint of

2 a juice **b** bottle **c** starter
  d delicious **e** selection

3 a you like to, with
  b to, main course
  c recommend
  d recommend
  e sounds, take
  f Would you like

4 a offering **b** having **c** ordering
  d having **e** eating **f** starting

5 a 3 **b** 4 **c** 1 **d** 2

6 a False **b** False **c** False **d** False **e** True

7 a 7 **b** 3 **c** 4 **d** 2 **e** 6 **f** 1 **g** 5

1 a True **b** False **c** True **d** True
e True **f** True **g** False

2 a 4 **b** 6 **c** 1 **d** 3 **e** 7 **f** 5 **g** 2

3 a broken **b** shoulder **c** entrance
d health club **e** hospital **f** twisted

4 8 (fore)arm 13 ankle 15 foot 4 shoulder

5 a fell, broke **b** twisted (hurt)
c hurting **d** swollen

6 a coming **b** doing **c** filling in **d** having
e interrupting **f** looking **g** phoning
h reading **i** signing **j** writing

7 a are, doing
b am going
c am having
d am inviting
e Is, coming too?
f is planning
g are trying

8 a doing **b** going **c** watching **d** working
e having **f** will have

9 b We're having a breakfast brunch.
c We're visiting the Tate Gallery.
d We're going to a night club.
e We're meeting Tom at the Film Museum.
f We're eating a pub lunch and having afternoon
tea.
g We're catching the train to Manchester.

10 COMING – SIGNING – WRITING – HELPING –
READING – OPERATING – PUTTING – PHONING –
GETTING – MEETING – EATING – GOING

11 a 5 **b** 10 **c** 9 **d** 6 **e** 7
f 3 **g** 1 **h** 4 **i** 2 **b** 8

Unit 15

1 a I'd like some tea, please. – *Certainly. How much
would you like?*
b I'd like some bananas, please. – *Certainly. How
many would you like?*
c I'd like some wine, please. – *Certainly. How many
bottles would you like?*
d I'd like some rolls, please. – *Certainly. How many
would you like?*
e I'd like some sausages, please. – *Certainly. How
many would you like?*

2 a – third floor tea basement fourth

2 b a 4 **b** 5 **c** 2 **d** 1 **e** 3

3 a a me, where **b** on, next **c** get/buy **d** them/
food **e** thing **f** there

3 b a False **b** True **c** False **d** True **e** False

4 a a pair of **b** any **c** men's **d** men
e three pairs of **f** three (some) **g** some
h a

5 a 4 **b** 1 **c** 5 **d** 6 **e** 3 **f** 7 **g** 2

Unit 16

2 a long **b** cheapest **c** small **d** expensive

3 a here **b** shorter **c** cheaper
d dark black **e** these

4 a tennis shorts **b** a pair of jeans **c** a pound of
cheese **d** a pair of shoes **e** a book

5 a 9 **b** 3 **c** 2 **d** 1 **e** 5 **f** 10 **g** 4 **h** 8
i 7 **j** 6

6 b small **c** smaller **d** bigger
e comfortable **f** expensive **g** cheaper

7 THAT: cheese pullover T-shirt
THESE: jeans shorts shoes

8 a second **b** left **c** expensive **d** fashion
e floor **f** that **g** rooms **h** size
i information **j** try **k** department

9 a False **b** False **c** True **d** False
e False **f** True **g** True **h** False

10 a 5 **b** 1 **c** 4 **d** 3 **e** 2

11 a 6 **b** 5 **c** 4 **d** 1 **e** 3 **f** 7 **g** 2

Unit 17

1 a Hello, Sue. How are you?
b I'm watching TV.
c I'd love to. Are you sure it is not too much
trouble?
d I arrive on the 17.30 train.

2 a call evening sorry speaking visiting

2 b How are you, Tom? – I'd love to. – Can I call you
later?

3 a He is in Edinburgh.
b He is calling Jack.
c He is staying at his uncle's / visiting his uncle.
d (They going to have a drink) On Saturday.
e (He is going to call back) In about one hour.

4 a Peter wants to improve his English.
  b Jack wants Suzie to tell Mr Jackson that Peter is here.
  c Suzie wants Mr Hoffmann to wait a moment.
  d Peter wants to return some of Natalie's hospitality.
  e Natalie wants Peter to ring (her) back tomorrow.

5 a True **b** False **c** False
  d False **e** False **f** False

6 a 4 **b** 5 **c** 7 **d** 1 **e** 6 **f** 2 **g** 2/3

Unit 18

1 a 4 **b** 2 **c** 3 **d** 1

2 a Can you tell me where the toilets are?
  b Where is the airport, please?
  c Take the second turning and it is on your left.
  d Go along here and the bus stop is in George Street.
  e Yes, the bank (travel agency) is next to the travel agency (bank).

3 a Is the station next to the airport?
  b Is the bank the second left turning and on the left?
  c Where is the shopping centre, please?

4 a sports arena, along, take, turning
  b stranger
  c your, turn, traffic, opposite

5 a post office **b** sports centre
  c John Dickins Memorial Centre **d** hospital

6 a 4 **b** 1 **c** 7 **d** 5 **e** 2 **f** 3 **g** 6

Unit 19

1 a When do the coaches from London to Manchester run? – They run every two hours.
  b How long does the train from Manchester to London take?
    – It takes two hours and 13 minutes.
  c How often do the trains run from London to Manchester?
    – They run every 1 ½ hours.
  d At what time/When does the five o'clock train get to Manchester?
    – At 19.34.
  e Do I have to change (on the 5.55 to London)?
    – No, it is a direct service.
  f What about the coach, is that any quicker/faster?/Is the coach faster than the train?
    – No, it isn't. It takes 4 hours 30 minutes/4 1/2 hours.

g How much is a single ticket to London?
    – It is £33.20.

2 a How do you want to travel to London?
  b When is he leaving for Manchester?
  c Where are they/Sam and Betty flying to?
  d How often do you go to Edinburgh?
  e How long does is take (to get there)?
  f What do they want to see in London?

3 a saver **b** takes **c** train **d** run
  e are **f** one **g** return

4 a best/fastest/cheapest **b** long **c** faster
  d longer/longest **e** good/ cheap **f** best/cheapest
  g better, cheaper/cheaper, better

5 a 3 **b** 4 **c** 5 **d** 2 **e** 1

6 a 2 **b** 1 **c** 4 **d** 4 **e** 2 **f** 2

7 a False **b** True **c** True
  d False **e** True **f** True

8 a Which **b** What **c** Which **d** Which
  e what **f** What **g** Which

9 a 6 **b** 1 **c** 2 **d** 3 **e** 4 **f** 5

Unit 20

1 a had **b** met **c** saw **d** were **e** took
  f knew **g** ate **h** gave

2 asked – be – changed – eaten – get – gave – gone
  – have – knew – met – played – seen – took

3 a 5 **b** 4 **c** 1 **d** 2 **e** 3

4 a *didn't, went*
  b *Did, show, didn't, showed*
  c *Did, eat, didn't, ate*
  d *Did, see, didn't, saw*
  e *Did, play, didn't, played*

5 a When did you leave Manchester?
  b Where did you take the train to?/ Where did you go?
  c What did you eat?
  d Who did you meet at the station?
  e How did you get to the restaurant?
  f Why did you bring Natalie flowers?

6 Across: worked – went – got– saw – played – picked
  Down: were – brought – arrived – knew – was – ate – had – met– noticed

7 a went **b** took **c** met
  d didn't see, saw
  e didn't eat, ate **f** had

8 c He saw Tower Bridge.

9 a 5 **b** 3 **c** 4 **d** s1 **e** 2

Unit 21

Aussprache
at – head – met – sad

1 a 4 **b** 1 **c** 1 **d** 1 **e** 1 **f** 3

2 a nobody **b** nothing **c** Somehow
d anything **e** Something **f** nothing
g somebody

3 a Everybody **b** Somebody **c** Anybody
d Everybody **e** Anybody **f** Everybody
g Nobody

4 a isn't **b** didn't **c** doesn't
d wasn't **e** doesn't

5 a gets up **b** has **c** takes **d** took **e** ate
f drank, ate **g** met **h** works, lives
i travels, took, picked

6 a tell **b** told **c** say **d** told **e** said

7 a … if/whether he liked his work at Winthrops.
b … if/whether Peter wanted to/would go to
London again.
c … when Mr Hoffman would return to Germany.
d …told (Jack) that he was going to Scotland the
following week.
e … Peter where he comes/came from in
Germany.
f … that he loves/loved a good old English
breakfast.
g … how Peter travelled to Manchester.

8 a 3 **b** 7 **c** 1 **d** 6 **e** 2 **f** 5 **g** 4 **h** 8

Unit 22

1 a any **b** any **c** some **d** some **e** any
f any **g** some **h** any, some **i** any, some
j any **k** some

2 a should **b** shouldn't **c** should
d Shouldn't **e** shouldn't **f** should

3 a Should **b** Shouldn't **c** should
d shouldn't **e** Shouldn't

4 a will **b** Would (Will *möglich, klingt aber
unhöflich*) **c** will **d** should/will **e** shouldn't
f should **g** wouldn't, will **h** won't

5 a Where will I work when I have finished my
internship at Winthrops? – You will work (for a
big international company).

b Where will I live? – You will live (in Frankfurt).
c Will I find a wife? – (Yes,) you will find (a
wonderful wife).
d Will I have (any) children? – (No,) you will not/
won't have (any children).
e Will I be happy? – (Yes,) you will be (very happy).
f Will I be successful? – (Yes,) you will be (very
successful).

6 Sue: can't come
Jack: can come
Sam: doesn't know yet

7 a (Peter wanted to know) where he would work
when he had finished his internship at
Winthrops? (Madame Maxine said) (that) he
would work (for a big international company).
b (Peter asked her) where he would live? (She told)
him he would (live in Frankfurt).
c (Peter wanted to know) if he would (find a wife).
(Madame Maxine thought), he would find
(a wonderful wife).
d (He then asked Madame Maxine) if he would
(have children)? (She said that, unfortunately,) he
wouldn't (have any children).
e (He also wanted to know) if he would be (happy)?
(She was pleased to tell) him that he would be
(very happy).
f (He also asked) if he would (be successful). (She
replied that, yes,) he would be (very successful).

8 a 3 **b** 2 **c** 1 **d** 10 **e** 6 **f** 5
g 8 **h** 7 **i** 9 **j** 11 **k** 4

Unit 23

1 a travels, will be
b take, will get
c call, will pick
d see, will ask
e visit, will buy
f don't understand, will help
g don't book, won't be
h drink, won't
i don't stop, will leave
j will be, doesn't go

2 b If you can't find a parking space near your office,
you should to take the bus to work.
c If you want to improve your English, you should
go to evening classes.
d If you can't find a babysitter for tonight, you
should ask your mother to babysit for you.
e If you are having a big party, you should buy a
lot of drinks.

3 a I will introduce you to some friends.

b What are you doing in London?

c Did I just hear my name?

d That is very strange.

e Did you find out what happened?

4 a False **b** True **c** False **d** True

e True **f** False **g** False

5 a Ah, I see, he was speaking to Janet when he saw an old friend.

b Ah, I see, she was telling Peter about her boyfriend when he came into the room.

c Ah, I see, he was travelling to London when he lost the present.

d Ah, I see, she was living in London when her mother visited her.

e Ah, I see, you were living in London when you had your first baby.

f Ah, I see, they were trying to contact his family when he disappeared.

6 a travel, takes **b** will pay, pay

c won't like, are **d** will have to, wants

7 a Clare was talking to Dennis and Susanne.

b Jack was having a drink with Janet.

c Janet's mother was making sandwiches.

d Harry was leaving to pick up friends at the station.

8 a present **b** single **c** trainee

d mentor **e** invitation

9 a 4 **b** 5 **c** 3 **d** 6 **e** 1 **f** 2

Unit 24

1 a who **b** that **c** who **d** which/whose **e** who

f which **g** which **h** which/that **i** whose

2 a Oh, so that's the woman that came to help you.

b Oh, so that's your friend that lives in Berlin.

c Oh, so that's the car that your farther bought.

d Oh, so that's the man that found your passport.

e Oh, so that's the lady that takes the children to school.

3 a Who **b** Whose **c** Where **d** Where **e** Which

f How **g** What **h** Why **i** Which **j** Whose

k Why **l** Where ('Which' if there are a lot of similar cars there!) **m** What/How **n** When **o** What

4 a What sports do you play?

b Why don't you buy these shorts?

c When do you have to leave?

d Who is driving to Edinburgh with you?

e Where are you going (to)?

f What are you doing on Saturday? / Where are you going on Saturday?

g How are you travelling to Paris?

h When did you buy them?

i How long have you been working for this company?

j Whose coat is this?

k Who were you talking to in the pub?

l What are you looking for?

m How long will you need the room for?

n Why are you so happy?

o How old is your sister?

5 a How many people are coming to the party?

b Where is the nearest post office, please?

c Why didn't you close the door?

d What is the man's name?

e Who did you see last night at the theatre?

6 a True **b** True **c** False

d True **e** True **f** False

7 ID 2

8 a who

b who – The man standing over there, who is looking at the photos, is my husband.

c which/that

d whose – There are three shops, whose employees are very knowledgeable, that I can recommend.

9 a 4 **b** 5 **c** 3 **d** 2 **e** 1 **f** 8 **g** 6 **h** 7

Test 2

1 a 4 **b** 5 **c** 1 **d** 2 **e** 3 **f** 6

2 a near **b** on top **c** on the right

d next to **e** under **f** opposite

g on the left **h** turn right **i** straight ahead

j turn left

3 a earlier **b** latest **c** good **d** fatter **e** worst

4 a exotic, as good as **b** cold, better / nicer

c most expensive **d** widest, wider

5 <u>Dear</u> Susan,

I <u>really</u> enjoyed my <u>visit to</u> your house. I <u>walked on</u> the beach every day. I <u>missed</u> you very much, but fine <u>weather helped</u> me. I <u>watched</u> the sun go down every night. <u>I can't</u> wait for you to <u>arrive</u> and I have <u>arranged everything</u> for you.

See you soon,

Yours,

Tom

6 a tried **b** were not **c** did, call
  d was **e** was babysitting **f** Did, want
  g was, wondering **h** would like
  i am playing **j** Have, seen
  k is working **l** will be back
  m is/was going (to go) **n** will ring **o** like
  p plays **q** give **r** will phone

7 a a pair of **b** any **c** some **d** are **e** are
  f some **g** any **h** some **i** as nice as

8 a 9 **b** 12 **c** 11 **d** 10 **e** 6 **f** 5
  g 8 **h** 7 **i** 1 **j** 4 **k** 3 **l** 2

Unit 25

1 a have to **b** must **c** has to **d** mustn't
  e must **f** mustn't **g** has to **h** must
  i have to **j** mustn't

2 b Yes, why don't you get a second job?
  c Yes, why don't you join a club?
  d Yes, why don't you take a holiday?
  e Yes, why don't you go to France?

3 a Everyone **b** Everywhere **c** everyone
  d Everything **e** everything **f** Everywhere
  g everywhere **h** everyone **i** Everyone
  j everything

4 b Oh, I see. You used to teach French, but you
    don't any more.
  c Oh, I see. You used to work in London, but you
    don't any more.
  d Oh, I see. You used to earn a good salary, but
    you don't any more.

5 a False **b** False **c** True **d** False **e** False
  f False **g** True

6 a used to drink, are used to drinking
  b never used to/didn't use to speak, are used to
    speaking
  c used to start, are used to starting
  d used to live, are used to living
  e never used to/didn't use to watch, are used to
    watching

7 a used to **b** use to **c** didn't use to
  d used to **e** used to **f** used to
  g use to, used to **h** didn't use to

8 a 3 **b** 6 **c** 1 **4 d** **e** 2 **5 f**

9 a teacher **b** team **c** recommend
  d join **e** earn

10 a 3 **b** 5 **c** 2 **d** 1 **e** 4

Unit 26

1 a honest **b** quite **c** enough **d** about
  e will **f** obejct **g** mind

2 a True **b** False **c** True **d** True **e** False

3 a, d positive **b** negative **c** indifferent

4 a was, would be able to
  b would be like, would have
  c closed down, would be
  d would go, had
  e would buy, wanted
  f would be, won
  g was, would not have to worry
  h would fly, was not

5 a lived, would visit
  b come, will help / came, would help
  c had, would fly
  d are, will invite
  e practised, would be
  f were, would stop

6 a 1 **b** 4 **c** 3 **d** 6 **e** 5 **f** 2

Unit 27

1 a Do you have any rooms free for the 14th July?
  b A double room, please.
  c I'd prefer a shower, please.
  d Do you accept Eurocard?
  e It's 593 876 4218.

2 a False **b** True **c** True **d** False **e** True

3 a 3 **b** 1 **c** 4 **d** 6 **e** 5 **f** 2

4 a minute **b** speaking **c** calling
  d booking **e** might **f** official

5 a I'd like to speak to Mr Black, please.
  b Sorry? I didn't quite catch that.
  c I'm sorry, I don't understand.
  d Could Mr Black call me back?
  e Great, thank you.

6 a Why don't you try a Scottish dish when you are in
    Edinburgh?
  b Do you think I will need a coat? (Do I need a
    coat?)
  c We had better make a reservation. (Had we
    better make a reservation?)
  d Let's visit all the sights. (Shall we visit all the
    sights?)
  e Do you think we (will) need our passports in
    Scotland / (Will we need our passports in

Scotland? / Do we need our passports in Scotland?)

7 a tell **b** during **c** recommend
 d put **e** booked

8 a if Peter is coming the next day
 b when he would arrive
 c if he would get her a cup of coffee
 d what his/her name was
 e to repeat his/her name
 f who was calling
 g to put the books on the desk

9 a 8 **b** 4 **c** 6 **d** 2 **e** 1 **f** 3 **g** 7 **h** 5 **i** 9

Unit 28

1 d 1 **g** 2 **a** 3 **f** 4 **c** 5 **b** 6 **e** 7

2 a recommend **b** mileage **c** accept **d** charge
 e insurance

3 a 1 **b** 3 **c** 1 **d** 2 **e** 4 **f** 3

4 a True **b** False **c** False **d** False
 e False **f** False **g** True **h** True

5 a What type of car can you recommend?
 b Do you need to see my driving licence?
 c Does that include mileage?
 d Do you accept cheques?
 e When will the car be ready?
 f Can I pay by credit card?

6 a will be writing
 b will be helping
 c will be reading and checking
 d will be helping
 e will be taking
 f will be doing
 g will be having

7 a 3 **b** 4 **c** 5 **d** 2 **e** 6 **f** 1 **g** 7 **h** 8

Unit 29

1 a hear **b** sign **c** fill **d** check **e** put

2 a have **b** had **c** has **d** have **e** have – had
 f have

3 a I had better reserve a room.
 b We had better buy some oil.
 c He has a good idea.
 d I will use the opportunity and fill up the car.
 e We had better stop at the next service station.

4 a fix **b** boot **c** call **d** has

5 a Are you wearing blue jeans?
 b Shall I fill your car / the car / her up?
 c Shall I check the tyres? / Do the tyres need checking?
 d What petrol does it / the car take?
 e Where are the toilets, please?
 f Had I better stop? / Do you want me to stop? / Should I stop?

6 a True **b** False **c** False **d** False **e** False
 f False **g** False

7 warning smoke engine member call phone

8 a 4 **b** 8 **c** 1 **d** 6 **e** 7 **f** 2 **g** 5 **h** 3

9 a Let's go to the theatre.
 b Let me finish the job.
 c Let's have lunch in town
 d Let me buy you a drink, Natalie.
 e Let's travel to London by coach, Peter.
 f Let me help you across the street.

10 a isn't there **b** hasn't it **c** hadn't you
 d hadn't I **e** have you **f** shall I

11 a 3 **b** 5 **c** 1 **d** 2 **e** 4 **f** 6

Unit 30

1 a False **b** False **c** True
 d False **e** False **f** False

2 a We managed to come up with an idea.
 b Many companies are in the same situation.
 c Thank you for giving up your time for me and for showing me around.
 d It is bigger than I had expected.
 e You should have been here a few years ago.
 f We had to rationalise because of costs.

3 a drew **b** covers **c** showing **d** fantastic
 e rationalise **f** manager **g** many **h** economy

4 plant – production site – kind – nice – 700 – 1700
 – very – quite – rationalise – cut back – see – understand.

5 a 29,029 ft   **b** 1.7 miles
 c 20 US gallons   **d** 6 US quarts
 e 40 pints   **f** 172 acres
 g 115 yds, 75 yds, 8,625 square yards

 1 20 US gallons
 2 29,029 ft
 3 1.7 miles
 4 40 pints

5 8,625 square yards

6 115 yds x 75 yds

7 172 acres

8 6 US quarts

6 a The plans were finished six months ago.

b Plans for a new machine were being designed (by engineers).

c The building materials are sent from Manchester to the plant in Scotland.

d The engineers have been told (by management) that they must cut costs.

e The new factory will be opened next year (by Winthrops).

f Nothing can be done about the problem.

g Everyone is being told to be careful.

7 a Peter doesn't like Chinese food and Natalie doesn't (like Chinese food) either. Peter doesn't like Chinese food and neither does Natalie. Neither Peter nor Natalie like Chinese food.

b Peter likes squash and Jack likes squash, too. Peter likes squash and so does Jack. Peter likes squash and Jack also likes squash.

c I don't speak Spanish and Jack doesn't (speak Spanish) either. I don't speak Spanish and neither does Jack. Neither I nor Jack speak Spanish.

d Mr Jackson likes Indian food and Mrs Jackson likes Indian food, too. Mr Jackson likes Indian food and so does Mrs Jackson. Mr Jackson likes Indian food and Mrs Jackson also likes Indian food.

8 a 2   **b** 4   **c** 5   **d** 1   **e** 3

Unit 31

1 a if he knew Christian Fauré

b how long he had known him

c where he had first met him

d if he had seen him since he had met him on the plane

e what he was/had been doing when he last saw him

f if he would be able to report everything to the police

2 a quite sure   **b** understand   **c** don't know

3 a I'm not quite sure I understand.

b So, what is the matter?

c I saw him at Winthrops' headquarters in Manchester.

c I don't know what to say.

d Let's call Jack back with the news.

4 a If you can read this short message, you have made a good start.

b As far as I know, all my mates are using text messages in business.

c Anyone can learn texting very quickly. If you want to save time and costs, texting is great.

d On the other hand, you have to be careful, in my opinion, because no one wants to be rude. For what it's worth, I believe more and more people will use this in future.

e Hi, P [name], where are you? Are you OK? I want to invite you to lunch tomorrow. Can you text me as soon as possible if you are OK?

f Hi, J [name]. Thank you for the invitation, but I'm sorry I can't make it tomorrow. Can we speak tonight? See you later, P [name].

5 a 4   **b** 5   **c** 6   **d** 1   **e** 2   **f** 3   **g** 8   **h** 7

Unit 32

1 a How much is that coat?   *It is £95.*

b How much is that pullover?   *It is £69.*

c How much is that blanket?   *It is £55.*

d How much is that skirt?   *It is £35.90.*

e How much is that blazer?   *It is £183.50.*

2 a 4   **b** 5   **c** 2   **d** 3   **e** 6   **f** 1

3 a That will be   **b** colour   **c** quite

d waiter   **e** go

4 a False   **b** False   **c** False

d True   **e** True   **f** True

5 a True   **b** False   **c** True   **d** False

e True   **f** True   **g** False   **h** False

6 a ~~good~~ well   **b** ~~terribly~~ terrible

c ~~necessary~~ necessarily   **d** ~~usual~~ usually

g ~~hardly~~ hard   **h** ~~friendly~~ in a friendly way

i ~~seriously~~ serious   **k** ~~well~~ good

7 a more, the most   **b** harder

c fewer, the fewest

d hardly   **e** faster, fastest, slowest

f bad, good, as well as   **g** comfortable

h further, furthest

8 a 7   **b** 4   **c** 6   **d** 5   **e** 1   **f** 2   **g** 3

Unit 33

1 a 3 **b** 2 **c** 7 **d** 6 **e** 5 **f** 1 **g** 4

2 a That will be £5.22.
b That will take two days.
c May I borrow your pen?
d That will be £2.50.
e They cost 50p.

3 a letter **b** 50 pence **c** postcards **d** same
e case, 50p **f** £2,50 **g** welcome

4 a scales **b** parcel **c** document **d** attach

5 a would **b** place **c** weighs **d** will

6 1 f **2** i **3** l **4** n **5** j **6** e **7** g **8** m
9 c **10** h **11** d/a **12** a/d **13** k **14** b

Übersetzungsvorschlag

7 Lösungsvorschlag

Svenja Grünhage
Beethovenstraße 70
45218 Essen

NSI
Unit 14A
Chorley Industrial Estate
Southport Road
Chorley PR/2NB
Lancashire
England   24 May, 20XX

Dear Sir/Madam

Application for an internship

I am writing to you on the recommendation of Heinrich Löwe, your agent in Germany.

I am a 25-year-old systems engineer and am at present employed as an assistant to the development manager at Westerhagen GmbH in Essen, Germany.

I would like to apply for an internship at NSI from 1st September to 30th November.
I would like to gain some experience in the marketing department.

I do not expect any remuneration for the internship, but would welcome a contribution to my board and lodging while in Chorley. By way of compensation, I would be pleased to offer my skills and know-how in the field of system engineering.

Please find attached my CV for further information.

I would particularly like to have the opportunity to …

Hoping that my application is of interest to you, I remain,

Yours faithfully

Svenja Grünhage

Enc. Curriculum Vitae, Letter of recommendation

8 a 9 **b** 6 **c** 2 **d** 1 **e** 10 **f** 4 **g** 8 **h** 7
i 3 **j** 5

Unit 34

1 a How about lunch?
  b That sounds interesting.
  c Shall we go in?
  d What have you got to eat?
  e I would like to try that.
  f It tastes disgusting.

2 a quite **b** typically **c** order **d** got **e** would

3 a True **b** False **c** False **d** False **e** True

4 roast lamb – chips – fresh salmon (2x) – boiled potatoes (2x)

5 a quite **b** So **c** about **d** sounds
  e Shall **f** let's **g** would **h** let

6 a serve **b** choice **c** haggis **d** warn
  e disgusting **f** hungry **g** shandy

7 a So am I **b** So do I **d** So have I
  e Neither am I **f** Neither have I
  g Neither do I.

8 a have been walking **b** has been working
  c has been going **d** have been painting
  e have been coming **f** has been learning

9 a had been shopping all morning
  b had been drinking all evening
  c had been smoking all evening
  d had been raining all afternoon
  e had been driving all morning
  f had been watching TV all morning

10 a They had been driving …
  b She had been working …
  c They had been playing tennis …
  d He had been cooking …
  e They had been walking …
  f She had been waiting …

11 a 6 **b** 4 **c** 1 **d** 7 **e** 2 **f** 5 **g** 3

Unit 35

1 a 2 **b** 1 **c** 4 **d** 3 **e** 6 **f** 5

2 a ~~cat~~ – car
  b ~~Tower Bridge~~ – Buckingham Palace
  c ~~cheese~~ – milk
  d ~~Ted~~ – Tom
  e ~~have~~ – drink

3 sailing dinner stealing police pullover
  vase

4 Lösungsvorschlag
  Dear X,
  I am spending my holiday in London. I am visiting Buckingham Palace and all the other well-known sights. When I am in London I usually (go to) eat in an Indian Restaurant. On Monday I am going to visit the Tate Art Gallery. I like the people here, but I don't like the food.
  Best wishes / Regards / All the best / See you soon / (With) Love
  X

5 a 4 **b** 1 **c** 2 **d** 6 **e** 3 **f** 5

6 a 3 **b** 1 **c** 4 **d** 2 **e** 8 **f** 5 **g** 7 **h** 6

Unit 36

1 d 1 **b** 2 **c** 3 **e** 4 **a** 5 **g** 6 **f** 7

2 a ~~thankful~~ – grateful **b** ~~programme~~ – plans
  c ~~suitcase~~ – case **d** ~~thank~~ – present
  e ~~take~~ – accept **f** ~~giving~~ – offering

3 a grateful **b** pleasure **c** gratitude **d** accept
  e enjoyed **f** thank you

4 a 4 **b** 5 **c** 1 **d** 2 **e** 3

5 a with **b** at **c** to **d** for **e** by

6 a I can't possibly accept that.
  b We hope you found your time with us useful and worthwhile.
  c Thank you very much for bringing me to the airport.
  d You will come and visit me in Germany, won't you?
  e I have enjoyed my stay very much.

7 a avoided meeting
  b succeeded in arresting
  c insisted on offering
  d complained of having had
  e forward to hearing
  f chance of going
  g talking about skiing
  h worried about spying
  i way of thinking
  j interested in meeting
  k mind not smoking
  l suggested eating
  m tired of writing

8 a to close **b** to eat **c** to eat **d** to open
  e kicking **f** asking **g** visiting **h** to work

9 a 3 **b** 6 **c** 1 **d** 5 **e** 2 **f** 4

Test 3

1 a 3   **b** 5   **c** 1   **d** 6   **e** 2   **f** 4

2 a has been living   **b** began
c had already been playing
d leaves   **e** will be working

3 a must have missed   **b** will have to apply
c will have to help   **d** had to help
e had to promise   **f** must come

4 a haven't written
b moved
c have been working
d are you?/have you been
e stayed
f moved
g have been living
h travelled
i fell/have fallen
j have you ever visited
k was taking place
l were
m saw
n will finish
o am going
p will be travelling
q hearing

5 a had been, would have been able
b had known, would never have employed
c would go, invited
d need, phone
e had not remembered, would not have caught

6 a is used to drinking
b used to watch
c because   **d** because of
e when he left/would leave/was leaving for
Germany.   **f** to help him with a business letter.

7 a aren't you   **b** haven't you   **c** hadn't you
d haven't you   **e** isn't it   **f** shall I
g weren't you   **h** can't you   **i** is it

8 a The factory was finished one year ago.
b A new design was developed for the XR23
(by the engineers).
c A new plant is being built in Scotland.
d Management was/were told to cut costs.
e A new trainee will be employed (by Winthrops)
next year.
f All the staff have been given more pay this year.
g A lot can be done to solve the problem.

9 a … neither/nor does Natalie./…Natalie doesn't
either.
b … so does Jack./… Jack also likes learning
languages./… Jack likes learning languages, too.
c … so do I./… I also come from Australia./ …
and I come from Australia, too.
d My friend likes working neither on Saturdays
nor on Sundays.

10 a well   **b** usually   **c** hard   **f** in a very friendly
way   **h** easy

11 a normally, more quickly, (the) fastest
b more carefully   **c** more clearly
d harder   **e** slower, faster

12 a to see   **b** driving   **c** skiing/to ski   **d** speaking
e seeing   **f** to buy   **g** smoking   **h** to be   **i** seeing
j to get   **k** to practise

KURZGRAMMATIK

Vorbemerkung

Sie haben in diesem Selbstlernkurs zwei Grammatiken:

- Die eine ist über die Units verteilt und bezieht sich direkt auf die Hörtexte. Dort werden jeweils die sprachlichen und grammatischen Strukturen vorgestellt und erklärt, die in der betreffenden Unit neu vorkommen. Damit ist eine unmittelbare Verbindung zu den Texten – oft mit Beispielen – und auch zu den Übungen gegeben. Dort und bei den Übungen selbst finden Sie auch Hinweise, wo Sie Erklärungen in der hier folgenden Kurzgrammatik und in anderen Units zum gleichen Thema finden. Ob und inwieweit Sie die Querverweise nutzen wollen, bleibt natürlich Ihre Entscheidung.
- Eine zweite Grammatik finden Sie hier. Sie stellt keine komplette Grammatik der englischen Sprache dar, sondern bietet Ihnen einen Überblick über die wichtigsten grammatischen Regeln, die Sie für die Beherrschung der Alltagssprache benötigen. Verweise innerhalb der Grammatik werden nur mit Pfeil und der entsprechenden Nummer gekennzeichnet.

Im Lesebuch finden Sie eine Auflistung der Unregelmäßigen Verben.

Pronomen und Begleiter *(pronouns and determiners)*

1 Personalpronomen *(personal pronouns)*

Subjektform		Objektform	
I	ich	me	mir, mich
you	du; Sie	you	dir, dich; Ihnen, Sie
he	er	him	ihm; ihn
she	sie	her	ihr, sie
it	es; er; sie	it	ihm, es; ihm, ihn; ihr, sie
we	wir	us	uns
you	ihr; Sie	you	euch; Ihnen, Sie
they	sie	them	ihnen, sie

Die Objektform des Personalpronomens steht nach Verben und nach Präpositionen. Im Gegensatz zum Deutschen gibt es im Englischen für jede Person nur eine Objektform:

> *You can phone **me** or send **me** an e-mail.*

Das deutsche ‚man'

Für das deutsche ‚man' können *you* und *one* verwendet werden, wenn man von Leuten im Allgemeinen sprechen will. *One* ist formell und wird nicht mehr häufig verwendet.

> *You can buy cheap tickets on the Internet.*
> *One never knows what the future will bring.*

2 Possessivpronomen und Possessivbegleiter (adjektivische Possessivpronomen) *(possessive pronouns and possessive determiners)*

Possessivpronomen		Possessivbegleiter	
mine	meine/r/s	my	mein/e
yours	deine/r/s; Ihre/r/s	your	dein/e; Ihr/e
his	seine/r/s	his	sein/e
hers	ihre/r/s	her	ihr/e
–	–	its	sein/e; ihre
ours	unsere/r/s	our	unser/e
yours	eure/r/s; Ihre/r/s	your	euer/eure; Ihr/e
theirs	ihre/r/s	their	ihr/e

Possessivpronomen stehen allein, d. h. ohne Substantiv. Sie werden verwendet, wenn man ein schon genanntes Substantiv nicht nochmal aufführen will:

> *Whose book is this?*   *– It is my book.*
>   *– It is **mine**.*

Possessivbegleiter stehen immer vor einem Substantiv und werden daher auch adjektivitische Possessivpronomen genannt:

> *Whose book is this?*   *– It is **my** book.*

Man kann Possessivpronomen auch wie folgt verwenden:

> *They are friends **of mine**. = **my** friends*
> *They are friends **of his**. = **his** friends*

3 Demonstrativpronomen und Demonstrativbegleiter *(demonstrative pronouns and demonstrative determiners)*

Singular		Plural
this	diese/r/s (hier)	these
that	jene/r/s (dort)	those

This, that, these und *those* können unterschiedlich verwendet werden:
- als Demonstrativpronomen, das heißt, sie stehen allein:
  > Are **those** your suitcases? – No, **these** are.
- als Demonstrativbegleiter, das heißt, zusammen mit einem Substantiv:
  > **This suitcase** is mine and **that suitcase** is yours.

Vom Sprecher aus gesehen, weisen *this* und *these* im Allgemeinen auf das räumlich oder zeitlich Nähere und *that* und *those* auf das Entferntere hin.

4 *a lot of / lots of – much – many*

a lot of / **lots of**	There is **a lot of / lots of** *(viel)* industry there. There are **a lot of / lots of** *(viele)* people. There's **a lot / lots** to do.	= mit nicht zählbaren Substantiven = mit zählbaren Substantiven im Plural Wenn kein Substantiv oder Pronomen folgt, fällt das *of* weg.
how much **how many**	**How much** *(wie viel)* money do we need? And **how many** *(wie viele)* eggs would you like?	= mit nicht zählbaren Substantiven = mit zählbaren Substantiven

5 *some – any* + Zusammensetzungen *(compounds)*

Some ist eine unbestimmte Mengenangabe, die bei zählbaren oder nicht zählbaren Substantiven in Aussagesätzen steht. In Fragesätzen oder negativen Aussagesätzen wird *any* gebraucht:

+	-	?
We do have **some** darker shorts in blue.	I'm sorry, but there are**n't any** here.	Do you need **any** help?

Zusammensetzungen *(compounds)* von *some* und *any*

somebody/someone	anybody/anyone
something	anything
somewhere	anywhere

Die Verwendung der Zusammensetzungen entspricht der von *some* und *any*.

6 *no* + Zusammensetzungen *(compounds) – nothing*

No *(kein)* dessert for me. **Nobody / No one** *(niemand/keiner)* came to pick me up. I had no money and **nowhere** *(nirgendwo)* to live. No, there is **nothing** *(nichts)* missing.	*No* steht immer vor einem Substantiv.

7 *every* + Zusammensetzungen *(compounds) – all*

He goes to work **every** day.	jede/r/s
Yes, and **everybody** is so busy.	jeder, alle
Everyone is so nice in the group.	
Everything was packed away in boxes.	alles
She followed me **everywhere**.	überall(hin)
All the **buses** are full.	*All* + **Plural** bedeutet ‚alle' …
I worked **all day**.	*All* + **Singular** bedeutet ‚ganz' …

8 *one*

Is there a department store in town? No, there is not, but there is **one** in Preston. Not that skirt, this **one**.	Um zu vermeiden, dass Substantive zu oft wiederholt werden, gebraucht man die Ersatzform *one*.

Artikel *(article)*

9   Bestimmter Artikel *(definite article)*

the man	der Mann	Im Gegensatz zum Deutschen gibt es
the woman	die Frau	im Englischen nur eine Form für den
the car	das Auto	bestimmten Artikel.
the teachers	die Lehrer	

The man's car.	Das Auto des Mannes.	(des, dem,	Auch die einzelnen Fälle des be-
The teachers' room.	Das Zimmer der Lehrer.	den, die)	stimmten Artikels im Singular und im
			Plural heißen im Englischen stets *the*.

Aussprache	the man	[ðə] vor Konsonanten
	the Englishman	[ði:] vor Vokalen

Gebrauch des bestimmten Artikels

Werden bestimmte Substantive mit Präpositionen verwendet, wird kein Artikel vorangestellt.

Kein Artikel	Artikel
by car/train/bus/coach	in the morning / afternoon / …
in summer/winter	in **the** summer/winter … *bezieht sich meistens auf einen besonderen Sommer/Winter und oft auf den vergangenen Sommer/Winter:* In the summer we moved to London. In the summer of '68 we …
on Monday/Tuesday/…	
in Manchester Road	
in Queen Street	in **the** High Street (= *Ausnahme*)

10   Unbestimmter Artikel *(indefinite article)*

a man	ein Mann	Im Englischen gibt es nur die Formen *a*
a woman	eine Frau	oder *an* für den unbestimmten Artikel.
a car	ein Auto	
an English car	ein englisches Auto	

Aussprache	a man	*a* vor Konsonanten [ə]	Nicht die Schreibung, sondern die Aus-
			sprache des Anfangslautes des folgenden
	an Englishman	*an* vor Vokalen [ən]	Wortes entscheidet darüber, ob *a* oder
			an verwendet wird.

half, quite, such, what + a/n

Der unbestimmte Artikel steht nach *half a, quite a* und *such a*. Beachten Sie die unterschiedliche Wortstellung im Deutschen und die Regel für *What a*.

half a bottle of beer	eine halbe Flasche Bier
quite a good CD	eine ziemlich gute CD
such a fool	ein solcher / so ein Dummkopf
What a lovely day!	Der unbestimmte Artikel steht nach *what* in Ausrufesätzen mit einem zählbaren Substantiv.
What nice weather!	Der unbestimmte Artikel steht aber **nicht** vor einem **nicht** zählbaren Substantiv.

Substantive *(nouns)*

11 Singular und Plural von Substantiven *(singular and plural of nouns)*

Singular	Plural	Aussprache	Schreibregeln
snack light month	snacks lights months	[s] nach den stimmlosen Konsonanten [f, k, p, t, θ]	
friend name family key	friends names families keys	[z] nach stimmhaften Konsonanten wie [b, d, g, l, m, n, r, v, y, ð]	Endet ein Substantiv im Singular mit einem geschriebenen Konsonanten und **-y**, bildet man den Plural mit **-ies**. Das **-y** bleibt erhalten, wenn es nach einem Vokal steht.
cheese village class	cheeses villages classes	[ɪz], wenn das Wort auf [s, z, ʃ, tʃ, ʒ oder dʒ] endet.	Nach einem Zischlaut bildet man den Plural durch Anhängen von **-(e)s**.
photo kilo	photos kilos	[əʊz]	Die meisten Substantive, die auf **-o** enden, bilden den Plural mit **-os**.
potato tomato	potatoes tomatoes		Einige Substantive, die auf **-o** enden, bilden aber den Plural mit **-oes**.

Einige Substantive haben eine unregelmäßige Pluralform, z. B.:
> *man – men • child – children • sheep – sheep*

12 Zählbare und nicht zählbare Subtantive *(countable and uncountable nouns)*

Man unterscheidet zwischen **zählbaren Substantiven** wie beispielsweise:
> *a friend – two friends, a car – three cars*

und **nicht zählbaren Substantiven** wie beispielsweise:
> *water, paper, sugar.*

Nicht zählbare Substantive stehen gewöhnlich **im Singular** und dürfen **nicht mit** *a/an* oder Zahlwörtern wie *one, two, three* usw. verwendet werden. → 5
Abweichend vom Deutschen gibt es im Englischen Substantive, die **nur im Singular** stehen. Dazu gehören z. B.:

advice	Rat, Ratschläge
damage	Schaden, Schäden
furniture	Möbel
information	Information(en)
knowledge	Wissen, Kenntnis(se)
shopping	Einkauf, Einkäufe

Will man **bestimmte Mengen** nicht zählbarer Substantive nennen, setzt man Ausdrücke wie *a / two / … piece(s) / bottle(s) / litre(s) / cup(s) of* davor:

two bottles of water
a piece of information

Einige Substantive werden **trotz** der **Pluralform** auf **-s** als **Singulare** verwendet. Dazu gehören z. B.:

athletics	Leichtathletik
economics	(Volks-)Wirtschaft
news	Nachricht(en)
politics	Politik

13 Substantive, die nur im Plural verwendet werden *(plural nouns)*

Paarwörter (*pair nouns*) bezeichnen Dinge, die aus zwei gleichen Teilen bestehen. Paarwörter werden **nur im Plural** verwendet. Sie dürfen **nicht mit** *a/an* **oder Zahlwörtern** stehen. Will man eine genaue Anzahl nennen, setzt man Ausdrücke wie *a/one pair of* oder *two/three … pairs of* davor. Dazu gehören z. B:

glasses	Brille	**shorts**	Shorts
headphones	Kopfhörer	**scissors**	Schere
jeans	Jeans	**trousers**	(lange) Hosen

Es gibt im Englischen auch Substantive, die **keinen Singular** haben. Die dazugehörigen Bestimmungswörter, Verben und Pronomen sehen anders aus als im Deutschen **im Plural**. Dazu gehören z. B.:

clothes	Kleidung, Kleider	**manners**	Benehmen
earnings	Verdienst	**stairs**	Treppe(nstufen)
looks	Aussehen	**surroundings**	Umgebung.

Clothes are expensive in Great Britain.   *The stairs lead to the first floor.*

14 Sammelnamen *(collective nouns)*

Sammelnamen werden für eine bestimmte **Gruppe von Leuten** verwendet. Ist die **Gruppe als Einheit** gemeint, verwendet man den **Singular** für Verb und Pronomen. Sind die **einzelnen Mitglieder** der Gruppe gemeint, verwendet man eher den **Plural** des Verbs bzw. des Pronomens. Zu den Sammelnamen gehören z. B.:

band	Band, Kapelle
class	Klasse
club	Klub, Verein
couple	Paar
family	Familie
group	Gruppe
management	Management, (Geschäfts)Leitung
staff	Kollegium, Personal
team	Team, Mannschaft

Folgende Sammelnamen werden **immer im Plural** verwendet:

people	(die) Leute
the police	die Polizei(beamten)
cattle	Vieh, Rinder

15 Genitiv *(genitive)*

's	John**'s** car	bei einer Person
	Natalie**'s** name	
	the men**'s** department	bei Substantiven mit unregelmäßigem Plural
s'	the teachers**'** room	bei mehreren Personen und
	Winthrops**'** headquarters	wenn das Substantiv auf **-s** endet
of	the end **of** the film	bei Sachen und bei Datumsangaben
	the days **of** the week	
	the seventh **of** April *(gesprochen)*	
of	friends **of** mine	mit Possessivpronomen

Adjektive *(adjectives)*

16 Steigerung von Adjektiven *(comparison of adjectives)*

Positiv (Grundstufe)	Komparativ (1. Steigerungsstufe)	Superlativ (2. Steigerungsstufe)	
dark light simple	dark**er** light**er** simpl**er**	dark**est** light**est** simpl**est**	An alle einsilbig gesprochenen Adjektive hängt man **-er**, **-est** an, um die beiden Steigerungsstufen zu bilden.
big	big**ger**	big**gest**	Endet das kurze Adjektiv mit einem Vokal und einem Konsonanten, wird der Schlusskonsonant verdoppelt und dann **-er** oder **-est** angehängt.
early	earl**ier**	earl**iest**	An zweisilbige Adjektive, die auf einen Konsonanten und **-y** enden, wird **-y** zu **-i** und dann **-er** bzw. **-est** angehängt.
fine	fin**er**	fin**est**	Ein stummes **-e** entfällt.
beautiful interesting	**more** beautiful **more** interesting	**(the) most** beautiful **(the) most** interesting	Die Steigerungsstufen von den meisten zweisilbigen Adjektiven, die **nicht** auf **-y** enden, und von Adjektiven mit mehr als zwei Silben werden mit *more* und *(the) most* gebildet.

Ausnahmen:

good	better	best
bad	worse	worst
far	further	furthest

17 Adjektive in Vergleichssätzen *(adjectives in comparative clauses)*

These shorts are **as** expensive **as** the navy blue ones.   Diese Shorts sind genauso teuer wie die marineblauen.
A Golf is **not as** expensive **as** a Mercedes.   Ein Golf ist nicht so teuer wie ein Mercedes.
The coach is cheap**er than** the train.   Der Reisebus ist billiger als der Zug.
Edinburgh is **more** interesting **than** Manchester.   Edinburgh ist interessanter als Manchester.
Manchester is **less** interesting **than**Edinburgh.   Manchester ist weniger interessant als Edinburgh.
The coach is **the** cheap**est** way to travel.   Der Reisebus ist die billigste Art zu reisen.
A Rolls Royce is **the most** comfortable car I know.   Ein Rolls Royce ist das komfortabelste Auto, das ich kenne.

Adverbien *(adverbs)*

18 Bildung von Adverbien *(adverb formation)*

Adverbien der Art und Weise werden gebildet, indem man **-ly** an das Adjektiv anhängt:

usual	usual**ly**	bad	bad**ly**
slow	slow**ly**	serious	serious**ly**

Endet ein Adjektiv auf **-y**, so wird daraus im Adverb **-i**; endet ein Adjektiv auf **-ll**, wird das Adverb ebenfalls mit **-ll** geschrieben:

necessary	necessar**ily**	full	ful**ly**
funny	funn**ily**		

Wenn das Adjektiv auf *-le* endet, wird *-le* zu *-ly*:

> *terrible – terribly*   ABER   *whole – wholly*

Einige Adverbien haben die gleiche Form und Bedeutung wie das Adjektiv:

> *fast – fast*   *hard – hard*

Weitere Wörter dieser Art sind beispielsweise:

> *deep* (tief), *fair, high* (hoch), *late, right, wide, wrong*

ABER: Die *-ly* abgeleitete Form dieser Adverbien haben eine weitere Bedeutung.

Das Wort *hardly* (*That's hardly likely.* → Ⓤ Unit 24) bedeutet nicht ‚hart' sondern ‚kaum'.

> *He works hard.* = Er arbeitet hart.
> *He hardly works.* = Er arbeitet kaum.

Adjektive, die auf *-ly* enden (z. B. *lovely, friendly: The landlady is very friendly.* → Ⓤ Unit 8) brauchen eine Umschreibung, wenn sie als Adverb verwendet werden:

> *She spoke **in a friendly way.***

19   Steigerung von Adverbien *(comparison of adverbs)*

Adverb	Komparativ	Superlativ
slowly	more slowly (than) less slowly (than) as slowly as	the most slowly the least slowly
funnily	more funnily (than) less funnily (than) as funnily as	the most funnily the least funnily
terribly	more terribly (than) less terribly (than) as terribly as	the most terribly the least terribly

Unregelmäßige Formen

Adverb	Komparativ	Superlativ
a little	less	(the) least
well	better	(the) best
badly	worse	(the) worst
much / a lot	more	(the) most
far	further	(the) furthest

→ 16

Adjektiv statt Adverb

Nach einigen Ausdrücken verwendet man ein Adjektiv statt eines Adverbs:

> *That **seems** good.*
> *Yours **looks** safe.*
> *The engine is **getting** hot.*
> *I **feel** good.*

20   Adverbien der Art und Weise *(adverbs of manner)*

Für gewöhnlich stehen Adverbien der Art und Weise am Ende des Satzes:

> *He twisted his ankle **badly**.*

Im Gegensatz zum Deutschen stehen sie nie zwischen Verb und Objekt:

> *He speaks English perfectly.*   ⟷   *He speaks ~~perfectly~~ English.*

21 Adverbien der Häufigkeit *(adverbs of frequency)*

I **usually** get up at half past seven. I **often** go to a pub with friends.	Adverbien wie *often, usually* usw. stehen vor dem Vollverb.

Die Adverbien *already*, *ever*, *just*, *never* und *yet* werden häufig mit dem *present* und *past perfect* verwendet:

	I	have	never	been to England before.
	We	have	just	seen our friends.
	I	have	already	done a lot of sightseeing.
Have	you		ever	been to London before?
	They	have not		made plans for next week **yet**.

Präpositionen *(prepositions)*

22 Bedeutung *(meaning)*

Präpositionen sind Verhältniswörter wie *about, behind, by, in, on*. Sie können aber auch aus mehr als einem Wort bestehen, z. B. *next to, in front of*. Es gibt Präpositionen des Ortes, der Zeit und Präpositionen mit anderen Bedeutungen wie *because of* (kausal).

Präpositionen haben unterschiedliche Bedeutungen. Hier ist eine Auswahl mit ihren häufigsten Bedeutungen:

about – *über*	by – *bei; mit; von; durch*	on – *auf*
above – *oberhalb, über*	during – *während*	on top of – *auf*
after – *nach*	for – *für*	opposite – *gegenüber*
around – *um … (herum)*	from – *von, aus*	since – *seit*
at – *an; zu; bei; um*	in – *in*	through – *durch*
because of – *wegen*	in front of – *vor*	to – *nach*
before – *(be)vor*	near – *bei, in der Nähe von*	under – *unter*
behind – *hinter*	next to – *neben*	with – *mit*
between – *zwischen*	of – oft ohne Übersetzung (a piece of cheese = *ein Stück Käse*)	without – *ohne*

Hilfsverben *(auxiliaries)*

23 *be*

Be dient als Hilfsverb zur Bildung der *continuous*-Zeitformen und des Passivs (*The machine is built in Manchester*).

Present continuous:

I **am** going to Manchester.   We **are** not travelling to Edinburgh.

	+ Langform	+ Kurzform	- Langform	- Kurzform
I	am	'm	am not	'm not
you, we, they	are	're	are not	aren't / 're not
he, she, it	is	's	is not	isn't / 's not

Past continuous:

They **were** talking to Mr Jackson.   He **was**n't working at the weekend.

	+ Langform	- Langform	- Kurzform
I, he, she, it	was	was not	wasn't
we, you, they	were	were not	weren't

24 *have*

Have dient als Hilfsverb der Bildung der *perfect*-Zeitformen.

Present perfect:

    *I **have** been to Manchester.*　　　　　*I **have**n't been to Edinburgh.*

	+ Langform	+ Kurzform	– Langform	– Kurzform
I, you, we, they	have	've	have not	haven't / 've not
he, she, it	has	's	has not	hasn't / 's not

Past perfect:

    *I **had** been to London before.*　　　*I **had** not been to Manchester before.*

	+ Langform	+ Kurzform	- Langform	- Kurzform
I, you, he, she, it, we, you, they	had	'd	had not	hadn't

25 *do*

Mit dem Hilfsverb *do* werden Verneinungen und Fragen in den *simple*-Zeitformen gebildet.

Simple present:

    ***Do** I need a new car?*　*I **don't** need a new TV.*

	+ Langform	- Kurzform
I, you, we, they	do not	don't
he, she, it	does not	doesn't

Do	I, you, we, they …?
Does	he, she, it …?

Simple past:

    ***Did** you see the Canadian?*　　　*We **didn't** find the CV.*

	+ Langform	- Langform	- Kurzform
I, you, he, she, it, we, you, they	did	did not	didn't

Did	I, you, he, she, it, we, you, they …?

Modale Hilfsverben *(modal verbs)*

26 *can – could*

	- Langform	- Kurzform	
can	cannot	can't	**Can** you tell me where my room is?
			You **can** take the train or the coach.
could	could not	couldn't	**Could** you help me with the shopping?
			You **could** fly or you **could** hire a car.

27 *would – should*

+ Langform	+ Kurzform	- Langform	- Kurzform	
would	'd	would not	wouldn't	**I'd** like a steak. What **would** you like to start with? **Would** you like to come to the pub?
should	'd	should not	shouldn't	I **should** think so. **Shouldn't** you help them?

28 *must – have to – need*

Präsens	+ Langform	- Langform	- Kurzform	
I, we, you, they	must have to need	must not do not have to need not	mustn't don't have to needn't	**Must** you go? Do you **have to** go? We **have to / need to** wear these protective overalls and helmets
he, she	must has to need	must not does not have to need not	mustn't doesn't have to needn't	**Must** she speak English? Does he **have to** leave now? You **needn't** tidy up.
Futur				
I, he, she, it, we, you, they	will have to	will not have to	won't have to	You **will have to** come next weekend.
Präteritum				
I, he, she, it, we, you, they	had to needed to	did not have to did not need to	didn't have to didn't need to	He **had to** go home. He **didn't need / have to** come.

Must und *have to* drücken Verpflichtung oder Notwendigkeit aus. *You must* ist ein Befehl und wird nur von einer Person, die Autorität besitzt, verwendet. Dagegen bedeutet *I must*, dass man sich verpflichtet oder verantwortlich fühlt. Sonst verwendet man für gewöhnlich *have to* oder *need to*.
Außer im Präsens verwendet man fast immer eine Form von *have to*:

> You **will have to** come next weekend. / He **had to** go home.

Zeitformen *(tenses)*

29 *Simple present* (einfaches Präsens)

Das *simple present* gebraucht man, um:
- über Tatsachen zu reden: *I work for Winthrops.*
- Gewohnheiten auszudrücken: *I often play tennis at the weekend.*
- Meinungen und Gefühle wiederzugeben: *I like Chinese food.*
- allgemeingültige Aussagen zu machen: *What goes up must come down.*
- über feststehenden Termine in der Zukunft zu
  sprechen (Verabredungen, Fahrpläne etc.):   *The number 10 leaves at ten past eight.*

Das *simple present* wird oft mit Ausdrücken wie *always, every (every few minutes / every day / morning / evening / week), never, often, sometimes, usually* verwendet.

I, you, we, they	come watch try play like	Mit Ausnahme der 3. Person Singular lauten alle Formen wie der Infinitiv.

he, she, it	comes [z] watches [ɪz] tries [z] plays [z] likes [s]	Die 3. Person Singular ist durch ein angehängtes -s gekennzeichnet. Endet der Infinitiv aber auf geschriebenes -sh, -ch, -ss, -x oder -z, so wird -es angehängt. Endet der Infinitiv mit einem geschriebenen Konsonanten + y, so schreibt man -ies. Endet der Infinitiv jedoch mit einem geschriebenen Vokal + y, so wird nur -s angefügt.

Aussprache des -s-Lautes:

Wenn der Laut auf einen stimmlos gesprochenen Konsonanten [p, t, k, f] folgt, ist der Laut auch stimmlos [s].

Der Laut ist stimmhaft [z], wenn er auf die stimmhaft gesprochenen Konsonanten [b, d, g, l, m, n, v] oder auf einen Vokal folgt.

Nach den Zischlauten [s, z, ʃ, tʃ, dʒ] wird die -es-Endung [ɪz] gesprochen.

30 *Present continuous* (Verlaufsform des Präsens)

Das *present continuous* wird verwendet, um eine Handlung zu beschreiben, die zum gegenwärtigen Zeitpunkt vor sich geht, von der wir aber wissen, dass sie von vorübergehender Natur ist und bald enden wird.

> I *am washing* my hair.
> You *are going* to the pub.
> He *is writing* a letter.
> She *is studying* for her exams.
>
> We *are leaving* now.
> You *are learning* English.
> Peter and Liz *are going* to the pub.

Das *present continuous* wird auch verwendet, wenn man über fest Geplantes oder Verabredetes spricht.

> What *are* you *doing* on Saturday?
> I *am joining* some friends at my health club.
> We *are playing* squash from 10 until 11.

Das *present continuous* wird aus einer Form von *be* + *-ing*-Form des Vollverbs gebildet. → 23, 42

31 *Simple past* (Präteritum)

Das *simple past* verwendet man zur Beschreibung von:

- Handlungen und Ereignissen in der Vergangenheit, die beendet sind:
  Peter travelled to London last week.
- Zuständen, die eindeutig vorüber sind:
  When we were children we played a lot with our friends.
- Dingen, die über einen längeren Zeitraum in der Vergangenheit Gültigkeit hatten, aber jetzt nicht mehr:
  I worked in a tax office.

Unwichtig dabei ist es, wann die Handlung stattfand, nur abgeschlossen muss sie sein.

Bei **regelmäßigen Verben** wird *-ed* an den Infinitiv des Verbs angehängt, um das *simple past* zu bilden.

stayed travelled arrived phoned tried played	[d]	worked watched missed	[t] nach [k, helped tʃ, s, p]	visited landed wanted	[id] nach [d] und [t]

Unregelmäßige Verben siehe Liste im Lesebuch

Aussage

I, You, He, She, It, We, You, They	**missed** something.

Verneinung

I, You, He, She, It, We, You, They	**did not / didn't**	miss anything.

Frage und verneinte Frage

Did **Didn't**	I, you, he, she, it, we, you, they	miss anything?

32 *Past continuous* (Verlaufsform des Präteritums)

Diese Zeitform kennt man im Deutschen nicht. Das *past continuous* wird verwendet für:
- eine inzwischen abgeschlossene Handlung, die zu einem vergangenen Zeitpunkt gerade vor sich ging,
  d. h. **noch nicht abgeschlossen war**:
    *Where **was** Jack **working** yesterday afternoon?*
    *Yesterday afternoon Peter Hoffmann **was working** in the factory.*
    *The machines **were operating** slowly all day yesterday.*
- eine Handlung, die zu einem vergangenen Zeitpunkt vor sich ging, als eine andere Handlung einsetzte:
    *I **was** just **telling** young Peter here about the trainee **when you came in**.*

Im Deutschen wird das *past continuous* häufig durch Zeitbestimmungen gekennzeichnet oder erklärt sich durch die Situation:

Ich erzählte **gerade** dem jungen Peter hier, wie dein letzter Praktikant abhanden gekommen ist.
Die Maschinen arbeiteten gestern **den ganzen Tag** zu langsam.

→ 23, 30, 42

Aussage

I, He, She,	**was**	tell**ing** Peter about the new plant when Jack arrived.
It		rain**ing** all evening.
We, You, They	**were**	try**ing** to contact his family when he disappeared.

Verneinung

I, He, She	**was not/** **wasn't**	tell**ing** Peter about the new plant when Jack arrived.
It		rain**ing** all evening.
We, You, They	**were not/** **weren't**	try**ing** to contact his family when he disappeared.

Frage und verneinte Frage

Was **Wasn't**	I, he, she, it	wait**ing** for you when you arrived? rain**ing** when you arrived?
Were **Weren't**	we, you, they	try**ing** to contact his family when he disappeared?

Unterschiede zwischen dem *simple past* und dem *past continuous*

Das *simple past* wird verwendet für Handlungen oder Vorgänge, die **zu einem bestimmten Zeitpunkt** oder **in einem bestimmten Zeitraum** in der Vergangenheit vor sich gingen. Die Handlung / Der Vorgang ist **abgeschlossen**:

> *On Saturday / Yesterday / This morning* Peter **went** *for a run.*

Das *past continuous* wird verwendet für Handlungen oder Vorgänge, die zu einer **bestimmten Zeit in der Vergangenheit gerade im Verlauf** waren. Es drückt aus, dass die Handlung **noch nicht abgeschlossen war**.

> *Mr Jackson* **was playing golf** *when it started to rain.*

33 *Past perfect* (Plusquamperfekt)

Das *past perfect* verwendet man, um auszudrücken, dass ein Ereignis vor einem anderen vergangenen Ereignis stattfand. Für das zeitlich frühere Ereignis verwendet man das *past perfect*, für das spätere Ereignis das *simple past*.

> *He* **went** *to Scotland after he* **had been** *to Manchester.*
> *If only I* **had realised** *what he was up to, I* **could have** *reacted sooner.*

	+ Lang-/Kurzform	- Lang-/Kurzform	regelmäßige Form = Infinitiv + *-ed*	unregelmäßige Form
I, you, he, she, it, we, you, they	had / 'd	had not / hadn't	realis**ed**	done

→ 24, 39

34 *Past perfect continuous* (Verlaufsform des Plusquamperfekts)

Das *past perfect continuous* wird verwendet, wenn man ausdrücken will, dass eine Handlung oder ein Vorgang vor einem bestimmten Zeitpunkt in der Vergangenheit begonnen hatte und bis (oder fast bis) zu diesem Zeitpunkt andauerte:

> *Peter* **had been** work**ing** *at Winthrops for several weeks before he visited the factory in Edinburgh.*

Es wird häufig in indirekter Rede und in Bedingungssätzen verwendet:

> *She wanted to know what he* **had been** *doing since she last saw him.*

Das *past perfect continuous* wird für alle Personen gebildet mit **had + been** und **Infinitiv + *-ing***.

	+ Lang-/Kurzform	- Lang-/Kurzform	Infinitiv + -ing
I, You, He, She, We, You, They	had been / 'd been	had not been / hadn't been	working.
It			raining.

35 *Will-future* (Futur mit *will*)

Die Zukunftsform mit *will* drückt oft eine spontane Entscheidung aus:

> *I* **will** *try the car rental company.* – **Ich werde die Autovermietung probieren.**

… oder auch ein Versprechen:

> *I* **will** *get the beer.* – **Ich werde das Bier holen.**

	+ Lang-/Kurzform	- Lang-/Kurzform	Infinitiv
I, you, he, she, it, we, you, they	will / 'll	will not / won't	get

Das *will-future* wird gebildet aus dem Hilfsverb *will* + **Infinitiv** des Vollverbs.

36 *Future with present continuous* (Futur mit Verlaufsform des Präsens)

Das *present continuous* wird verwendet, wenn man über fest Geplantes oder Verabredetes in der Zukunft spricht:

> What **are** you **doing** on Saturday?
> I **am joining** some friends at my health club.
> We **are playing** squash from 10 until 11.

37 *Going to-future* (Futur mit *going to*)

Wenn man über persönliche Absichten und Pläne spricht, verwendet man das *going to-future*:
> We are **going to** sell the idea to American investors.

Der Unterschied zwischen festem Plan (z. B. eine Fahrkarte ist schon gebucht) oder Abmachungen (z. B. eine Konferenz ist einberufen worden), wo man das *present continuous* verwenden würde (→ 30, 36), und persönlicher Absicht ist nicht immer klar ersichtlich. Deshalb kann man in solchen Fällen sowohl das *present continuous* als auch das *going to-future* verwenden:

> We are going to meet tomorrow morning.   I'm going to join some friends in the pub.

38 *Future continuous* (Verlaufsform des Futurs)

Diese Form wird verwendet:
- für Handlungen oder Vorgänge, die zu einem bestimmten Zeitpunkt in der Zukunft im Verlauf sein werden:
  > We'**ll be talking** to Mr Jackson tomorrow.   I'**ll be visiting** Natalie all next weekend.
- um sich höflich nach jemandes Absichten oder Plänen zu erkündigen:
  > **Will** you **be paying** by credit card or in cash?
- um über Handlungen und Vorgänge zu sprechen, die zwangsläufig passieren werden:
  > I **will be seeing** Jack tomorrow at work.

	+ Lang-/Kurzform	- Lang-/Kurzform	Infinitiv + *-ing*
I, he, she, we, you, they	will be/'ll be	will not be/won't be	seeing…
It			raining.

39 *Present perfect* (Perfekt)

Das *present perfect* drückt eine Handlung aus …,
- die zu einem vergangenen Zeitpunkt begonnen hat und noch andauert.
  > They **have done** business with Germany for over ten years.
- die zu einem vergangenen Zeitpunkt begonnen hat und auch beendet wurde, deren Ergebnis und Folgen aber für die Gegenwart bedeutsam oder relevant sind.
  > They **have arranged** for us to visit a company.
  > I **have not been** to Edinburgh before.
- Das *present perfect* kommt besonders häufig bei Fragen vor, die sich auf die Vergangenheit bis hin zur Gegenwart beziehen.
  > **Have** you ever **visited** an English company?

	+ Lang-/Kurzform	- Lang-/Kurzform	regelmäßige Form = Infinitiv + *-ed*	unregelmäßige Form
I, we, you, they	have/'ve	have not/haven't	visited	done
he, she, it	has/'s	has not/hasn't	tr**ied** sto**pp**ed	been

Present perfect und Adverbien

Die Adverbien *already*, *ever*, *just*, *never* und *yet* werden häufig mit dem *present perfect* verwendet (→ 24):

I	have	never	been to England before.
We	have	just	seen our friends.
I	have	already	done a lot of sightseeing.
Have	you		never	been to London before?
	They	have not		made plans for next week **yet**.

Present perfect mit *since* und *for*

I have known John **since** 1990.	*since* = **von** einem bestimmten **Zeitpunkt** bis zur Gegenwart
We have not been to London **for** more than two years.	*for* = **während** einer bestimmten **Zeitspanne** bis zur Gegenwart

40 *Present perfect continuous* (Verlaufsform des Perfekts)

Das *present perfect continuous* drückt eine Handlung oder einen Vorgang aus, die bzw. der zu einem vergangenen Zeitpunkt begonnen hat und noch andauert. Diese Form des Perfekts hebt besonders vor, dass die Handlung oder der Vorgang noch andauert.

	have + been	Infinitiv + *-ing*	
I	**have** (not) **been**	learn**ing**	English all my life.
He	**has** (not) **been**	work**ing**	all morning.

41 Infinitiv (*infinitive*)

Infinitiv ohne *to*

Der Infinitiv ohne *to* wird verwendet nach:

• modalen Hilfsverben wie beispielsweise:

can	He **can speak** French.
should	But why **should** he **strike** tonight?
will	He **will tell** you what he is doing here.
had better	You **had better stop**.

• nach gewissen Verben:

let	**Let** me **have** a look at the engine.
see	Peter **saw** Jack's car **drive** round the corner.
hear	I **heard** Jack **say** something.
help*	I **helped** Janet **tidy up**.

* **help** auch möglich mit **to**

Infinitiv mit *to*

Der Infinitiv mit *to* wird verwendet nach:

• gewissen Adjektiven:

sorry	I am **sorry to hear** that.
glad	I'm **glad to hear** that.
ready	Mr Jackson is **ready to see** you.
able to	They might be **able to help** you.
difficult	The instructions are **difficult to follow**.

• gewissen Verben:

Verb + Infinitiv + *to*		Verb + <u>Objekt</u> + Infinitiv + *to*	
agree			
arrange	They **arranged to visit** a company.	arrange	They have **arranged** <u>for us</u> **to visit** a company.
choose			
decide			
offer	Thanks for **offering to show** me around		
plan			
promise	She **promised to come** to Germany.		
want	Peter **wants to try** the shorts on.	want	I don't **want** <u>you</u> **to go** to any trouble.**
would like/ love	I **would like to buy** a pair of running shorts.	would like	

** Im Deutschen ≈ „Ich will nicht, dass du dir Umstände machst."
Im Englischen ist *don't want that* nicht möglich.

42 *-ing*-Form *(-ing form)*

	+ Lang-/Kurzform	- Lang-/Kurzform	regelmäßige Form = Infinitiv + *-ing*	unregelmäßige Form
I	am/'m	am not/'m not	visiting	trave**lling**
he, she, it	is/'s	is not/isn't/'s not	tr**ying** hop**ing**	
you, we, they	are/'re	are not/aren't/'re not	shop**ping**	

Die *-ing*-Form wird verwendet sowohl als Teil der *continuous*-Form (→ 30, 32, 34), sowie:

• als Substantiv:

running	**Running** is what I like doing most. It's my favourite sport.
cooking	Chinese **cooking**.
living	What do you do for a **living**?

• nach gewissen Verben:

to avoid	(es) vermeiden	He **avoided** look**ing** at her.
to finish	fertig sein mit, aufhören mit, beenden	Have you **finished** eat**ing**?
to mind	etwas dagegen haben	Would you **mind** wait**ing** a moment?
to suggest	vorschlagen	Jack **suggested** go**ing** to the cinema.

• nach gewissen Adjektiven, Verben und Substantiven + Präposition:

be fond of	gern tun	I am not so **fond of** eat**ing** Chinese food.
be interested in	interessiert sein an, sich interessiern für	
be tired of	genug haben von, es leid sein zu	
to complain of	sich beschweren über	
to insist on	bestehen auf	
to look forward to	sich freuen auf	I **look forward to** meet**ing** you.
to succeed in	Erfolg haben bei/mit	

to talk about	sprechen über	
to thank sb for	jmdm. danken für	Thank you for mak**ing** my stay so interesting.
to think of	denken an, in Betracht ziehen	I'm **thinking of** travell**ing** to Scotland.
to worry about	sich Sorgen machen wegen/um	
chance of	Chance/Gelegenheit (zu)	
way of	Art und Weise	

• nach gewissen Ausdrücken:

can't help …	einfach müssen	I **couldn't help** laugh**ing**.
How about …?	Wie wäre es …?	**How about** go**ing** there for lunch?
It is no use/good …	es hat keinen Zweck	**It is no use / no good** ask**ing** me. I don't know.
There is no point …	es ist zwecklos	**There is no point** ask**ing** me. I don't know.

• statt eines Nebensatzes:

You can check my story **by calling** Jack	You can check my story if you call Jack.

43 *-ing*-Form und *to*-Infinitiv *(-ing form and to-infinitive)*

Einige Verben können sowohl mit der *-ing*-Form als auch mit dem Infinitiv verwendet werden. Dann haben sie allerdings eine andere Bedeutung. Hier sind einige Beispiele:

Will you **remember to invite** Peter?	daran denken, (in der Zukunft) etwas zu tun
Do you **remember inviting** Peter?	sich daran erinnern, dass man (in der Vergangenheit) etwas getan hat
He **stopped to ask** the way.	anhalten, um etwas anderes zu tun
If I had a lot of money, I would **stop working**.	aufhören, etwas zu tun
Please **try to remember**.	sich bemühen
You could **try calling** the Scottish Tourist Board.	ausprobieren, es probieren mit

Satzarten *(sentence types)*

44 Positive Aussagesätze *(positive statements)*

In positiven (bejahenden) Aussagesätzen gleicht die Wortstellung der des Deutschen (→ 23, 26):

Subjekt	Prädikat		Ergänzung
	Hilfsverb	**Verb**	
I		am	German.
This		is	Natalie.
They		are	Scottish.
Jack		works	at Winthrops.
Martina		comes	from Frankfurt.
Peter	is	visiting	Natalie.
They	can	help	you.

45 Imperativ (*imperative*)

Go along King Street. **Turn** left.	= Infinitiv des Verbs
Do not (**Don't**) turn right.	= **Do not** + Infinitiv des Verbs

46 Negative Aussagesätze mit Hilfsverb (*negative statements with auxiliary*)

Simple present (**Präsens**)

Subjekt	Hilfsverb	Verneinung	Verb	Ergänzung
I	do	not	work	at Winthrops.
Jack	does		come	from Frankfurt.
We	do		like	Chinese food.
They	do		work	on Sundays.

Simple past (**Präteritum**)

Subjekt	Hilfsverb	Verneinung	Verb	Ergänzung
I	did	not	work	at Winthrops.
Jack			go	to Newcastle.
We			like	the food.
They			work	last Sunday.

47 Negative Aussagesätze mit dem Vollverb *be* (*negative statements with the main verb 'be'*)

I	am		German.
This	is	not	Natalie.
They	are		Swiss.

→ 23

48 Frageanhängsel (*question tags*)

In der Umgangssprache werden Feststellungen häufig kurze Fragen angehängt, die inhaltlich dem deutschen ‚nicht wahr …?' bzw. ‚oder …?' ähnlich sind. Zur Bildung eines solchen Frageanhängsels (*question tag*) werden das erste Hilfsverb + Personalpronomen verwendet. Enthält der Satz kein Hilfsverb wird *do*, *does* oder *did* verwendet. Es handelt sich hier aber nicht um eine Frage, sondern um eine Aufforderung zur Zustimmung oder wenn man aus Unsicherheit nachfragen will.

Wenn der Aussagesatz positiv ist, ist das Frageanhängsel negativ und wenn der Aussagesatz negativ ist, ist das Frageanhängsel positiv.

You **are** German,	**aren't** you?
He **can** speak English,	**can't** he?
They **work** for Winthrops,	**don't** they?
We **don't** leave until two o'clock,	**do** we?
I'm right,	**aren't** I?
He **couldn't** come,	**could** he?
You **had better** listen to him,	**hadn't** you?
Peter and Jack **didn't play** squash yesterday,	**did** they?

49 Fragesätze mit dem Hilfsverb *do (questions with the auxiliary 'do')*

Wenn kein Hilfsverb im Aussagesatz vorhanden ist, wird im Fragesatz eine Form des Hilfsverbs *do – do/does* im simple *present* und *did* im *simple past* – vor das Subjekt gestellt, wenn nicht nach dem Subjekt gefragt wird. Das Hauptverb steht im Infinitiv.

Hilfsverb	Subjekt	Hauptverb	Ergänzung
Do	you	speak	English?
Does	Peter	visit	Natalie?
Do	they	play	squash?
Did	Peter	visit	Natalie?
Did	they	play	squash?

→ 25

50 Fragesätze ohne Fragewörter *(questions without question words)*

Es gibt zwei Arten von Fragen: Ja/Nein-Fragen und Fragen mit einem Fragewort.

In Ja/Nein-Fragen mit dem Vollverb *be* sind – wie im Deutschen – Subjekt und Verb vertauscht:

> **Are you** *Martina Glass?*
> **Is this** *your name?*

In Fragesätzen, in denen nicht wie oben nach dem Subjekt gefragt wird, steht das Hilfsverb des Aussagsatzes vor dem Subjekt.

Hilfsverb	Subjekt	Hauptverb	Ergänzung
Is	Ursula	washing	her hair?
Are	Jack and Peter	playing	badminton?
Has	Peter	bought	a kilt?
Can	you	tell	me where the bar is?
Must	you	go	now?
Will	Peter	go	to London?
Would	you	like	a cup of coffee?

Bei **zwei oder mehr Hilfsverben** wird das erste Hilfsverb vor das Subjekt gestellt:

> *Jack* **has been** *waiting long. –* **Has** *Jack been waiting long?*
> *The plan* **might have been** *stolen. –* **Might** *the plan have been stolen?*

51 Negative Fragen *(negative questions)*

Negative Fragen, in denen nicht nach dem Subjekt gefragt wird, werden mit der verneinten Form des Hilfsverbs gebildet.

Hilfsverb + *n't*	Subjekt	Hauptverb	Ergänzung
Isn't	Peter	working	today?
Aren't	Jack and Peter	playing	badminton?
Hasn't	Ursula	phoned?	
Don't	you	like	Chinese food?
Didn't	Jack	pick up	Peter?

Negative Fragen sind oft keine echten Fragen. Sie werden vewendet, um Vorschläge, Missbilligung, Erstaunen und andere Sprechabsichten zum Ausdruck zu bringen.

> *Isn't it nice?*
> *Aren't you Mr Brown?*

52 Fragesätze mit Fragewort und Hilfsverb *(questions with question word and auxiliary)*

Fragesätze mit einleitendem Fragewort und Hilfsverb werden genauso gebildet wie Fragesätze ohne Fragewort, indem man das Hilfsverb des Aussagesatzes vor das Subjekt stellt.

Fragewort	Hilfsverb	Subjekt	Verb
What	are	you	doing?
What	has	Peter	done?
When	will	the parcel	arrive?

53 Fragesätze mit Fragewort und dem Hilfsverb *do (questions with question word and the auxiliary 'do')*

Wenn kein anderes Hilfsverb vorhanden ist, muss stattdessen im Fragesatz eine Form des Hilfsverbs *do* vor das Subjekt gesetzt werden. Das Hauptverb steht im Infinitiv.

Fragewort	Hilfsverb	Subjekt	Verb
What	do	I	need?
Where	does	she	live?
When	did	he	arrive?

54 Negative Fragen mit Fragewort *(negative questions with question word)*

Negative Fragen mit Fragewort werden mit der verneinten Form des Hilfsverbs gebildet.

Fragewort	Hilfsverb + *n't*	Subjekt	Verb	Ergänzung
Why	don't	you	ask	Mr Brown?
Why	doesn't	Suzie	play	squash?
Why	didn't	you	ask	the boss?
Why	haven't	you	phoned?	

55 Ja/Nein-Fragen mit Kurzantworten *(yes/no questions with short answers)*

Hilfsverb	Subjekt	Verb	Ergänzung	Kurzantworten	
				+	−
Is	it	raining?		Yes, it is.	No, it isn't.
Can	you	use	the Internet?	Yes, I can.	No, I can't.
Have	they	got	a DVD player?	Yes, they have.	No, they haven't.
Do	you	like	cheese?	Yes, I do.	No, I don't.
Does	Peter	play	squash?	Yes, he does.	No, he doesn't.
Did	they	enjoy	the trip?	Yes, they did.	No, they didn't.

56 Kurzantworten *(short answers)*

Hier eine Auflistung der am häufigsten verwendeten Kurzantworten.

Yes, I am. / No, I am not.
Yes, it is. / No, It is not.
Yes, he/she is. / No, he/she is not.
Yes, I do. / No, I do not.
Yes, he/she does. / No, he/she does not.
Yes, I did. / No, I didn't.
Yes, I have. / No, I have not.
Yes, he/she has. / No, he/she has not.
Yes, I can. / No, I cannot.
Yes, I would. / No, I would not.

57 Sätze mit *There is / There are (sentences with There is / There are)*

There is an Indian restaurant in Park Road.
There are a lot of interesting things to see in Edinburgh.

Is there a post office near here?
Are there any pubs here?

There is/are entspricht dem Deutschen ,Es gibt' und drückt allgemein das Vorhandensein von etwas aus.

Komplexe Sätze *(complex sentences)*

58 Bedingungssätze *(conditional sentences)*

Bedingungssatz Typ 1 *(conditional sentence type 1)*
Dieser Typ Bedingungssatz (*if*-Satz Typ 1) enthält im *if*-Satz eine Voraussetzung bzw. Bedingung, die erfüllbar oder erfüllt ist, und im Hauptsatz die mögliche Folge (Was ist, wenn …?):

> *They can help you if you want.*

Der Bedingungssatz Typ 1 kann sich auch auf die Zukunft beziehen. Solche Sätze werden häufig verwendet, um Versprechungen zu machen:

> *If there **are** no trains, we **will travel** by car.*
> *If I **come** to Germany, **I'll visit** you.*

Im *if*-Satz steht das *simple present* und im Hauptsatz *will-future* oder ein modales Hilfsverb (→ 29, 35):

> ***if + simple present – will future* oder modales Hilfsverb + Infinitiv**

Will steht im britischen Englisch immer im Hauptsatz, **nie im *if*-Satz**.

Bedingungssatz Typ 2 *(conditional sentence type 2)*
Der Bedingungssatz Typ 2 (*if*-Satz Typ 2) enthält im *if*-Satz eine Voraussetzung bzw. Bedingung, von der der Sprecher es für unwahrscheinlich hält, dass sie erfüllt wird (Was wäre, wenn …?):

> *If I won the lottery, I would buy a big house.*

Es kann aber auch eine Bedingung genannt werden, die nicht erfüllbar ist, weil sie den Tatsachen widerspricht:

> *If I was younger, I would travel more.*

Im Alltagsgebrauch werden Bedingungssätze dieser Art oft verwendet, um einen Rat zu geben oder um einen Wunsch zu äußern:

> *If I **were** you, **I would shorten** it a little.*
> *If I **had** a lot of money, **I would stop** working.*

Im *if*-Satz steht das *simple past* und im Hauptsatz *would, could* oder *might* + Infinitiv (→ 31, 26, 27):

> ***if + simple past – would/could/might* + Infinitiv**

Would, could und *might* stehen immer im Hauptsatz, **nie im *if*-Satz**.

Bedingungssatz Typ 3 *(conditional sentence type 3)*
Bedingungssätze des Typ 3 (*if*-Satz Typ 2) beziehen sich auf die Vergangenheit. Sie beschreiben, was passiert wäre, wenn eine Bedingung erfüllt worden wäre (Was wäre gewesen, wenn …?), die aber in Wirklichkeit nicht erfüllt wurde.

> *If he **had** already **taken** them, he **would have disappeared** quickly.*
> *If only I **had realised** what he was up to, I **could have reacted** sooner.*

Im *if*-Satz steht das *past perfect* und im Hauptsatz *would/could/might* + *have* + Partizip Perfekt (→ 33, 26, 27, 24):

> ***if + past perfect – would/could/might + have* + Partizip Perfekt**

Mit Bedingungssätzen vom Typ 3 kann man u. a. Vorwürfe oder Rechtfertigungen ausdrücken.

59 Relativsätze *(relative clauses)*

Relativsätze sind Nebensätze, die ein Bezugswort (meist ein Substantiv) näher bestimmen.

> *That's Peter's friend who lives in London.   I can't find the CV which he sent us.*

Relativpronomen

Die Relativpronomen *who* und *whose* beziehen sich auf eine Person.
Das Relativpronomen *which* bezieht sich auf eine Sache.
Das Pronomen *that* kann oft für beides verwendet werden.

> **Merke:**
> Das deutsche ‚was' im Relativsatz entspricht **nicht** dem englischen **what**:
> Alles, **was** Sie sehen, ist verkäuflich. . . . . *Everything **that**/**which** you see is for sale.*

Bestimmende und nicht bestimmende Relativsätze

Ein bestimmender Relativsatz gibt unentbehrliche Information über die Person/Sache, über die gesprochen wird:

> *Have you got a photo of the man **who** was on the plane?*

Der Relativsatz beantwortet in diesem Fall die Frage: „Von welchem Mann sprichst du?"

Dagegen ist in dem folgenden Satz die Information darüber, was der Mann getragen hat, nicht notwendig, um zu verstehen, welche Person gemeint ist.

> *The man you met in the factory, who was wearing a dark blue coat, is Mr Jackson's brother.*

Das Pronomen *that* darf in nicht bestimmenden Relativsätzen nicht als Ersatz für *who* oder *which* verwendet werden.

60 Indirekte Rede *(indirect speech)*

Indirekte Rede verwendet man, um wiederzugeben, was jemand gesagt, geschrieben oder gedacht hat:

> Guard: *"The drawers were closed when I began my rounds on Friday evening."*
> Jack to Peter: *The guard said the drawers were closed when he began his rounds on Friday evening*

Steht das einleitende Verb im *simple present* (hier *says*), ändert sich die Zeitform des Verbs in der indirekten Rede (hier: *am*) nicht.

> Peter: *"I am not so fond of Chinese food."*
>   *Peter **says** he **is** not so fond of Chinese food.*

Steht das einleitende Verb aber im simple past, wird die Zeitform dieses Verbs in der indirekten Rede um eine „Stufe" zurück in die Vergangenheit verschoben, also wird in diesem Fall aus „am" „was":

> *Peter said he **was** not so fond of Chinese food.*

Man verwendet das *present* aber in der eigentlichen Aussage, wenn man meint, dass sie zum Zeitpunkt des Berichtens noch gültig ist:

> *Peter said he **is** not so fond of Chinese food.*

Überblick über die Zeitverschiebungen in der indirekten Rede:

Direkte Rede	Indirekte Rede
simple present	*simple past*
"I **don't** want you to go to any trouble."	He said he **didn't** want her to go to any trouble.
present continuous	*past continuous*
"Well, I **am going** for a run."	He said he **was going** for a run.
present perfect	*past perfect*
"So far they **have** not **been** successful."	He said that so far they **had** not **been** successful.

present perfect continuous	*past perfect continuous*
"I **have been living** in Manchester for ten years."	He said he **had been living** in Manchester for ten years.
simple past	*past perfect*
"I **didn't** actually **lose** him."	He said he **hadn't** actually **lost** him.
past continuous	*past perfect continuous*
"I **was travelling** to London when I saw him."	He said he **had been travelling** to London when he saw him.

<table>
<tr><td colspan="2" align="center">**Modale Hilfsverben**</td></tr>
<tr><td colspan="2" align="center">will → would • can → could • must → had to • may → might</td></tr>
</table>

Nicht nur die Zeitformen ändern sich in der indirekten Rede, sondern oft auch die Personalpronomen und *this* und *that* sowie Zeit- und Ortsbestimmungen.

Indirekte Fragesätze

What's the man's name?	→	He asked me **what** the man's name **was**.
When do you **leave** for work?	→	They wanted to know **when** I **left** for work.
Do you **walk** to work, Mr Brown?	→	She asked Mr Brown **if/whether** he **walked** to work.

- Wenn das einleitende Verb im *simple past* steht, wird die Zeitform genauso zurückverschoben (oder nicht zurückverschoben) wie bei Aussagessätzen.
- Fragewörter wie *how, what, when* usw. werden in der indirekten Rede beibehalten.
- Ist in der direkten Rede kein Fragewort vorhanden (Ja/Nein-Frage), wird die indirekte Frage mit *if* oder *whether* (= ob) eingeleitet.

61 Passiv *(passive)*

Wie im Deutschen verwendet man das Passiv, wenn derjenige, der etwas getan hat, nicht bekannt oder unwichtiger ist als die Handlung selbst:

> The machine **was built** in Manchester.

Wenn man besonders hervorheben will, wer etwas getan hat, so verwendet man das Passiv mit dem Zusatz *by*:

> It was found **by** the guard, not the police.

Das Passiv wird gebildet mit einer Form von **be** und dem **Partizip Perfekt**. Für die Verwendung der Zeitform gelten die gleichen Regeln wie im Aktiv.

		Regelmäßige Verben	Unregelmäßige Verben	
Simple present	am/are/is	recommended		
Present continuous	is/are being		written	Reports are being written.
Present perfect	have/ has been		stolen	It must have been stolen.
Simple past	was/were		built	It was built in Manchester.
Past continuous	was/were being	planned		
Past perfect	had been		worn	Helmets had been worn at all times.
Will-future	will be	trapped		He will be trapped.

In Sätzen mit einem modalen Hilfsverb kann *be* + Partizip Perfekt *(be worn)* oder die *perfect*-Form mit *have been* + Partizip Perfekt *(have been seen)* stehen:

You **must** wear helmets.   → Helmets must be **worn**.

Someone **should** have seen to it. → should **have been seen** to.

Bildquellenverzeichnis

lex:tra

Sprachkurs *Premium*

Englisch
Lesebuch

Anthony Fitzpatrick
Leah Fitzpatrick

Cornelsen

Englisch
von Anthony Fitzpatrick, Leah Fitzpatrick

Konzept und Koordinierung: Anthony Fitzpatrick
Redaktion: Sigrid Janssen
redaktionelle Mitarbeit: Sinéad Butler, Tina Harnischfeger
Projektleitung: Rebecca Syme
Layout und technische Umsetzung: sign, Berlin
Umschlaggestaltung: Cornelsen Verlag Design
Umschlagfoto: Purestock/Alamy; Blue Jean Images/Alamy

Weitere Lextra Englisch-Titel:
978-3-589-01539-9 Lextra Großes Themenwörterbuch Englisch
978-3-589-01561-0 Lextra Grund- und Aufbauwortschatz Englisch
978-3-589-22264-3 Lextra Lerngrammatik Englisch + CD-ROM

www.cornelsen.de
www.lextra.de

Die Links zu externen Webseiten Dritter, die in diesem Lehrwerk angegeben sind, wurden vor Drucklegung sorgfältig auf ihre Aktualität geprüft. Der Verlag übernimmt keine Gewähr für die Aktualität und den Inhalt dieser Seiten oder solcher, die mit ihnen verlinkt sind.

Dieses Werk berücksichtigt die Regeln der reformierten Rechtschreibung und Zeichensetzung. Bei den mit ® gekennzeichneten Texten haben die Rechteinhaber einer Anpassung widersprochen.

1. Auflage, 1. Druck 2010

Alle Drucke dieser Auflage sind inhaltlich unverändert und können im Unterricht nebeneinander verwendet werden.

© 2010 Cornelsen Verlag, Berlin

Druck: CS-Druck CornelsenStürtz, Berlin

ISBN 978-3-589-01571-9

 Inhalt gedruckt auf säurefreiem Papier aus nachhaltiger Forstwirtschaft.

Inhaltsverzeichnis

Einleitung

Dieses Lesebuch bietet Ihnen die englischen Dialoge und deutschen Übersetzungen, die eine interessante Geschichte bilden. Der englische Sprechtext und die deutsche Übersetzung sind so in Zeilen unterteilt, dass sich sprachliche Sinneinheiten ergeben. Sie können die Geschichte selber lesen und als Hörversion anhören. Weitere Informationen zum Lextra Sprachkurs Premium Englisch finden Sie in der Einleitung des Lernbuchs.

Hier sind einige Tipps, wie Sie die englische Sprache am besten und effektivsten lernen können, um Ihre Arbeit mit dem Lextra Sprachkurs Premium zu unterstützen.

Wir wünschen Ihnen viel Spaß damit.

Ihr
Sprachkurs Premium Englisch Team

Tipps

Wenn Sie die Empfehlungen auf Ihre Weise umsetzen, werden Sie eine breite Grundlage für das Verstehen von gesprochenen und geschriebenen Texten, sowie für den mündlichen und schriftlichen Ausdruck erwerben. Allerdings ist dieser Kurs für unterschiedlichste Lerner konzipiert und beinhaltet möglicherweise nicht alles, was für Sie persönlich wichtig ist. Ihr persönliches Englisch müssen Sie daher von Anfang an mit Hilfe eines Wörterbuchs abrunden, indem Sie sich z. B. folgende Fragen stellen:

- Wie heißen meine Lieblingssportarten auf Englisch?
- Was esse ich besonders gern, was mag ich überhaupt nicht, worauf bin ich allergisch? Wie heißen diese Ausdrücke auf Englisch?
- Was sind meine Hobbys, wie heißen sie auf Englisch?
- Sind einige meiner Freunde vielleicht Italiener, Schweizer oder Dänen? Wie sagt man das auf Englisch?
- Welches Instrument spiele ich oder mag ich besonders gern? Wie heißt es auf Englisch?
- Welches Vokabular benötige ich, um Menschen von mir zu erzählen?

Wenn Sie sich auf diese Weise in den Mittelpunkt Ihres Lernens stellen, fehlen Ihnen beim Sprechen oder Schreiben über für Sie selbstverständliche Dinge des Lebens und Ihres Alltages nicht die Worte.

Suchen Sie jede Gelegenheit zu beweisen, dass Sie bereits einiges verstehen und auf Englisch sagen können. Das motiviert Sie zum Weiterlernen und gibt Ihnen die nötige Sicherheit beim Sprechen. Der Schritt vom Lernen zum selbstverständlichen Sprechen ist psychologisch gesehen nicht immer leicht. Hier einige Vorschläge, wie Sie solche Gelegenheiten wahrnehmen können:

- Gehen Sie an Plätze, an denen Sie englische, australische, kanadische oder amerikanische Touristen treffen. Sprechen Sie sie an, bieten Sie Ihre Hilfe an, erklären Sie ihnen den Weg oder begleiten Sie sie ein kurzes Stück. Wenn sich an Ihrem Wohnort eine solche Gelegenheit selten bietet, stellen Sie sich solche Situationen bildlich vor und sagen Sie ein paar Dinge laut, die Sie in der realen Situation sagen könnten.
- Stellen Sie sich einen englischen Freund, eine australische Freundin vor und schreiben Sie ihnen eine Karte, einen kurzen Brief und erzählen Sie, was Sie im Moment tun, was Ihnen Freude oder Kummer macht, was Sie im Sommer vorhaben und was Ihre Pläne sind.
- Kaufen Sie sich eine englische Zeitschrift. Zeitschriften sind leichter zu verstehen als Zeitungen, die Bilder erleichtern das Lesen und Sie können den Inhalt auf vielen Seiten vorher erraten: die schönsten Reiseziele, Klatsch über bekannte Personen, das Horoskop für Liebe, Geld und Gesundheit, Werbung für die Produkte X und Y.
- Riskieren Sie es, sich einen englischen Film in der Originalfassung anzusehen. Auch wenn Sie beim ersten Mal den Eindruck haben, dass Sie „überhaupt nichts" verstehen, wird das nicht stimmen. Ein englischer Film auf DVD bietet oft die zusätzliche Möglichkeit, Untertitel im Deutschen einzublenden oder aber den Film zuerst auf Deutsch zu sehen. Eine gute Möglichkeit, das Hörverstehen zu verbessern ist, englische Untertitel zum englischen Original zuzuschalten und mitzulesen, während Sie den Film schauen.
- Vielleicht können Sie über Kabel, Satellit oder Internet auch englisches Radio oder Fernsehen empfangen und sich dadurch mit Tempo und Klang der englischen Sprache vertraut machen.

Peter Hoffmann	Excuse me, is this row 10, seat G?
Passenger	Yes, it is. My seat is 10 H.
Peter Hoffmann	Thanks. Are you from America?
Passenger	No, I am not. I am Canadian –
	French Canadian.
	I am from Quebec.
Peter Hoffmann	Ah, I see.
	Are you on holiday in Europe?
Passenger	No, my company is here in London.
	What about you? Are you English?
Peter Hoffmann	No, I am not. I am German.
	I am here to improve my English.
Passenger	But your English is excellent.
Peter Hoffmann	That's very kind of you to say so.
Passenger	But it is true. Are you here on holiday?
Peter Hoffmann	No, I am with a company in Manchester.
	I am a trainee.

Hören Sie und sprechen Sie nach.

Now listen and repeat.

Peter Hoffmann	Entschuldigung, ist dies hier Reihe 10, Sitz G?
Passagier	Ja, (das stimmt / ist es). Mein Sitz ist 10 H.
Peter Hoffmann	Danke. Sind Sie aus Amerika?
Passagier	Nein, das bin ich nicht. Ich bin Kanadier – Französischkanadier. Ich komme aus Quebec.
Peter Hoffmann	Ah, ich verstehe. Sind Sie in Europa im Urlaub?
Passagier	Nein, meine Firma ist hier in London. Was ist mit Ihnen? Sind Sie Engländer?
Peter Hoffmann	Nein, das bin ich nicht. Ich bin Deutscher. Ich bin hier, um meine Englischkenntnisse zu verbessern.
Passagier	Aber Ihr Englisch ist hervorragend.
Peter Hoffmann	Das ist sehr nett von Ihnen, das zu sagen.
Passagier	Aber es ist wahr. Sind Sie hier im Urlaub?
Peter Hoffmann	Nein, ich bin bei einer Firma in Manchester. Ich bin Praktikant.

007

Flight attendant	Can Mr P. Hoffmann, H–O–F–F–M–A–N–N, come to the front of the plane, please?
Patrick Hoffmann	Good morning. My name is Hoffmann. Can I help you?
Flight attendant	Yes, is your name Peter Hoffmann, sir?
Patrick Hoffmann	No, sorry. I am Patrick Hoffmann.
Flight attendant	Sorry to bother you, but we are looking for a Mr Peter Hoffmann.
Peter Hoffmann	Hello. I am Peter Hoffmann.
Flight attendant	Is this your passport, Mr Hoffmann?
Peter Hoffmann	Oh. Yes, it is.
Flight attendant	Then this is your ticket.
Peter Hoffmann	Thank you very much. I am lucky!
Flight attendant	Excuse me, sir. Can you please put your hand luggage here, under your seat?
Peter Hoffmann	Yes, of course.
Peter Hoffmann	Can I have a German newspaper, please?
Flight attendant	I am sorry, but the newspapers are only for business class travellers.
Peter Hoffmann	Oh, really?
Flight attendant	Would you like an English magazine, sir?
Peter Hoffmann	No, thank you. I can read my book.

008

Hören Sie und sprechen Sie nach.

Now listen and repeat

Flugbegleiterin	Kann Herr P. Hoffmann, H–O–F–F–M–A–N–N, bitte nach vorne / zum vorderen Ende des Flugzeuges kommen?
Patrick Hoffmann	Guten Morgen. Mein Name ist Hoffmann. Kann ich Ihnen helfen?
Flugbegleiterin	Ja, sind Sie Herr Peter Hoffman?
Patrick Hoffmann	Nein, tut mir leid. Ich bin Patrick Hoffmann.
Flugbegleiterin	Bitte entschuldigen Sie die Umstände, aber wir suchen (gerade) einen Herrn Peter Hoffmann.
Peter Hoffmann	Hallo. Ich bin Peter Hoffmann.
Flugbegleiterin	Ist dies Ihr Reisepass, Herr Hoffmann?
Peter Hoffmann	Oh. Ja, (ist er).
Flugbegleiterin	Dann ist dies Ihr Flugschein.
Peter Hoffmann	Vielen Dank. Ich habe (wirklich) Glück!
Flugbegleiterin	Entschuldigen Sie, mein Herr, können Sie bitte Ihr Handgepäck hier unter Ihrem Sitz verstauen?
Peter Hoffmann	Ja, natürlich.
Peter Hoffmann	Kann ich bitte eine deutsche Zeitung haben?
Flugbegleiterin	Es tut mir leid, aber die Zeitungen sind nur für Reisende der Businessklasse.
Peter Hoffmann	Ach, wirklich?
Flugbegleiterin	Möchten Sie eine englische Zeitschrift?
Peter Hoffmann	Nein, danke. Ich kann mein Buch lesen.

▶ 012

Jack	Excuse me, are you Mr Hoffmann?
Stranger	No, I am not.
Jack	Oh, I am sorry.
Stranger	That's all right.
Jack	Excuse me, are you Mr Hoffmann from Germany?
Peter Hoffmann	Yes, I am.
Jack	My name is Jack Baker.
	I am the personnel director's assistant.
Peter Hoffmann	How do you do, Mr Baker?
	Nice to meet you.
Jack	How do you do? Please call me Jack.
	Can I help you with your luggage?
Peter Hoffmann	Yes, thanks. I am Peter by the way.
Jack	Are those your suitcases?
Peter Hoffmann	No, these are my suitcases,
	this one and that one.
Jack	Great. Let's see.
	Is there a trolley around?
Peter Hoffmann	Yes. There are lots over there.
Jack	Fine.
Peter Hoffmann	Here we are.

▶ 013

Hören Sie und sprechen Sie nach.

Now listen and repeat.

Jack	Entschuldigung, sind Sie Herr Hoffmann?
Fremder	Nein, (das) bin ich nicht.
Jack	Oh, Entschuldigung.
Fremder	Keine Ursache.
Jack	Entschuldigung, sind Sie Herr Hoffmann aus Deutschland?
Peter Hoffmann	Ja, (das) bin ich.
Jack	Mein Name ist Jack Baker.
	Ich bin der Assistent des Personaldirektors.
Peter Hoffmann	Sehr erfreut, Herr Baker.
	Nett, Sie kennenzulernen.
Jack	Sehr erfreut. Bitte nennen Sie mich Jack.
	Kann ich Ihnen mit Ihrem Gepäck behilflich sein?
Peter Hoffmann	Ja, bitte. Ich heiße übrigens Peter.
Jack	Sind das Ihre Koffer?
Peter Hoffmann	Nein, diese hier sind meine Koffer,
	dieser hier und jener da drüben.
Jack	Prima. So, schauen wir mal.
	Gibt es hier (einen) Gepäckwagen?
Peter Hoffmann	Ja, da drüben sind ganz viele.
Jack	Fein.
Peter Hoffmann	So, das hätten wir.

018	Peter Hoffmann	Wow! What a fantastic car, Jack.
	Jack	Yeah, the only problem is that it is a company car.
	Peter Hoffmann	Well, I am grateful that you are here to pick me up, anyway.
	Jack	It's a pleasure.
		By the way, your English is very good, Peter.
	Peter Hoffmann	That is very kind of you to say so.
	Jack	Look, this is the programme for your first day at Winthrops.
		First, you meet our human resources director. His name is Mr Jackson.
	Peter Hoffmann	Oh, yes, I remember his letter to me.
	Jack	Right, off we go.
	Jack	Where are you from in Germany, Peter?
	Peter Hoffmann	Well, I live in Frankfurt now, but I come from Düsseldorf.
	Jack	That's interesting. I have got a friend in Frankfurt.
	Peter Hoffmann	Have you?
	Jack	Yes, her name is Martina. Martina Glass. She is very nice, too.
	Peter Hoffmann	Has she got a sister, Andrea?
	Jack	Yes, she has.
	Peter Hoffmann	Then I know her. And I know her brother, Oliver, too. They are very good friends of mine.
	Jack	Really? What a coincidence!
	Peter Hoffmann	Yes, and their father is my father's best friend.
	Jack	So your mothers are probably good friends, too?
	Peter Hoffmann	Yes, our families are all good friends. It is a small world, isn't it?

Hören Sie und sprechen Sie nach.

Now listen and repeat.

12

Peter Hoffmann	Wow! Was für ein tolles Auto, Jack.
Jack	Ja, das einzige Problem ist, dass es ein Firmenwagen ist.
Peter Hoffmann	Tja, ich bin dir trotzdem dankbar, dass du hier bist, um mich abzuholen.
Jack	Es ist mir ein Vergnügen. Übrigens, dein Englisch ist sehr gut, Peter.
Peter Hoffmann	Das ist nett, dass du das sagst.
Jack	Schau mal, hier ist das Programm für deinen ersten Tag bei Winthrops. Zuerst triffst du unseren Personaldirektor. Sein Name ist Herr Jackson.
Peter Hoffmann	Ach, ja. Ich erinnere mich an seinen Brief an mich.
Jack	So, los geht's.
Jack	Woher in Deutschland kommst du, Peter?
Peter Hoffmann	Also, ich wohne jetzt in Frankfurt, aber ich komme aus Düsseldorf.
Jack	Das ist ja interessant. Ich habe eine Freundin in Frankfurt.
Peter Hoffmann	Ach ja? / Hast du?
Jack	Ja, ihr Name ist Martina. Martina Glass. Sie ist auch sehr nett.
Peter Hoffmann	Hat sie eine Schwester, die Andrea heißt?
Jack	Ja, hat sie.
Peter Hoffmann	Dann kenne ich sie. Und ihren Bruder Oliver kenne ich auch. Sie sind sehr gute Freunde von mir.
Jack	Wirklich? Was für ein Zufall!
Peter Hoffmann	Ja, und ihr Vater ist der beste Freund meines Vaters.
Jack	Und eure Mütter sind wohl auch gute Freunde?
Peter Hoffmann	Ja, unsere ganzen Familien sind befreundet. Es ist eine kleine Welt, nicht wahr?

025

Jack	Hi Suzie! This is Peter Hoffmann from Germany. He is here to see Mr Jackson.
Suzie	Hi Jack! How do you do, Mr Hoffmann. Pleased to meet you.
Peter Hoffmann	Nice to meet you too, Suzie.
Suzie	May I take your coat?
Peter Hoffmann	Thanks. That's very kind of you.
Suzie	Can I tell Mr Jackson you are here?
Peter Hoffmann	Yes, please do.
Suzie	Oh, the line is engaged. He is on the phone at the moment. Would you mind waiting a moment?
Peter Hoffmann	Of course not. It is no problem at all.
Suzie	Would you like a drink? Tea? Coffee?
Peter Hoffmann	No, thank you, but could you tell me where the toilets are?
Suzie	Yes, certainly. They are over there.

(*outside the toilets*)

Peter Hoffmann	Excuse me, is this the men's?
Man	Yes, it is.
Peter Hoffmann	Oh, aren't you the Canadian from the plane?
Man	I am sorry, but you are mistaken.
Peter Hoffmann	Oh, but I am sure …
Man	Excuse me.

Suzie	Mr Jackson is ready to see you now, Mr Hoffmann.
Jack	This way, Peter. Let's take the lift. It's on the fourth floor.
Peter Hoffmann	After you, Jack.

Hören Sie und sprechen Sie nach.

Now listen and repeat.

026

14

Jack	Hi Suzie! Dies ist Peter Hoffmann aus Deutschland. Er ist hier, um Herrn Jackson zu sehen.
Suzie	Hi Jack! Sehr erfreut, Herr Hoffmann. Nett, Sie kennenzulernen.
Peter Hoffmann	Ganz meinerseits, Suzie.
Suzie	Darf ich Ihnen Ihren Mantel abnehmen?
Peter Hoffmann	Danke. Das ist sehr freundlich von Ihnen.
Suzie	Kann ich Herrn Jackson sagen, dass Sie hier sind?
Peter Hoffmann	Ja, bitte (tun Sie das).
Suzie	Oh, sein Apparat ist besetzt. Er spricht gerade. Macht es Ihnen etwas aus, einen Moment zu warten?
Peter Hoffmann	Natürlich nicht. Überhaupt kein Problem.
Suzie	Möchten Sie etwas trinken? Tee? Kaffee?
Peter Hoffmann	Nein danke, aber könnten Sie mir sagen, wo die Toiletten sind?
Suzie	Ja natürlich. Sie sind dort drüben.

(vor den Toiletten)

Peter Hoffmann	Entschuldigung, ist dies die Herrentoilette?
Mann	Ja, das ist sie.
Peter Hoffmann	Ach, sind Sie nicht der Kanadier aus dem Flugzeug?
Mann	Es tut mir leid, aber Sie irren sich.
Peter Hoffmann	Aber ich bin sicher …
Mann	Entschuldigen Sie mich.

Suzie	Herr Jackson kann Sie jetzt empfangen, Herr Hoffmann.
Jack	Hier entlang, Peter. Nehmen wir den Aufzug. Es ist im vierten Stock.
Peter Hoffmann	Nach dir, Jack.

(in the lift)

Jack	Up we go!
Peter Hoffmann	Jack, is there a Canadian here in the company?
Jack	No, why? What is the matter? You look puzzled.
Peter Hoffmann	Oh, it is nothing really, but there was a Canadian in the men's. I am sure I have seen him before.
Jack	So?
Peter Hoffmann	He was on the plane.
Jack	Really? I am surprised. What a coincidence!
Peter Hoffmann	Yes, it is.
Jack	Well, here we are.
Mr Jackson	Come in.
Jack	Good morning, Mr Jackson. This is Peter Hoffmann from Germany.
Mr Jackson	Ah, yes! Do come in. Have a seat.
Peter Hoffmann	Thank you.
Mr Jackson	Have you been to Manchester before?
Peter Hoffmann	No, this is the first time I have been to the north of England. But I have been to Glasgow in Scotland and I think it is very similar to Manchester.
Mr Jackson	Yes, you are right. There is a lot of industry there and here. Has Jack shown you around yet?
Peter Hoffmann	Well, I think we have looked at almost all the offices since I have been here.
Jack	Yes, and I want to show him the production site as soon as we have finished here.
Mr Jackson	Good. Well, I hope you enjoy your stay here. I am sure you are in good hands with Jack. Please don't hesitate to call me, if you need my help.
Peter Hoffmann	That is very kind of you, but I have not had any problems so far.
Mr Jackson	Well, good bye, Mr Hoffmann.
Peter Hoffmann	Goodbye.

Hören Sie und sprechen Sie nach.

Now listen and repeat.

(im Aufzug)

Jack	So, hoch geht's!
Peter Hoffmann	Jack, gibt es hier in der Firma einen Kanadier?
Jack	Nein, wieso? Was ist los? Du siehst etwas verwirrt aus.
Peter Hoffmann	Ach, nichts Wichtiges, aber auf der Herrentoilette war ein Kanadier. Ich bin mir sicher, dass ich ihn schon mal gesehen habe.
Jack	Ja, und?
Peter Hoffmann	Er war im Flugzeug.
Jack	Ach wirklich? Das überrascht mich. Was für ein Zufall!
Peter Hoffmann	Ja, das ist es.
Jack	Also, wir sind da.
Herr Jackson	Herein.
Jack	Guten Morgen, Herr Jackson. Dies ist Peter Hoffmann aus Deutschland.
Herr Jackson	Ah, ja! Kommen Sie doch herein. Nehmen Sie Platz.
Peter Hoffmann	Danke schön.
Herr Jackson	Sind Sie schon einmal in Manchester gewesen?
Peter Hoffmann	Nein, dies ist mein erster Besuch in Nordengland. Aber ich war schon einmal in Glasgow in Schottland, und ich glaube, es ähnelt Manchester sehr.
Herr Jackson	Ja, da haben Sie recht. Es gibt dort wie hier viel Industrie. Hat Jack Ihnen schon alles gezeigt?
Peter Hoffmann	Nun, ich glaube, dass wir uns fast alle Büros angeschaut haben, seitdem ich hier bin.
Jack	Ja, und ich werde ihm die Fertigungsstätte zeigen, sobald wir hier fertig sind.
Herr Jackson	Gut. Ich hoffe, Sie haben einen angenehmen Aufenthalt. Ich bin sicher, dass Sie bei Jack in guten Händen sind. Rufen Sie mich bitte an, wenn Sie meine Hilfe brauchen.
Peter Hoffmann	Das ist sehr freundlich von Ihnen, aber bisher habe ich keine Probleme gehabt.
Herr Jackson	Also, auf Wiedersehen, Herr Hoffmann.
Peter Hoffmann	Auf Wiedersehen.

Jack	We are going down to the production line now, so we need to wear these protective overalls and helmets.
Peter Hoffmann	Oh, really? Do we have to?
Jack	Yes, it is company policy, and it's better for your clothes. Let me see. You are taller than me. This might fit you.
Peter Hoffmann	Sorry, but it is too small.
Jack	How tall are you? What size do you take?
Peter Hoffmann	I am not sure in feet, but in metres I am 1.90.
Jack	Ah, 1.90 m. That is 6'3" (six foot three inches). Try this overall.
Peter Hoffmann	Yes, that is better.
Jack	Right, here we are. Please put your helmet on now.
Peter Hoffmann	Do they do all the manual work here?
Jack	Yes, that's right. Do you see those metal rods?
Peter Hoffmann	Yes, I do. Those next to the green machine?
Jack	Yes. Well, the worker feeds them into the machine at this end. Now watch, the machine is going to cut them to size.
Peter Hoffmann	But why are some rivets bigger and some smaller?
Jack	That is because the computer which operates the machine can change the size and thickness of the rivets.
Peter Hoffmann	I have never seen anything like that before.
Jack	First, it measures the length of the rod then produces rivets of a certain size. That way it uses as little metal as possible.
Peter Hoffmann	Wow! That is clever!
Jack	Yes, we are very proud of it. We are going to sell the idea to American investors.
Peter Hoffmann	Do you have a patent on it?
Jack	Yes, but our competitors have tried to copy this model. So far they have not been successful.

Hören Sie und sprechen Sie nach.

Now listen and repeat.

Jack	Wir gehen jetzt zur Fertigungsstraße hinunter, also müssen wir diese Schutzanzüge und Helme tragen.
Peter Hoffmann	Ach ja? Müssen wir das?
Jack	Ja, es ist Firmenvorschrift und es ist besser für deine Kleidung. Lass mich mal sehen. Du bist größer als ich. Dies könnte dir passen.
Peter Hoffmann	Tut mir leid, aber es ist zu klein.
Jack	Wie groß bist du denn? Welche Größe hast du?
Peter Hoffmann	In Fuß bin ich mir nicht sicher, aber in Meter bin ich 1,90.
Jack	Ah, 1,90. Das ist 6'3" (sechs Fuß drei Zoll). Probier mal diesen Schutzanzug an.
Peter Hoffmann	Ja, der ist besser.
Jack	So, da wären wir. Bitte setz jetzt deinen Helm auf.
Peter Hoffmann	Machen sie hier die ganze manuelle Arbeit?
Jack	Ja, das ist richtig. Siehst du die Metallstäbe dahinten?
Peter Hoffmann	Ja. Die neben der grünen Maschine?
Jack	Ja. Also, der Arbeiter führt sie an diesem Ende in die Maschine ein. Jetzt schau mal, die Maschine wird sie jetzt zurechtschneiden.
Peter Hoffmann	Aber warum sind einige Bolzen größer und einige kleiner?
Jack	Das kommt daher, weil der Computer, der die Maschine steuert, die Größe und Dicke der Bolzen verändern kann.
Peter Hoffmann	Ich habe so etwas noch nie gesehen.
Jack	Zuerst misst er die Länge des Metallstabs und produziert dann Bolzen einer bestimmten Größe. So wird so wenig Metall wie möglich verwendet.
Peter Hoffmann	Wow! Das ist schlau!
Jack	Ja, wir sind darauf sehr stolz. Wir werden die Idee an amerikanische Investoren verkaufen.
Peter Hoffmann	Habt ihr denn ein Patent dafür?
Jack	Ja, aber unsere Konkurrenz hat versucht, dieses Modell zu kopieren. Bis jetzt waren Sie noch nicht erfolgreich.

▶ 043

Peter Hoffmann	Good afternoon.
Estate Agent	Good afternoon. How may I help you?
Peter Hoffmann	My name is Peter Hoffmann.
	I believe you have a reservation for me for an apartment in Castle Heights?
Estate Agent	Just a minute, I will check.
	Ah, here we are.
	I am afraid that there is a small problem, Mr Hoffmann.
Peter Hoffmann	Oh?
Estate Agent	The flat won't be ready until the day after tomorrow.
Peter Hoffmann	Oh, dear! That is very unfortunate.
Estate Agent	We are very sorry, but we can offer you accommodation in a hotel or bed & breakfast for today and tomorrow.
Peter Hoffmann	What bed & breakfast places can you recommend?
Estate Agent	I think this one would suit you.
	It is a large house in King Street on the river.
	The landlady is very friendly and it is not far from Winthrops.
Peter Hoffmann	That sounds fine. I will take it for two days then.
Estate Agent	I will call immediately and book you in.
Peter Hoffmann	No, that's all right.
	Just give me the number and I'll phone.

▶ 044

Hören Sie und sprechen Sie nach.

Now listen and repeat.

Peter Hoffmann	Guten Tag.
Makler	Guten Tag. Wie kann ich Ihnen behilflich sein?
Peter Hoffmann	Mein Name ist Peter Hoffmann.
	Ich glaube, Sie haben für mich eine Reservierung für ein Appartement in Castle Heights.
Makler	Einen Moment, ich sehe mal nach.
	Ah, hier haben wir es.
	Ich fürchte, es gibt da ein kleines Problem, Herr Hoffmann.
Peter Hoffmann	Oh?
Makler	Die Wohnung wird erst übermorgen fertig sein.
Peter Hoffmann	Oh je! Das ist aber unerfreulich.
Makler	Es tut uns sehr leid, aber wir können Ihnen eine Unterkunft in einem Hotel oder in einer Pension für morgen und übermorgen anbieten.
Peter Hoffmann	Welche Pensionen können Sie empfehlen?
Makler	Ich glaube, dies hier wird Ihnen zusagen.
	Es ist ein großes Haus in der King Street am Fluss.
	Die Vermieterin ist sehr freundlich und es ist nicht weit von Winthrops.
Peter Hoffmann	Das klingt gut. Ich werde es dann für zwei Tage nehmen.
Makler	Ich rufe sofort an und reserviere für Sie.
Peter Hoffmann	Nein, das ist schon in Ordnung.
	Geben Sie mir einfach die Nummer und ich werde anrufen.

▶ 048	Voice	Hello?
	Peter Hoffmann	Is that 496 325 77?
	Voice	No, this is 496 325 78.
	Peter Hoffmann	Oh, sorry. Wrong number.
	Mrs Bambridge	496 325 77.
	Peter Hoffmann	Can I speak to Mrs Bambridge, please?
	Mrs Bambridge	Speaking. Who is calling?
	Peter Hoffmann	My name is Peter Hoffmann.
		I have your number from the estate agent's in Newmarket Street.
	Mrs Bambridge	Oh, yes! How may I help you?
	Peter Hoffmann	Have you any rooms free for tonight and tomorrow night?
	Mrs Bambridge	Just a moment. Yes, I have. Do you want a single or double room?
	Peter Hoffmann	A single with bath, please.
	Mrs Bambridge	Oh, I am sorry, but the singles are only with shower. There is a double room with bath, but it is on the third floor.
	Peter Hoffmann	How much are the rooms, please, Mrs Bambridge?
	Mrs Bambridge	The single is £ 35 for bed and breakfast and the double with bath, bed and breakfast is £ 55.
	Peter Hoffmann	I think I would prefer the double room, please.
	Mrs Bambridge	Fine. So that is one double with bath for two nights for Monday, 25th and Tuesday, 26th May.
	Peter Hoffmann	Yes, please. My name is Hoffmann, Peter Hoffmann.
	Mrs Bambridge	Can you spell Hoffmann, please?
	Peter Hoffmann	Certainly. H–O–FF–M–A–NN.
	Mrs Bambridge	Thank you. When will you arrive?
	Peter Hoffmann	I will be there in about twenty minutes to half an hour.
	Mrs Bambridge	Good. I look forward to meeting you, Mr Hoffmann. Goodbye.
	Peter Hoffmann	Goodbye.

 Now listen and repeat.
049

Stimme	Hallo?
Peter Hoffmann	Ist das 496 325 77?
Stimme	Nein, dies ist 496 325 78.
Peter Hoffmann	Oh, Entschuldigung. Ich habe mich verwählt.
Frau Bambridge	496 325 77.
Peter Hoffmann	Kann ich bitte Frau Bambridge sprechen?
Frau Bambridge	Am Apparat. Wer spricht bitte?
Peter Hoffmann	Mein Name ist Peter Hoffmann.
	Ich habe ihre Telefonnummer von dem Immobilienmakler in Newmarket Street.
Frau Bambridge	Ach, ja! Wie kann ich Ihnen helfen?
Peter Hoffmann	Haben Sie für heute Abend und morgen Abend noch Zimmer frei?
Frau Bambridge	Einen Moment bitte. Ja, habe ich.
	Möchten Sie ein Einzel- oder Doppelzimmer?
Peter Hoffmann	Einzel mit Bad, bitte.
Frau Bambridge	Oh, es tut mir leid, aber die Einzelzimmer haben nur eine Dusche.
	Es gibt noch ein Doppelzimmer mit Bad, aber es ist im dritten Stock.
Peter Hoffmann	Was bitte kosten die Zimmer, Frau Bambridge?
Frau Bambridge	Das Einzelzimmer kostet mit Frühstück £ 35 und das Doppelzimmer mit Bad und Frühstück £ 55.
Peter Hoffmann	Ich glaube, das Doppelzimmer wäre mir lieber.
Frau Bambridge	Fein. Das wäre also ein Doppelzimmer mit Bad für zwei Nächte für Montag, den 25. und Dienstag, den 26. Mai.
Peter Hoffmann	Ja, bitte. Mein Name ist Hoffmann, Peter Hoffmann.
Frau Bambridge	Können Sie bitte Hoffmann buchstabieren?
Peter Hoffmann	Natürlich. H–O–FF–M–A–NN.
Frau Bambridge	Vielen Dank. Wann werden sie ankommen?
Peter Hoffmann	Ich werde in ungefähr zwanzig Minuten bis einer halben Stunde da sein.
Frau Bambridge	Gut. Ich freue mich, Sie kennenzulernen, Herr Hoffmann. Auf Wiedersehen.
Peter Hoffmann	Auf Wiedersehen.

058

Mrs Bambridge	What time would you like breakfast, Mr Hoffmann?
Peter Hoffmann	Well, in Germany I don't often eat breakfast because I usually leave home at ten past seven.
Mrs Bambridge	You know, it only takes about five minutes to the bus stop from here.
Peter Hoffmann	Oh, really?
Mrs Bambridge	Yes, you could leave with Mr Brown.
Peter Hoffmann	Mr Brown? When does he leave?
Mrs Bambridge	Well, he usually leaves for work at a quarter to eight. He takes the 7.57.
Peter Hoffmann	Three minutes to eight? But my working day at Winthrops doesn't start until 9 o'clock.
Mrs Bambridge	I see. But Mr Brown works at Winthrops, too. He always goes to work at 7.45.
Peter Hoffmann	OK. That seems a good idea, then. Yes, we can leave together.
Mrs Bambridge	Do you prefer English or Continental, Mr Hoffmann?
Peter Hoffmann	I beg your pardon?
Mrs Bambridge	Breakfast. What do you prefer, an English or Continental breakfast?
Peter Hoffmann	Oh, I would love a good old English breakfast.
Mrs Bambridge	Do you like fried eggs or poached eggs with your bacon?
Peter Hoffmann	Fried, please.
Mrs Bambridge	And how many eggs would you like?
Peter Hoffmann	Two, please.

Now listen and repeat.
059

Frau Bambridge	Um wie viel Uhr möchten Sie frühstücken?
Peter Hoffmann	Tja, in Deutschland frühstücke ich nicht oft, weil ich das Haus normalerweise um zehn nach sieben verlasse.
Frau Bambridge	Wissen Sie, man braucht nur fünf Minuten zur Haltestelle von hier.
Peter Hoffmann	Ach wirklich?
Frau Bambridge	Ja, sie könnten zusammen mit Herrn Brown weggehen.
Peter Hoffmann	Herr Brown? Wann geht er denn weg?
Frau Bambridge	Nun, er geht normalerweise um Viertel vor acht zur Arbeit. Er nimmt den Bus um 7.57.
Peter Hoffmann	Drei Minuten vor acht? Aber bei Winthrops fängt mein Arbeitstag erst um 9 Uhr an.
Frau Bambridge	Ich verstehe. Aber Herr Brown arbeitet auch bei Winthrops. Er geht immer um 7.45 zur Arbeit.
Peter Hoffmann	OK. Dann scheint das ja eine gute Idee zu sein. Ja, wir können zusammen gehen.
Frau Bambridge	Möchten Sie lieber Englisch oder Kontinental?
Peter Hoffmann	Wie bitte?
Frau Bambridge	Frühstück. Was möchten Sie lieber, ein englisches oder ein kontinentales Frühstück?
Peter Hoffmann	Ach, ich hätte liebend gern ein echtes englisches Frühstück.
Frau Bambridge	Mögen Sie Spiegeleier oder pochierte Eier mit Ihrem Schinken?
Peter Hoffmann	Spiegeleier, bitte.
Frau Bambridge	Und wie viele Eier möchten Sie?
Peter Hoffmann	Zwei, bitte.

065	Mrs Bambridge	Good morning, Mr Hoffmann. Did you sleep well?
	Peter Hoffmann	Good morning.
		Yes, fine, thank you, Mrs Bambridge.
	Mrs Bambridge	It is a lovely day today. Very warm for May, isn't it?
	Peter Hoffmann	Yes, it is. A wonderful morning.
	Mrs Bambridge	Are you ready for your first day?
	Peter Hoffmann	Yes, I am. What do you think, Mrs Bambridge? Is it better to walk or go by bus?
	Mrs Bambridge	Why don't you ask Mr Brown?
	Peter Hoffmann	Does he walk to work?
	Mrs Bambridge	He usually goes by bus, but he sometimes walks.
	Peter Hoffmann	How often do the buses run from here to Winthrops?
	Mrs Bambridge	They run very frequently at this time of the morning.
	Peter Hoffmann	Does the number 5 go to Winthrops?
	Mrs Bambridge	Yes, but the number 10 is best. It runs every ten minutes.
	Peter Hoffmann	When does Mr Brown leave the house when he walks to work?
	Mrs Bambridge	He usually leaves at the same time – at a quarter to eight.
	Peter Hoffmann	Fine, I can go with Mr Brown, then. That sounds like him now.
	Mrs Bambridge	Yes. I think you are right.

Now listen and repeat.
066

26

Frau Bambridge	Guten Morgen, Herr Hoffmann. Haben Sie gut geschlafen?
Peter Hoffmann	Guten Morgen.
	Ja, gut, danke Frau Bambridge.
Frau Bambridge	Es ist ein herrlicher Tag heute. Sehr warm für Mai, nicht wahr?
Peter Hoffmann	Ja (das ist es). Ein wunderschöner Morgen.
Frau Bambridge	Sind Sie für Ihren ersten (Arbeits-)Tag bereit?
Peter Hoffmann	Ja, das bin ich. Was meinen Sie, Frau Bambridge?
	Ist es besser, zu Fuß zu gehen oder mit dem Bus zu fahren?
Frau Bambridge	Warum fragen Sie nicht Herrn Brown?
Peter Hoffmann	Geht er zu Fuß zur Arbeit?
Frau Bambridge	Er fährt für gewöhnlich mit dem Bus, aber manchmal läuft er.
Peter Hoffmann	Wie oft fahren die Busse von hier zu Winthrops?
Frau Bambridge	Sie verkehren sehr häufig morgens um diese Uhrzeit.
Peter Hoffmann	Fährt die Nummer 5 zu Winthrops?
Frau Bambridge	Ja, aber die Nummer 10 ist am besten. Die fährt alle zehn Minuten.
Peter Hoffmann	Wann geht Herr Brown aus dem Haus, wenn er zur Arbeit läuft?
Frau Bambridge	Normalerweise verlässt er das Haus zur selben Zeit – um Viertel vor acht.
Peter Hoffmann	Prima, dann kann ich mit Herrn Brown gehen. Es hört sich so an, als käme er gerade.
Frau Bambridge	Ja. Ich glaube, Sie haben recht.

27

068

Peter Hoffmann	Hi, Jack. How are you?
Jack	Hello, Peter. Very well, thanks.
	And what about you? Are you settling in?
Peter Hoffmann	Yes, fine, thanks.
Jack	Look, we have to inspect the machines this morning.
	There is a slight problem.
Peter Hoffmann	Oh, really?
Jack	Yes, they are operating a little slowly
	and I need to find out why.
Peter Hoffmann	OK. I will be pleased to come along.
Jack	Fine. I can introduce you to some more people
	down there.
Peter Hoffmann	On the factory floor?
Jack	Yes, they are working on the machines at the moment.
Peter Hoffmann	Suits me fine.
Jack	And at one o'clock we can go for lunch.
	Do you like Chinese cooking?
Peter Hoffmann	Not really. I am not so fond of Chinese food.
Jack	Well, we needn't eat Chinese.
	Are you keen on Indian food?
Peter Hoffmann	Oh yes, I love trying Indian dishes,
	especially curries.
Jack	Well, there is an Indian restaurant near here,
	just down the road.
	How about going there for lunch?
Peter Hoffmann	Sounds perfect.

Now listen and repeat.
069

Peter Hoffmann	Hi, Jack. Wie geht es dir?
Jack	Hallo, Peter. Sehr gut, danke.
	Und wie steht es mit dir? Hast du dich eingelebt?
Peter Hoffmann	Ja, danke gut.
Jack	Hör mal, wir müssen die Maschinen heute morgen überprüfen.
	Es gibt ein kleines Problem.
Peter Hoffmann	Ach wirklich?
Jack	Ja, Sie laufen ein bisschen langsam und ich muss herausfinden warum.
Peter Hoffmann	OK. Ich werde gerne mitgehen.
Jack	Prima. Ich kann dich da unten noch einigen Leuten vorstellen.
Peter Hoffmann	In der Fabrikhalle?
Jack	Ja, sie arbeiten im Moment an den Maschinen.
Peter Hoffmann	Das passt mir gut.
Jack	Und um ein Uhr können wir Mittagessen gehen.
	Magst du die chinesische Küche?
Peter Hoffmann	Eigentlich nicht. Ich mag chinesisches Essen nicht so gern.
Jack	Nun ja, wir müssen nicht Chinesisch essen.
	Schmeckt dir indisches Essen?
Peter Hoffmann	Oh ja, ich probiere gerne indische Gerichte aus, besonders Curries.
Jack	Also, es gibt ein indisches Restaurant hier in der Nähe, nur die Straße runter.
	Wie wäre es, wenn wir zum Mittagessen dorthingehen?
Peter Hoffmann	Klingt ausgezeichnet.

Waiter	Would you like to order your drinks now?
Jack	What would you like, Peter?
Peter Hoffmann	I am not sure. What have you got?
Waiter	Orange juice, lager, bitter, red or white wine …
Peter Hoffmann	I would like half of lager, please.
Jack	For me half a bottle of red wine, please. No, a pint of bitter, please.
Waiter	What would you like to start with? Melon, fruit juice, soup, or a mixture of Indian starters?
Jack	No, thank you, not for me. What about you, Peter?
Peter Hoffmann	No, just a main course will do.
Waiter	If I may suggest something?
Peter Hoffmann & Jack	Yes?
Waiter	We have an excellent chicken korma as dish of the day served with pilau rice and poppadums.
Jack	Oh, that sounds delicious. I will take that. What about you, Peter?
Peter Hoffmann	Yes, I think I will try that, too.
Waiter	So, that's two chicken kormas. Would you like some naan bread with that?
Jack	Yes, please. Oh, and knives and forks, please.
Waiter	Yes, of course, sir.
Waiter	Would you care for a dessert? There is a wide selection of desserts on the sweets trolley.
Peter Hoffmann	Yes, I think I would like to try that cake, please.
Jack	No sweet for me. Just a cup of coffee instead.
Waiter	Certainly, sir.

Now listen and repeat.
074

30

Bedienung	Möchten Sie jetzt Ihre Getränke bestellen?
Jack	Was möchtest du, Peter?
Peter Hoffmann	Ich bin nicht sicher. Was haben Sie?
Bedienung	Orangensaft, Lagerbier, Bitterbier,
	Rot- oder Weißwein …
Peter Hoffmann	Ich hätte gern einen halben Pint Lagerbier.
Jack	Für mich bitte eine halbe Flasche Rotwein.
	Nein, ein Pint (= 0,568 l) Bitterbier, bitte.
Bedienung	Was möchten Sie als Vorspeise?
	Melone, Fruchtsaft, Suppe
	oder eine Auswahl an indischen Vorspeisen?
Jack	Nein danke, nicht für mich.
	Was ist mit dir, Peter?
Peter Hoffmann	Nein, nur ein Hauptgang reicht (mir).
Bedienung	Wenn ich etwas empfehlen darf?
Peter Hoffmann & Jack	Ja?
Bedienung	Wir haben als Tagesgericht ein ausgezeichnetes
	Hühnerfleisch Korma,
	serviert mit Pilaureis und Poppadums.
Jack	Oh, das klingt lecker. Ich werde das nehmen.
	Was ist mit dir, Peter?
Peter Hoffmann	Ja, ich glaube, das werde ich auch probieren.
Bedienung	So, das sind dann zweimal Hühnerfleisch Korma.
	Möchten Sie dazu Naan-Brot?
Jack	Ja, bitte. Und Messer und Gabeln, bitte.
Bedienung	Ja, natürlich, mein Herr.
Bedienung	Möchten Sie einen Nachtisch?
	Es gibt eine große Auswahl an Nachspeisen
	auf dem Dessertwagen.
Peter Hoffmann	Ja, ich glaube, ich würde gerne den Kuchen da
	probieren.
Jack	Kein Nachtisch für mich.
	Stattdessen nur eine Tasse Kaffee.
Bedienung	Gerne, mein Herr.

077

Jack	What are you doing on Saturday?
Peter Hoffmann	Well, I am going for a run. What about you?
Jack	I am joining some friends at my health club.
	Would you like to come along?
Peter Hoffmann	Yes, I'd love to.
Jack	We're playing squash from ten until eleven.
Peter Hoffmann	Great. See you on Saturday.
Jack	Excuse me for interrupting the game.
	I am taking Jim to hospital.
Peter Hoffmann	Oh, no! What has happened? Has he hurt himself?
Jack	Well, he twisted his ankle badly and fell on his hand.
	Maybe his foot is broken.
	And his hand is swollen.
	We do not know ourselves yet.
Peter Hoffmann	I am sorry to hear that.
	Look, I am coming with you, you may need help.
Jack	Thanks.

(at the hospital)

Jim	Peter could you please fill in the form for me.
	I cannot write it myself.
Peter Hoffmann	Yes, of course. Let's see.
	It says: 'What part of your body is hurt?'
Jim	My right hand and right ankle.
Peter Hoffmann	'Do you suspect a fracture?' What does that mean?
Jim	That means: 'Is it broken?' Mmmh. Write 'Yes'.
Peter Hoffmann	When was your last x-ray?
Jim	Oh, I do not remember. I think it was twelve years ago
	when I fell off my motorbike.
	I broke my arm and my shoulder.
Peter Hoffmann	OK. Look, you have to sign here
	to say that you have not got any contagious diseases
	like aids, hepatitis, syphilis and so on.
Jim	Perhaps I can sign with my left hand.
	What do you think?

Now listen and repeat.
078

Jack	Was machst du Samstag?
Peter Hoffmann	Also, ich gehe laufen. Und du?
Jack	Ich treffe einige Freunde in meinem Fitnessklub.
	Hättest du Lust mitzukommen?
Peter Hoffmann	Ja, sehr gerne.
Jack	Wir spielen von zehn bis elf Squash.
Peter Hoffmann	Prima. Wir sehen uns Samstag. / Bis Samstag.

Jack	Entschuldigt bitte, dass ich das Spiel unterbreche.
	Ich werde Jim ins Krankenhaus fahren.
Peter Hoffmann	Oh nein! Was ist passiert? Hat er sich verletzt?
Jack:	Also, er hat sich das Fußgelenk schlimm verdreht und ist auf seine Hand gefallen.
	Vielleicht ist sein Fuß gebrochen.
	Und seine Hand ist geschwollen.
	Wir wissen es selbst noch nicht.
Peter Hoffmann	Es tut mir leid, das zu hören.
	Hör mal, ich komme mit euch, vielleicht braucht ihr Hilfe.
Jack	Danke.

(*im Krankenhaus*)	
Jim	Peter, könntest du bitte dieses Formular für mich ausfüllen.
	Ich kann es selbst nicht schreiben.
Peter Hoffmann	Ja, natürlich. Lass mal sehen.
	Hier steht: ‚Welcher Körperteil ist verletzt?'
Jim	Meine rechte Hand und mein rechtes Fußgelenk.
Peter Hoffmann	‚Vermuten Sie einen (Knochen-)Bruch?' Was heißt das?
Jim	Das heißt: ‚Ist es gebrochen?' Mmm. Schreib ‚Ja'.
Peter Hoffmann	Wann war deine letzte Röntgenaufnahme?
Jim	Oh, ich erinnere mich nicht. Ich glaube, das war vor zwölf Jahren, als ich von meinem Motorrad gefallen bin.
	Ich habe mir den Arm und die Schulter gebrochen.
Peter Hoffmann	OK. Guck mal, du musst hier unterschreiben und bestätigen, dass du keine ansteckenden Krankheiten wie Aids, Hepatitis, Syphilis und so weiter hast.
Jim	Ich kann vielleicht mit meiner linken Hand unterschreiben. Was meinst du?

(at the information desk)

Peter Hoffmann	Excuse me.
	Can you tell me where the men's department is?
Information Desk	Yes, it is on the second floor,
	next to the children's department.
Peter Hoffmann	Near the children's department?
Information Desk	Yes. It's on the left-hand side as you leave the lift.
Peter Hoffmann	Thank you. Oh, and where can I get jeans?
Information Desk	Also in the men's department.
	Or you can buy them in the fashion boutique on the ground floor.
Peter Hoffmann	I'm also looking for food. Cheese, actually.
Information Desk	You can find food in the food hall
	in the basement.
Peter Hoffmann	Thank you for your help.
Information Desk	Not at all.

(in the food hall)

Peter Hoffmann	I would like some of that Cheshire cheese, please.
Male sales assistant	Certainly, sir. How much would you like?
	About a pound?
Peter Hoffmann	No, just 250 grams, please.
Male sales assistant	That is £3.20. And 80 p change.
Peter Hoffmann	Thank you.

(on the second floor)

Female sales assistant	Can I help you?
Peter Hoffmann	Well, I would like to buy a pair of running shorts, but I cannot see any here.
Female sales assistant	I'm sorry, but there aren't any here.
	There are some in the sports department.
Peter Hoffmann	Aren't there any sports clothes here?
Female sales assistant	No, I'm afraid that sports clothing is on the fourth floor, next to ladies' hairdressing.
Peter Hoffmann	Oh, I see. Well, thank you.
Female sales assistant	You are welcome.

Now listen and repeat.

34

(an der Information)

Peter Hoffmann	Entschuldigung.
	Können Sie mir sagen, wo die Herrenabteilung ist?
Information	Ja, sie ist im zweiten Stock,
	neben der Kinderabteilung.
Peter Hoffmann	Bei der Kinderabteilung?
Information	Ja. Sie ist auf der linken Seite, wenn Sie aus dem Aufzug kommen.
Peter Hoffmann	Danke. Oh, und wo bekomme ich Jeans?
Information	Ebenfalls in der Herrenabteilung.
	Oder aber Sie können sie in der Modeboutique im Erdgeschoss kaufen.
Peter Hoffmann	Ich suche auch Lebensmittel. Käse, um genau zu sein.
Information	Sie finden Lebensmittel in der Lebensmittelabteilung im Kellergeschoss.
Peter Hoffmann	Vielen Dank für Ihre Hilfe.
Information	Keine Ursache.

(in der Lebensmittelabteilung)

Peter Hoffmann	Ich hätte gerne etwas von dem Chesterkäse, bitte.
Verkäufer	Selbstverständlich, mein Herr. Wie viel möchten Sie gerne? Etwa ein Pfund?
Peter Hoffmann	Nein, nur 250 Gramm bitte.
Verkäufer	Das macht £3,20. Und 80 Pence Wechselgeld.
Peter Hoffmann	Danke schön.

(im zweiten Stockwerk)

Verkäuferin	Kann ich Ihnen behilflich sein?
Peter Hoffmann	Also, ich möchte gerne Laufshorts kaufen,
	aber ich kann hier keine sehen.
Verkäuferin	Es tut mir leid, aber hier es gibt keine.
	Es gibt welche in der Sportabteilung.
Peter Hoffmann	Gibt es denn hier gar keine Sportbekleidung?
Verkäuferin	Nein, es tut mir leid, Sportbekleidung ist im vierten Stock neben dem Damenfriseursalon.
Peter Hoffmann	Ach, ich verstehe. Ja also, danke.
Verkäuferin	Gern geschehen.

087

(on the fourth floor)

Female sales assistant	Yes, how may I help you?
Peter Hoffmann	I am looking for a pair of running shorts.
Female sales assistant	Certainly, what colour would you like?
Peter Hoffmann	Navy blue, please.
Female sales assistant	What about these?
Peter Hoffmann	No, I am afraid they are too long.
Female sales assistant	Well, how about those over there?
Peter Hoffmann	Yes, I think they look shorter.
Female sales assistant	Yes, they are the shortest we have. What size do you take?
Peter Hoffmann	Oh, I don't know. In Germany I take size 48.
Female sales assistant	These should be your size. Size 38. It sounds smaller in a British size.
Peter Hoffmann	How much are they?
Female sales assistant	They are £50.
Peter Hoffmann	That is too expensive, I am afraid, and I would really like a darker pair.
Female sales assistant	We do have some darker shorts in blue, but they are even more expensive.
Peter Hoffmann	Do you have any in other colours, which are less expensive?
Female sales assistant	Yes, we do have some cheaper shorts, but we don't have any cheaper ones in dark blue or navy.
Peter Hoffmann	Oh, that is a pity.
Female sales assistant	We have dark green, black, red, yellow and light blue. They are £25 each. Those are the cheapest we have.
Peter Hoffmann	Can I see the black ones, please?
Female sales assistant	Yes, of course. Here you are.
Peter Hoffmann	OK, they are not as nice as the navy blue ones, but they are less expensive and not too bad either.
Female sales assistant	Would you like to try them on?
Peter Hoffmann	Yes, please.
Female sales assistant	The changing rooms are this way.

Now listen and repeat.

088

(im vierten Stock)

Verkäuferin	Wie kann ich Ihnen helfen?
Peter Hoffmann	Ich suche Laufshorts.
Verkäuferin	Sicher, welche Farbe möchten Sie gerne?
Peter Hoffmann	Marineblau, bitte.
Verkäuferin	Wie wäre es mit diesen?
Peter Hoffmann	Nein, ich fürchte, die sind zu lang.
Verkäuferin	Wie wäre es mit denen dort drüben?
Peter Hoffmann	Ja, ich glaube, die sehen kürzer aus.
Verkäuferin	Ja, das sind die kürzesten, die wir haben. Welche Größe haben Sie?
Peter Hoffmann	Oh, das weiß ich nicht. In Deutschland habe ich Größe 48.
Verkäuferin	Diese sollten in Ihrer Größe sein. Größe 38. Es klingt kleiner in der britischen Größe.
Peter Hoffmann	Was kosten die?
Verkäuferin	Die kosten £ 50.
Peter Hoffmann	Ich fürchte, das ist zu teuer, und eigentlich hätte ich lieber ein dunkleres Paar.
Verkäuferin	Wir haben noch einige dunklere Shorts in blau, aber die sind noch teurer.
Peter Hoffmann	Haben Sie welche in anderen Farben, die preiswerter sind?
Verkäuferin	Ja, wir haben billigere Shorts, aber wir haben keine billigeren in dunkel- oder marineblau.
Peter Hoffmann	Oh, das ist schade.
Verkäuferin	Wir haben dunkelgrün, schwarz, rot, gelb und hellblau. Sie kosten £ 25 das Stück. Das sind die billigsten, die wir haben.
Peter Hoffmann	Kann ich bitte die schwarzen einmal sehen?
Verkäuferin	Ja, natürlich. Hier, bitte schön.
Peter Hoffmann	OK, die sind zwar nicht so schön wie die marineblauen, aber sie sind billiger und auch nicht so schlecht.
Verkäuferin	Möchten Sie sie anprobieren?
Peter Hoffmann	Ja, bitte.
Verkäuferin	Die Umkleidekabinen sind hier entlang.

094	Natalie	Hello?
	Peter Hoffmann	Hello, Natalie?
		This is Peter Hoffmann from Germany speaking.
	Natalie	Peter! How are you?
		It's ages since we last met!
	Peter Hoffmann	Yes, it is. I'm fine. How are you?
	Natalie	Great, thanks. What are you doing now? Where are you?
	Peter Hoffmann	I'm working in Manchester for a company
		called Winthrops for six months.
	Natalie	Great! You must come and visit me.
	Peter Hoffmann	I'd love to.
		In fact, that's why I'm phoning.
		I'm coming to London next weekend.
	Natalie	Super! Would you like to stay at my place?
	Peter Hoffmann	That sounds great.
		Are you sure it's not too much trouble?
	Natalie	Oh, don't be silly. Of course not.
		I'd be delighted to have you here.
	Peter Hoffmann	That's perfect. It's very kind of you.
	Natalie	When do you arrive? I'll pick you up at the station.
	Peter Hoffmann	Look, I don't want you to go to any trouble.
	Natalie	It's no trouble at all.
		I can return some of your hospitality at last.
	Peter Hoffmann	Look, can I ring you back tomorrow?
		I'll have all my travel details then.
	Natalie	Yes, please do. At about the same time, OK?
	Peter Hoffmann	Fine. Until tomorrow then. And thanks again, Natalie.
	Natalie	Bye, Peter.

Now listen and repeat.

095

Natalie	Hallo?
Peter Hoffmann	Hallo, Natalie?
	Hier spricht Peter Hoffmann aus Deutschland.
Natalie	Peter! Wie geht es dir?
	Es ist eine Ewigkeit her seit wir uns das letzte Mal gesehen haben.
Peter Hoffmann	Ja, das ist es. Mir geht es gut. Wie geht es dir?
Natalie	Großartig, danke. Was machst du jetzt? Wo bist du?
Peter Hoffmann	Ich arbeite für sechs Monate in Manchester für eine Firma namens Winthrops.
Natalie	Prima! Du musst mich unbedingt besuchen.
Peter Hoffmann	Das würde ich liebend gerne.
	Eigentlich rufe ich dich deswegen auch an.
	Ich komme nächstes Wochenende nach London.
Natalie	Super! Würdest du gerne bei mir übernachten?
Peter Hoffmann	Das klingt gut.
	Bist du sicher, dass es dir nicht zu viele Umstände macht?
Natalie	Ach, sei doch nicht albern. Natürlich nicht.
	Ich würde mich sehr freuen, dich hier zu haben.
Peter Hoffmann	Das ist toll. Das ist sehr nett von dir.
Natalie	Wann kommst du an? Ich hole dich am Bahnhof ab.
Peter Hoffmann	Hör mal, ich möchte dir keine Umstände machen.
Natalie	Es macht mir überhaupt keine Umstände.
	Ich kann mich endlich etwas für deine Gastfreundschaft revanchieren.
Peter Hoffmann	Hör mal, kann ich dich morgen zurückrufen?
	Dann habe ich meine Reisedaten.
Natalie	Ja bitte, mach das. Etwa um die gleiche Uhrzeit, OK?
Peter Hoffmann	Gut. Dann bis morgen. Und vielen Dank nochmal, Natalie.
Natalie	Tschüs, Peter.

099

Peter Hoffmann	Excuse me. Can you tell me how to get to Cook's, the travel agent's?
Stranger 1	I'm sorry, but I'm a stranger here myself.
Peter Hoffmann	Excuse me. Can you tell me the best way to get to Cook's, the travel agent's?
Stranger 2	Yes, of course. It is in the High Street. You go along this street until you get to the crossing.
Peter Hoffmann	Which crossing?
Stranger 2	The zebra crossing.
Peter Hoffmann	The one with the flashing lights?
Stranger 2	That's right. Do you see the traffic lights on the other side?
Peter Hoffmann	Yes, I do.
Stranger 2	Turn left at the lights, then take the second turning on the right to Market Square.
Peter Hoffmann	So, that's left at the traffic lights and then the second turning on the right.
Stranger 2	Yes, into Market Square. Go across Market Square, straight ahead and then turn left into the High Street. Cook's is on the right, opposite Barclays Bank.
Peter Hoffmann	Thank you very much.
Stranger 2	Don't mention it.

100

Now listen and repeat.

Peter Hoffmann	Entschuldigung. Können Sie mir sagen, wie ich zu Cook's, dem Reisebüro, komme?
Fremder 1	Es tut mir leid, aber ich bin selbst fremd hier.
Peter Hoffmann	Entschuldigen Sie. Können Sie mir sagen, wie ich am besten zu Cook's, dem Reisebüro, komme?
Fremder 2	Ja, natürlich. Es ist in der High Street. Sie gehen diese Straße entlang bis Sie zum Überweg kommen.
Peter Hoffmann	Welcher Überweg?
Fremder 2	Der Zebrastreifen.
Peter Hoffmann	Der mit dem Blinklicht?
Fremder 2	Genau. Sehen Sie die Ampel auf der anderen Seite?
Peter Hoffmann	Ja, sehe ich.
Fremder 2	Gehen Sie an der Ampel nach links, dann nehmen Sie die zweite Abzweigung rechts zum Market Square.
Peter Hoffmann	Also, links an der Ampel und dann die zweite Abzweigung rechts.
Fremder 2	Ja, zum Market Square. Gehen Sie über den Market Square, gerade aus und dann links in die High Street. Cook's ist auf der rechten Seite, gegenüber von Barclays Bank.
Peter Hoffmann	Ganz vielen Dank.
Fremder 2	Keine Ursache.

▶	Agent	Good afternoon. Can I help you?
105	Peter Hoffmann	Yes, please.
		I want to travel to London next weekend.
		Which is the best way to get there?
	Agent	Well, there are several options:
		by coach, by train or you could even fly.
		When do you want to leave?
	Peter Hoffmann	On Friday, early evening, at about 5 o'clock.
	Agent	The cheapest way is by coach,
		but it also takes longest.
	Peter Hoffmann	How much is it? And how long does it take?
	Agent	It is £35 return and it takes 4½ hours.
	Peter Hoffmann	When do the coaches from Manchester to London run?
	Agent	They run every two hours.
		There is one at 1600 hours or at 1800 hours.
		That is at 4 p.m. or at 6 p.m.
	Peter Hoffmann	At what time does the six o'clock coach get to London?
	Agent	At 22.30, half past ten.
	Peter Hoffmann	Oh, no! That is far too late.
		What about the train? Is that any quicker?
	Agent	It takes two hours and 13 minutes
		and there is one at 17.55.
	Peter Hoffmann	Do I have to change?
	Agent	No, it's a direct service.
	Peter Hoffmann	That sounds better.
		How much is it?
	Agent	It is £66.40 return normal fare or £33.20 single.
	Peter Hoffmann	Can I take a Supersaver?
	Agent	Supersaver tickets aren't called that any more.
		And I'm afraid an Off-Peak ticket is not valid at the time
		you wish to travel on Friday.
	Peter Hoffmann	OK. Then I'd like to book a normal return, please.

Now listen and repeat.

106

Reiseberaterin	Guten Tag. Kann ich Ihnen behilflich sein?
Peter Hoffmann	Ja, bitte.
	Ich möchte nächstes Wochenende nach London fahren.
	Wie komme ich am besten dahin?
Reiseberaterin	Also, es gibt mehrere Möglichkeiten:
	mit dem Reisebus, der Bahn oder Sie könnten sogar
	fliegen.
	Wann möchten Sie losfahren?
Peter Hoffmann	Am Freitag, am frühen Abend, etwa um 5 Uhr.
Reiseberaterin	Die billigste Möglichkeit ist mit dem Reisebus,
	aber das dauert auch am längsten.
Peter Hoffmann	Wie viel kostet das? Und wie lange dauert das?
Reiseberaterin	Es kostet £ 35 hin und zurück und dauert 4 ½ Stunden.
Peter Hoffmann	Wann fahren die Reisebusse von Manchester nach
	London?
Reiseberaterin	Sie fahren alle zwei Stunden.
	Es fährt einer um 16 Uhr oder um 18 Uhr,
	d. h. um vier oder um sechs Uhr am Nachmittag.
Peter Hoffmann	Um welche Uhrzeit kommt der Sechs-Uhr-(Reise-)Bus in
	London an?
Reiseberaterin	Um 22.30 Uhr, halb elf.
Peter Hoffmann	Oh, nein! Das ist viel zu spät.
	Wie ist es mit dem Zug?
	Ist das schneller?
Reiseberaterin	Das dauert zwei Stunden 13 Minuten
	und es fährt einer um 17.55.
Peter Hoffmann	Muss ich umsteigen?
Reiseberaterin	Nein, es ist eine direkte Verbindung.
Peter Hoffmann	Das klingt besser. Wie viel kostet das?
Reiseberaterin	Es kostet £ 66.40 hin und zurück Normalfahrpreis oder
	£ 33.20 die einfache Fahrt.
Peter Hoffmann	Kann ich einen Supersaver-Tarif nehmen?
Reiseberaterin	Der Supersaver-Tarif heißt so nicht mehr.
	Und leider ist ein Off-Peak Ticket nicht gültig zu der Zeit,
	wenn Sie am Freitag reisen wollen.
Peter Hoffmann	Na gut. Dann möchte ich bitte eine normale Hin- und
	Rückfahrkarte buchen.

110

Jack	How was your weekend in London, Peter?
	Did you have a good trip?
Peter Hoffmann	Fantastic! I visited an old friend.
	I am sure I saw all the sights in London.
	We walked everywhere:
	Big Ben, the Houses of Parliament,
	the Tower of London, Tower Bridge and so on.
Jack	Wow! Did you do the whole tourist programme?
Peter Hoffmann	Yes, we did, I'm afraid. We walked all day.
	I even watched the Changing of the Guard.
Jack	What did you think of it?
Peter Hoffmann	It was quite impressive, actually.
	There were thousands of people there.
	Some even waved little flags.
Jack	Really?
Peter Hoffmann	Yes. Natalie was a great hostess.
	She knows where the best restaurants are
	and we tasted some delicious food in Chinatown.
Jack	Didn't you say that you don't like Chinese cooking?
Peter Hoffmann	Yes, I did, but I liked this food. It was different.
Jack	I see. And what did you like best in London?
Peter Hoffmann	Oh, I enjoyed everything.
	But most of all the atmosphere
	and the mix of people I saw there.
	By the way, I recognised that Canadian again.
Jack	You must be joking!
Peter Hoffmann	No, seriously.
	I noticed him near the Houses of Parliament.
	He handed something over to a man there.
Jack	Oh, come on, Peter.
	I think you watch too many detective films.

▶ *Now listen and repeat*
111

Jack	Wie war dein Wochenende in London, Peter?
	Hattest du eine gute Reise?
Peter Hoffmann	Phantastisch! Ich habe eine alte Bekannte/Freundin besucht.
	Ich bin sicher, dass ich alle Sehenswürdigkeiten in London gesehen habe.
	Wir sind überallhin gelaufen:
	Big Ben, Parlamentsgebäude,
	Tower von London, Tower Bridge und so weiter.
Jack	Wow! Habt ihr das ganze Touristenprogramm absolviert?
Peter Hoffmann	Ja, ich fürchte, das haben wir. Wir sind den ganzen Tag gelaufen.
	Ich habe mir sogar die Wachablösung angesehen.
Jack	Wie fandst du das?
Peter Hoffmann	Es war eigentlich sehr beeindruckend.
	Es waren Tausende von Menschen da.
	Einige schwenkten sogar kleine Fähnchen.
Jack	Wirklich?
Peter Hoffmann	Ja. Natalie war eine großartige Gastgeberin.
	Sie weiß, wo die besten Restaurants sind
	und wir haben ganz leckeres Essen in Chinatown gegessen.
Jack	Hast du nicht gesagt, dass du chinesisches Essen nicht magst?
Peter Hoffmann	Ja, habe ich, aber ich mochte dieses Essen. Es war anders.
Jack	Ich verstehe. Und was hat dir in London am besten gefallen?
Peter Hoffmann	Ach, mir hat alles gefallen.
	Aber am meisten die Atmosphäre
	und die Vielfalt an Leuten, die ich dort gesehen habe.
	Übrigens, ich habe da den Kanadier wiedergesehen.
Jack	Du machst wohl Witze!
Peter Hoffmann	Nein, im Ernst.
	Ich habe ihn in der Nähe des Parlaments bemerkt.
	Er hat da einem Mann etwas übergeben.
Jack	Ach, komm schon, Peter.
	Ich glaube, du siehst zu viele Krimis.

116

Peter Hoffmann	Sorry, Jack, I forgot to ask you how your weekend went.
Jack	Friday evening was great, but on Saturday morning I got a call from the security guard at Winthrops.
Peter Hoffmann	Oh, why was that?
Jack	Well, the guard found the light on and some drawers in my office open.
Peter Hoffmann	Perhaps you forgot to close them?
Jack	No, the guard said they were closed when he began his rounds on Friday evening. There was nobody left in the office at that time.
Peter Hoffmann	So, you mean somebody went into your office during the night? But why? Was there anything missing?
Jack	No, there is nothing missing. Somehow it doesn't make sense.
Peter Hoffmann	But there must be something interesting enough for somebody to break in during the night.
Jack	No, not really, … unless … Oh, no! The blueprints to the machine – on my computer!
Peter Hoffmann	What? What is the matter?
Jack	Maybe your mysterious Canadian does exist.
Peter Hoffmann	What do you mean?
Jack	Espionage, industrial espionage. Follow me. We need to see Mr Jackson immediately. You can give him a description of the man you saw.
Peter Hoffmann	Yes, of course.

Now listen and repeat.

117

Peter Hoffmann	Tut mir leid, Jack, aber ich habe vergessen zu fragen, wie dein Wochenende war.
Jack	Freitag Abend war großartig, aber am Samstag Morgen bekam ich einen Anruf vom Winthrops' Wachmann.
Peter Hoffmann	Oh, wieso das denn?
Jack	Also, der Wachmann entdeckte, dass das Licht in meinem Büro an und einige Schubladen offen waren.
Peter Hoffmann	Vielleicht hast du vergessen, sie zuzumachen?
Jack	Nein, der Wachmann sagte, dass sie geschlossen waren, als er seine Rundgänge am Freitag Abend begann. Um die Uhrzeit war keiner mehr im Büro.
Peter Hoffmann	Du meinst also, dass jemand in der Nacht in dein Büro gegangen ist? Aber warum? Fehlte etwas?
Jack	Nein, es fehlt nichts. Irgendwie ergibt das keinen Sinn.
Peter Hoffmann	Aber es muss irgendetwas geben, das interessant genug ist für jemanden, um in der Nacht einzubrechen.
Jack	Nein, eigentlich nicht … es sei denn … Oh nein! Die Baupläne für die Maschine – auf meinem Computer!
Peter Hoffmann	Was? Was ist los?
Jack	Vielleicht existiert dein mysteriöser Kanadier doch.
Peter Hoffmann	Was meinst du damit?
Jack	Spionage, Industriespionage. Folge mir. Wir müssen sofort Herrn Jackson sprechen. Du kannst ihm eine Beschreibung des Mannes geben, den du gesehen hast.
Peter Hoffmann	Ja, natürlich.

120

Jack	By the way, Peter, my wife and I are having a little party this Saturday and we would like to invite you.
Peter Hoffmann	Oh, that is very kind. Will there be many people there?
Jack	Yes, there will be about 30 people.
Peter Hoffmann	Is it formal? Should I wear a suit?
Jack	No, no! It is just an informal occasion with friends and neighbours. There will be a buffet.
Peter Hoffmann	That will be quite a lot of work for you. Do you need any help?
Jack	It is very kind of you to offer, Peter, but it's really not necessary.
Peter Hoffmann	Well, shall I bring something along?
Jack	Well, actually, most people will bring a dish*.
Peter Hoffmann	Something to eat, you mean?
Jack	Yes, some kind of food. So all we will really need to do is buy the drinks and provide the music.
Peter Hoffmann	Then I will bring one, too – a dish, I mean. Should I bring anything special?
Jack	No, anything will do.
Peter Hoffmann	OK. I will see what I can do.

Now listen and repeat.
121

*Dish kann sowohl **das Gericht** als auch **Geschirr** heißen.

48

Jack	Übrigens, Peter,
	meine Frau und ich geben diesen Samstag eine kleine Party
	und wir würden dich gerne einladen.
Peter Hoffmann	Oh, das ist sehr nett.
	Werden viele Leute da sein?
Jack	Ja, es werden ungefähr 30 Leute da sein.
Peter Hoffmann	Ist es förmlich? Sollte ich einen Anzug tragen?
Jack	Nein, nein! Es ist nur ein informeller Anlass
	mit Freunden und Nachbarn.
	Es wird ein Büfett geben.
Peter Hoffmann	Das wird aber ziemlich viel Arbeit für euch.
	Braucht ihr Hilfe?
Jack	Das ist sehr nett, dass du deine Hilfe anbietest, Peter,
	aber es ist wirklich nicht nötig.
Peter Hoffmann	Na gut, soll ich etwas mitbringen?
Jack	Also, eigentlich bringen die meisten Leute ein Gericht mit.
Peter Hoffmann	Etwas zu essen, meinst du?
Jack	Ja, irgendetwas zum Essen.
	Also müssen wir eigentlich nur
	die Getränke kaufen und uns um die Musik kümmern.
Peter Hoffmann	Dann werde ich auch eins mitbringen – ein Gericht, meine ich.
	Soll ich irgendetwas Spezielles mitbringen?
Jack	Nein, einfach irgendetwas.
Peter Hoffmann	OK. Ich werde sehen, was ich tun kann.

124	Janet	Ah, Peter. I'm glad you could come.
	Peter Hoffmann	Thanks for the invitation, Janet.
		This is a little present for you.
	Janet	Oh, Peter, you shouldn't have!
		Oh, it's lovely, thanks.
		I had better put it somewhere safe.
	Peter Hoffmann	I'm glad you like it.
	Janet	Now, if you come this way,
		I will introduce you to some friends.
	Janet	Peter this is Clare, Dennis and Susanne.
	Peter Hoffmann	Nice to meet you.
	Clare & Susanne	Hello.
	Dennis	Quite a way to come –
		all the way from Germany for a party!
	Janet	Typical Dennis! If you give Peter a chance,
		he will tell you what he is doing here.
	Peter Hoffmann	Thank you, Janet.
	Dennis	What are you doing in Manchester then, Peter,
		if I may ask?
	Peter Hoffmann	I'm a trainee at Winthrops and Jack is my mentor.
	Dennis	Ho ho ho! If Jack is looking after you,
		we won't see you around much longer.
		He lost his last trainee.
	Jack	Did I just hear my name?
	Dennis	I was just telling young Peter here
		how your last trainee went missing.
	Jack	Well, I didn't actually lose him.
		He suddenly disappeared.
	Dennis	Did you ever find out what happened to him?
	Jack	No, we tried to contact his family in France,
		but the address was wrong.
	Peter Hoffmann	That is very strange.

Now listen and repeat.
125

Janet	Ah, Peter. Ich freue mich, dass du kommen konntest.
Peter Hoffmann	Vielen Dank für die Einladung, Janet.
	Dies ist ein kleines Geschenk für dich.
Janet	Oh, Peter, das sollst du doch nicht / das wäre nicht nötig
	gewesen. Oh, es ist wunderschön, danke.
	Ich stelle es besser an einen sicheren Platz.
Peter Hoffmann	Ich freue mich, dass es dir gefällt.
Janet	So, wenn du mir folgst,
	werde ich dich einigen Freunden vorstellen.
Janet	Peter, dies sind Clare, Dennis und Susanne.
Peter Hoffmann	Angenehm.
Clare & Susanne	Hallo.
Dennis	Eine ganz schöne Strecke bis hierher –
	extra aus Deutschland zu einer Party!
Janet	Typisch Dennis! Wenn du Peter eine Chance/Gelegenheit
	gibst, wird er euch erzählen, was er hier macht.
Peter Hoffmann	Danke Janet.
Dennis	Also, was machst du in Manchester, Peter,
	wenn ich fragen darf?
Peter Hoffmann	Ich bin Praktikant bei Winthrops und Jack ist mein Mentor.
Dennis	Ho ho ho! Wenn Jack sich um dich kümmert,
	werden wir dich hier nicht mehr lange sehen.
	Seinen letzten Praktikanten hat er verloren.
Jack	Habe ich gerade meinen Namen gehört?
Dennis	Ich habe gerade dem jungen Peter hier erzählt,
	wie dein letzter Praktikant abhanden gekommen ist.
Jack	Nun ja, ich habe ihn nicht wirklich verloren.
	Er verschwand plötzlich.
Dennis	Hast du je herausgefunden, was mit ihm passiert ist?
Jack	Nein, wir haben versucht, Kontakt zu seiner Familie in
	Frankreich aufzunehmen, aber die Adresse war falsch.
Peter Hoffmann	Das ist sehr merkwürdig.

128

Peter Hoffmann	Jack, I was wondering, have you got a photo of the man who was your 'lost' trainee?
Jack	Yes, I have his CV in my desk. Why do you ask?
Peter Hoffmann	Well, what if your lost trainee is the mysterious Canadian I have met so often?
Jack	That's hardly likely, but let's take a look. Mmm, that's strange.
Peter Hoffmann	What's wrong?
Jack	I can't find the CV which he sent us. It must have been stolen the other night.
Peter Hoffmann	But why?
Jack	Well, there must have been some important information in that CV.
Peter Hoffmann	But what? And what kind of man was he anyway?
Jack	He was the kind of person who is quiet, but friendly.
Peter Hoffmann	No, I mean what did he look like?
Jack	Well, he was quite tall, about 6' 5" and about 30 years old. Funnily enough, his date of birth was the same as Janet's, 2nd of April 1968.
Peter Hoffmann	What else do you remember about him?
Jack	He had fair hair and blue-green eyes. Oh, yes, and he had a beard. The women thought he was handsome.
Peter Hoffmann	Haven't you got copies of the CVs anywhere?
Jack	Of course! Why didn't I think of that? Mrs Kilbride keeps copies of all personnel records in her office. Let's take a look there.

Now listen and repeat.
129

Peter Hoffmann	Jack, ich habe mich gerade gefragt, ob du ein Foto von dem Mann hast, der dein ‚verlorener' Praktikant war.
Jack	Ja, ich habe seinen Lebenslauf in meinem Schreibtisch. Warum fragst du?
Peter Hoffmann	Also, was, wenn dein verlorener Praktikant der mysteriöse Kanadier ist, dem ich so oft begegnet bin?
Jack	Das ist unwahrscheinlich, aber lass uns nachsehen. Mmm, das ist merkwürdig.
Peter Hoffmann	Stimmt was nicht?
Jack	Ich kann den Lebenslauf nicht finden, den er uns geschickt hat. Er muss neulich nachts gestohlen worden sein.
Peter Hoffmann	Aber warum?
Jack	Also, der Lebenslauf muss eine wichtige Information enthalten.
Peter Hoffmann	Aber was? Und was war er überhaupt für ein Mann?
Jack	Er war die Art von Mensch, die ruhig, aber freundlich ist.
Peter Hoffmann	Nein, ich meine, wie sah er aus?
Jack	Also, er war recht groß, etwa 1,98 und etwa 30 Jahre alt. Komischerweise war sein Geburtsdatum das gleiche wie Janets, der 2. April 1968.
Peter Hoffmann	Was fällt dir noch zu ihm ein?
Jack	Er hatte blondes Haar und blaugrüne Augen. Oh ja, und er hatte einen Bart. Die Frauen fanden, dass er gut aussah.
Peter Hoffmann	Habt ihr nicht irgendwo Kopien der Lebensläufe?
Jack	Ja, natürlich! Warum habe ich nicht daran gedacht. Frau Kilbride bewahrt Kopien aller Personalunterlagen in ihrem Büro auf. Lass uns mal dort nachschauen.

133

Peter Hoffmann	What do you do for a living, Clare?
Clare	I am a secondary school teacher.
	I used to work in a tax office, but I had to stop.
Peter Hoffmann	Oh, I see. Do you enjoy your work?
Clare	Well, the working conditions aren't as good
	as people think.
Peter Hoffmann	You must have a lot of paperwork.
Clare	Yes, and everybody is so busy
	that there isn't much team work.
Peter Hoffmann	Yes, I can imagine that.
Clare	And the pay isn't very good.
Peter Hoffmann	That's interesting because in Germany teachers are
	civil servants and earn quite a good salary.
Clare	Do they really?
Peter Hoffmann	Yes, they do. Look, Clare, I have to improve my English.
	Can you recommend evening classes?
Clare	Why don't you join our theatre group?
Peter Hoffmann	Do you think I'm good enough?
Clare	Yes, of course you are.
	You should join us, practise your English
	and have fun at the same time.
Peter Hoffmann	Will I have to perform on stage?
Clare	You needn't, if you don't want to.
	Anyway, everyone is so nice in the group.
	You'll really enjoy it.

Now listen and repeat.
134

Peter Hoffmann	Was machst du beruflich, Clare?
Clare	Ich bin Lehrerin in an einer weiterführenden Schule.
	Früher habe ich in einem Finanzamt gearbeitet, aber ich
	musste aufhören.
Peter Hoffmann	Ah, ich verstehe. Macht dir deine Arbeit Spaß?
Clare	Tja, die Arbeitsbedingungen sind nicht so gut,
	wie die Leute glauben.
Peter Hoffmann	Du hast bestimmt viel Schreibarbeit.
Clare	Ja, und alle sind immer so beschäftigt,
	sodass es kaum Teamarbeit gibt.
Peter Hoffmann	Ja, das kann ich mir vorstellen.
Clare	Und die Bezahlung ist nicht sehr gut.
Peter Hoffmann	Das ist interessant, denn in Deutschland sind Lehrer
	Beamte und verdienen ein ganz gutes Gehalt.
Clare	Tun sie das wirklich?
Peter Hoffmann	Ja, das tun sie. Hör mal, Clare ich muss mein Englisch
	verbessern.
	Kannst du mir Abendkurse empfehlen?
Clare	Warum schließt du nicht unserer Theatergruppe an?
Peter Hoffmann	Glaubst du denn, dass ich dafür gut genug bin?
Clare	Ja, natürlich bist du das.
	Du solltest dich uns anschließen, dein Englisch üben
	und gleichzeitig Spaß haben.
Peter Hoffmann	Werde ich auf der Bühne auftreten müssen?
Clare	Das brauchst du nicht, wenn du nicht willst.
	Außerdem sind alle in der Gruppe so nett.
	Es wird dir wirklich Spaß machen.

137

Director	Right. Let's go through that last scene again. It's not good enough. In fact, it is terrible.
Clare	Why don't we ask Peter to watch us?
Sam	Yes, that is a good idea. He is an outsider and hasn't seen the play yet.
Director	Fine. Peter, would you please take a seat here?
Peter Hoffmann	To be honest, I have no idea what a good play should be like.
Director	OK. Just watch and tell us how you like it.

(a few minutes later)

Director	Well, what do you think of the first act, Peter?
Peter Hoffmann	I thought the fight was very good, but if I were you I would shorten it a little. It is too long.
Director	I quite agree. Let's try and …
Henry	I'm tired of doing that scene again and again.
Sam	I've had enough for one evening, too.
Clare	I'm all for going for a drink. Shall we go to the pub?
Sam	I'll go along with that.
Director	I'm quite satisfied with things so far, so, as you were saying, Clare, a drink sounds a good idea.
Henry	How do you feel about going to the "Crown"?
Sam	Anything will do. Do you like it here Peter?
Peter	Yes, I like it here. I'm very pleased with everything.
Clare	How do you guys feel about asking Peter along to the Fringe? Do you object?
Director	I don't mind.
Clare	Peter, do you want to come to Edinburgh with us and watch us perform our play at the festival?
Peter Hoffmann	I'd love to. I've never been to Edinburgh before.

Now listen and repeat.
138

Regisseur	So. Lasst uns die letzte Szene noch einmal durchgehen. Es ist nicht gut genug. Es ist sogar fürchterlich.
Clare	Warum bitten wir nicht Peter, uns zuzuschauen?
Sam	Ja, das ist eine gute Idee. Er ist ein Außenstehender und hat das Stück noch nicht gesehen.
Regisseur	In Ordnung. Peter, würdest du bitte hier Platz nehmen?
Peter Hoffmann	Um ehrlich zu sein, habe ich überhaupt keine Ahnung, wie ein gutes (Theater-)Stück sein sollte.
Regisseur	OK. Schau einfach zu und sag uns, wie es dir gefällt.

(*ein paar Minuten später*)

Regisseur	Also, wie findest du den ersten Akt, Peter?
Peter Hoffmann	Ich fand den Kampf sehr gut, aber wenn ich du wäre, würde ich ihn etwas kürzen. Er ist zu lang.
Regisseur	Dem stimme ich völlig zu. Lasst uns versuchen zu …
Henry	Ich bin es leid, die Szene immer wieder zu proben.
Sam	Mir reicht es auch für einen Abend.
Clare	Ich bin dafür, etwas trinken zu gehen. Wollen wir in die Kneipe gehen?
Sam	Dem schließe ich mich an.
Regisseur	Ich bin eigentlich bisher ziemlich zufrieden, also, wie du gerade sagtest, Clare, etwas trinken zu gehen, hört sich nach einer guten Idee an.
Henry	Was haltet ihr davon, in die „Krone" zu gehen?
Sam	Egal wohin. Gefällt es dir hier, Peter?
Peter Hoffmann	Ja, es gefällt mir hier. Ich bin mit allem sehr zufrieden.
Clare	Leute, was haltet ihr davon, Peter zu fragen, ob er mit zum „Fringe" kommen möchte? Habt ihr etwas dagegen?
Regisseur	Ich habe nichts dagegen.
Clare	Peter, möchtest du mit nach Edinburgh fahren und uns zuschauen, wenn wir unser Stück beim Festival aufführen?
Peter Hoffmann	Das würde ich liebend gerne. Ich war noch nie in Edinburgh.

▶ 140	Receptionist	Good evening. The Caledonian. Samantha speaking. How may I help you?
	Peter Hoffmann	I would like to speak to reservations, please.
	Receptionist	Certainly. One moment, please. I will put you through.
	Reservations	Reservations. Tricia speaking. How may I help you?
	Peter Hoffmann	I would like to make a booking for 16th August, please.
	Reservations	I am sorry, sir, but that is during the Edinburgh Festival and we are completely booked out then.
	Peter Hoffmann	Oh, dear. Can you recommend any other hotels?
	Reservations	I would think that all the hotels and guest houses are very busy at this time of the year.
	Peter Hoffmann	What shall I do? I can't go camping.
	Reservations	You could try calling the Scottish Tourist Board. They might be able to help you.
	Peter Hoffmann	Do you have their telephone number by any chance?
	Reservations	Yes, just a minute. Here it is: 0131–321 46 62.
	Peter Hoffmann	Thank you.
	Reservations	You are welcome.
	Tourist Board	Scottish Tourist Board. What can I do for you?
	Peter Hoffmann	I am looking for accommodation during the Festival.
	Tourist Board	I am very sorry, but all the boarding houses and hotels are fully booked.
	Peter Hoffmann	Oh, that is a pity!
	Peter Hoffmann	Jack, I can't get any accommodation in Edinburgh during the Festival.
	Jack	That is no problem. We will send you on an official visit to our subsidiary just outside Edinburgh and you can stay in the company's own guesthouse.
	Peter Hoffmann	Do you think that would be possible?
	Jack	Of course. Leave it to me.

Now listen and repeat.
141

Rezeptionistin	Guten Abend. Das Caledonian. Samantha am Apparat. Wie kann ich Ihnen helfen?
Peter Hoffmann	Ich möchte bitte mit der Reservierung sprechen.
Rezeptionistin	Natürlich. Einen Moment, bitte. Ich werde Sie durchstellen.
Reservierung	Reservierung. Tricia am Apparat. Wie kann ich Ihnen helfen?
Peter Hoffmann	Ich möchte bitte eine Buchung für den 16. August vornehmen.
Reservierung	Es tut mir leid, mein Herr, aber das ist während des Edinburgher Festivals und wir sind dann vollkommen ausgebucht.
Peter Hoffmann	Ach, herje. Können Sie mir andere Hotels empfehlen?
Reservierung	Ich denke, dass alle Hotels und Gästehäuser zu dieser Zeit des Jahres ausgebucht sind.
Peter Hoffmann	Was soll ich machen? Ich kann doch nicht zelten.
Reservierung	Versuchen Sie es mit einem Anruf beim Schottischen Fremdenverkehrsamt. Vielleicht können die Ihnen helfen.
Peter Hoffmann	Haben Sie zufällig deren Telefonnummer?
Reservierung	Ja, einen Moment. Hier ist sie: 0131–321 46 62.
Peter Hoffmann	Danke schön.
Reservierung	Gern geschehen.
Fremdenverkehrsamt	Schottisches Fremdenverkehrsamt. Was kann ich für Sie tun?
Peter Hoffmann	Ich suche nach einer Unterkunft während des Festivals.
Fremdenverkehrsamt	Es tut mir sehr leid, aber alle Pensionen und Hotels sind vollkommen ausgebucht.
Peter Hoffmann	Oh, das ist aber schade!
Peter Hoffmann	Jack, ich kann keine Unterkunft in Edinburgh während des Festivals finden.
Jack	Das ist kein Problem. Wir werden dich zu einem offiziellen Besuch in unsere Niederlassung gleich außerhalb Edinburghs schicken und du kannst im firmeneigenen Gästehaus übernachten.
Peter Hoffmann	Glaubst du, dass das möglich wäre?
Jack	Natürlich. Überlass das mir.

144

Peter Hoffmann	Good afternoon.
	I would like to hire a car for this weekend.
Agent	Certainly, sir. What type of car would you like?
Peter Hoffmann	Well, I am taking friends along
	so there are four of us.
	What can you recommend?
Agent	In this case, I would recommend category B.
Peter Hoffmann	What is the charge for B?
Agent	We have a special weekend rate.
	It is only £108.36.
	Normally it would be £60.11 per day.
Peter Hoffmann	Does that include mileage?
Agent	Yes, and third party insurance,
	VAT, theft and damage.
Peter Hoffmann	How much is comprehensive insurance?
Agent	There's no comprehensive insurance,
	but there is a waiver fee of £250
	in the third party insurance.
Peter Hoffmann	OK, that sounds fine.
Agent	Thank you. May I see your driving licence, please?
	Thank you. Oh, it is made out in Germany.
Peter Hoffmann	Yes, I am German. Is that a problem?
Agent	No, not at all.
	Will you be paying by credit card or in cash?
Peter Hoffmann	Do you accept Eurocard?
Agent	Yes, no problem.
	If you could just sign here and fill in this form.
Peter Hoffmann	When can I pick the car up?
Agent	It will be ready on Friday at 5 p.m.
Peter Hoffmann	Thank you. Goodbye.
Agent	Goodbye.

Now listen and repeat.
145

Peter Hoffmann	Guten Tag.
	Ich möchte gerne ein Auto für dieses Wochenende mieten.
Autovermieter	Natürlich, mein Herr. Was für einen Wagentyp möchten Sie haben?
Peter Hoffmann	Also, ich nehme Freunde mit,
	sodass wir vier Personen sind.
	Was können Sie empfehlen?
Autovermieter	In diesem Fall würde ich Kategorie B empfehlen.
Peter Hoffmann	Was ist die Leihgebühr für B?
Autovermieter	Wir haben einen speziellen Wochenendtarif.
	Er kostet nur £108,36.
	Normalerweise wären es £60,11 pro Tag.
Peter Hoffmann	Ist die Kilometerzahl inklusive?
Autovermieter	Ja, und Teilkasko/Haftpflichtversicherung,
	Mehrwertsteuer, Diebstahl und Schäden.
Peter Hoffmann	Was kostet Vollkaskoversicherung?
Autovermieter	Es gibt keine Vollkaskoversicherung,
	aber es gibt einen Freibetrag von £250
	in der Haftpflichtversicherung.
Peter Hoffmann	OK. Das klingt gut.
Autovermieter	Danke schön. Darf ich bitte Ihren Führerschein sehen?
	Danke schön. Oh, er ist in Deutschland ausgestellt.
Peter Hoffmann	Ja, ich bin Deutscher. Ist das ein Problem?
Autovermieter	Nein, überhaupt nicht.
	Werden Sie mit Kreditkarte zahlen oder in bar?
Peter Hoffmann	Akzeptieren Sie Eurocard?
Autovermieter	Ja, kein Problem.
	Wenn Sie bitte hier unterschreiben und dieses Formular ausfüllen könnten.
Peter Hoffmann	Wann kann ich das Auto abholen?
Autovermieter	Es wird am Freitag um 17 Uhr bereitstehen.
Peter Hoffmann	Vielen Dank. Auf Wiedersehen.
Autovermieter	Auf Wiedersehen.

▶ 148

Clare	There is a strange noise coming from the engine, Peter, isn't there?
Peter Hoffmann	Yes, and the engine is getting hot because the warning light has come on.
Sam	You had better stop and let me have a look at the engine, hadn't you?
Peter Hoffmann	OK. I'll just put the hazard warning lights on.
Sam	Mmh. It looks as though the fan belt has broken, doesn't it?
Peter Hoffmann	I think you are right. We'd better call the AA.
Sam	No, wait a moment. I have got an idea. Clare, have you got a pair of stockings?
Clare	I have some in my bag in the boot of the car. Why?
Sam	I could fix the fan belt with a pair of nylons and then we could drive to the next garage.

(*a few minutes later on the road*)

Peter Hoffmann	That was a great idea of yours, Sam.
Sam	Oh, don't mention it. That is a sign for the next service station, isn't it?
Peter Hoffmann	OK, I'll see if there is a mechanic around, shall I?
Sam	And I will fill her up while we are waiting in order to save time.
Peter Hoffmann	Fine. It takes super unleaded. About 30 litres, I think.
Sam	That's about eight gallons, isn't it? What about oil, and water?
Peter Hoffmann	No, they are OK. But you could check the tyres.

▶ 149 *Now listen and repeat.*

Clare	Da ist ein merkwürdiges Geräusch, das vom Motor kommt, Peter, oder?
Peter Hoffmann	Ja, und der Motor wird heiß, denn das Warnlicht ist angegangen.
Sam	Du hältst besser an und lässt mich mal einen Blick auf den Motor werfen, nicht wahr?
Peter Hoffmann	OK. Ich schalte nur noch die Warnblinkanlage ein.
Sam	Mmh. Es sieht so aus, als ob der Keilriemen gerissen ist, nicht wahr?
Peter Hoffmann	Ich glaube, du hast recht. Wir rufen besser den Automobilklub an.
Sam	Nein, warte einen Moment. Ich habe eine Idee. Clare, hast du Nylonstrümpfe?
Clare	Ich habe welche in meiner Tasche im Kofferraum des Wagens. Warum?
Sam	Ich könnte den Keilriemen mit Nylonstrümpfen reparieren und dann könnten wir zur nächsten Werkstatt fahren.

(*ein Paar Minuten später unterwegs*)

Peter Hoffmann	Das war eine großartige Idee von dir, Sam.
Sam	Ach, nicht der Rede wert. Das ist ein Schild für die nächste Tankstelle mit Werkstatt, oder?
Peter Hoffmann	OK, ich werde sehen, ob ein Mechaniker da ist, ja?
Sam	Und ich werde auftanken, während wir warten, um Zeit zu sparen.
Peter Hoffmann	Prima. Er nimmt Super bleifrei. Etwa 30 Liter, glaube ich.
Sam	Das sind ungefähr acht Gallonen, nicht wahr? Was ist mit Öl und Wasser?
Peter Hoffmann	Nein, das ist OK. Aber du könntest die Reifen prüfen.

Duncan Black	Pleased to meet you, Mr Hoffmann.
	My name is Duncan Black.
	I am the regional manager for Winthrops for Scotland.
Peter Hoffmann	Nice to meet you. Thanks for giving up your time
	and offering to show me around.
Duncan Black	It's a pleasure.
Peter Hoffmann	How big is the plant here?
Duncan Black	The plant employs 600 workers
	and covers about three acres of land.
Peter Hoffmann	Oh, that is bigger than I had expected.
Duncan Black	Oh, you should have been here a few years ago.
	We used to be even bigger,
	but when the economy started going downhill,
	we had to rationalise.
Peter Hoffmann	I understand. Many companies in Germany
	are in the same situation.
Duncan Black	Nevertheless, we managed to come up with the design
	plans for the Super 8 machine.
	You probably saw it in Manchester.
Peter Hoffmann	Oh, yes, I did.
	It is fantastic, but I didn't realise
	it was made here.
Duncan Black	Well, no, it isn't.
	One of our engineers had the idea and drew up the plans.
Peter Hoffmann	Ah, I see.
Duncan Black	So, as we had neither the building materials
	nor the capacity,
	the machine was built in Manchester.

Now listen and repeat.

Duncan Black	Ich freue mich, Sie kennenzulernen, Herr Hoffmann.
	Mein Name ist Duncan Black.
	Ich bin der Gebietsleiter von Winthrops für Schottland.
Peter Hoffmann	Sehr erfreut. Vielen Dank, dass Sie Ihre Zeit opfern
	und anbieten, mir alles zeigen.
Duncan Black	Es ist mir ein Vergnügen.
Peter Hoffmann	Wie groß ist das Werk hier?
Duncan Black	Das Werk beschäftigt 600 Arbeiter
	und umfasst ungefähr 1,2 Hektar.
Peter Hoffmann	Oh, das ist größer, als ich erwartet hatte.
Duncan Black	Oh, Sie hätten vor ein paar Jahren hier sein sollen.
	Wir waren noch größer,
	aber als es mit der Wirtschaft bergab ging,
	mussten wir rationalisieren.
Peter Hoffmann	Ich verstehe. In Deutschland
	sind viele Firmen in der gleichen Situation.
Duncan Black	Trotzdem haben wir es geschafft, die Baupläne für die
	Super-8-Maschine zu entwickeln.
	Sie haben sie wahrscheinlich in Manchester gesehen.
Peter Hoffmann	Oh ja, das habe ich.
	Sie ist phantastisch, aber mir war nicht bewusst,
	dass sie hier gebaut wurde.
Duncan Black	Tja, nein, das wird sie nicht.
	Einer unserer Ingenieure hatte die Idee und entwarf die
	Baupläne.
Peter Hoffmann	Ah, ich verstehe.
Duncan Black	Und da wir weder die Baumaterialien
	noch die Kapazität hatten,
	wurde die Maschine in Manchester gebaut.

155

Peter Hoffmann	Tell me, who is that man over there?
Duncan Black	Oh, that is Christian Fauré.
	He is from Belgium
	and is our new service manager.
	Why? Do you know him?
Peter Hoffmann	Well, I'm not quite sure,
	but could I talk to you in private?
Duncan Black	Ehr … I'm not quite sure I understand.
	Well, yes, let's go to my office.
Duncan Black	So, what is the matter?
Peter Hoffmann	Well, to cut a long story short,
	I suspect that your Mr Fauré is an industrial spy.
Duncan Black	A spy?
Peter Hoffmann	Yes, I saw him at Winthrops' headquarters
	in Manchester.
Duncan Black	Good grief! I don't know what to say.
	If you are right, then …
Peter Hoffmann	You can check my story by calling Jack.
	At the same time you can ask him whether they have
	found the missing CV yet.
Duncan Black	I don't quite understand, but I will call Jack.
Duncan Black	Jack confirmed your story and sent the CV by e-mail.
	He told me to ask you to look at the photograph
	which he has sent by fax.
Peter Hoffmann	He is like the missing trainee,
	my Canadian, your service manager,
	except now he hasn't got a beard.
	Let's call Jack back with the news.

 Now listen and repeat.
156

Peter Hoffmann	Sagen Sie mir, wer ist der Mann dort drüben?
Duncan Black	Oh, das ist Christian Fauré.
	Er ist aus Belgien
	und ist unser neuer Service Manager.
	Warum? Kennen Sie ihn?
Peter Hoffmann	Nun ja, ich bin mir nicht ganz sicher,
	aber könnte ich Sie unter vier Augen sprechen?
Duncan Black	Ehr … Ich bin nicht sicher, ob ich Sie verstehe.
	Nun, ja, gehen wir in mein Büro.

Duncan Black	Also, was ist los?
Peter Hoffmann	Um es kurz zu machen,
	ich vermute, dass Ihr Herr Fauré ein Industriespion ist.
Duncan Black	Ein Spion?
Peter Hoffmann	Ja, ich habe ihn in der Winthrops Zentrale
	in Manchester gesehen.
Duncan Black	Ach, du liebe Güte! Ich weiß nicht, was ich sagen soll.
	Wenn Sie recht haben, dann …
Peter Hoffmann	Sie können meine Geschichte überprüfen, indem Sie Jack anrufen.
	Sie können ihn auch gleichzeitig fragen, ob sie den verschwundenen Lebenslauf gefunden haben.
Duncan Black	Ich verstehe zwar nicht ganz, aber ich werde Jack anrufen.

Duncan Black	Jack hat ihre Geschichte bestätigt und den Lebenslauf per E-Mail geschickt.
	Er sagte mir, ich solle Sie bitten, sich das Foto anzusehen, das er per Fax geschickt hat.
Peter Hoffmann	Er gleicht dem verschwundenen Praktikanten, meinem Kanadier, Ihrem Service Manager,
	außer, dass er er jetzt keinen Bart mehr hat.
	Lassen Sie uns Jack zurückrufen mit der Neuigkeit.

158

Peter Hoffmann	It's my mother's birthday next week. I thought of buying her something that is typically Scottish.
Clare	Well, you could buy her a blanket, a knitted sweater or a kilt.
Peter Hoffmann	A kilt?
Clare	You know, one of those tartan skirts.
Peter Hoffmann	Now that's a good idea.
Clare	Look, there is a shop with traditional Scottish homespun clothes.
Shop assistant	Can I help you?
Clare	We are looking for kilts.
Shop assistant	Over here, please.
Peter Hoffmann	Goodness! I didn't know there were so many different colours.
Shop assistant	Every clan uses their own pattern and colouring. What size are you?
Clare	Oh, it's not for Peter*.
Peter Hoffmann	It's for my mother.
Shop assistant	I see. Well, what size and colour would you like?
Peter Hoffmann	Well, my mother takes a German size 40.
Shop assistant	Just a moment, I have a conversion table behind the counter. That would be size 14 in British size.
Peter Hoffmann	Fine. Do you have that blue one in a size 14?
Shop assistant	Yes, we do, but what length do you want?
Peter Hoffmann	Oh, I don't know. Perhaps you could try it on, Clare. You are about the same height as my mother, but much slimmer, of course.
Clare	Yes, I'd love to. There, it's just the right length.

Now listen and repeat.
159

* Kilts werden in Schottland nur von Männern getragen.

Peter Hoffmann	Nächste Woche hat meine Mutter Geburtstag.
	Ich dachte, ich kaufe ihr etwas,
	das typisch schottisch ist.
Clare	Also, du könntest ihr eine Decke,
	einen gestrickten Pullover oder einen Kilt kaufen.
Peter Hoffmann	Einen Kilt?
Clare	Du weißt schon, einen dieser karierten Schottenröcke.
Peter Hoffmann	Also, das ist eine gute Idee.
Clare	Schau mal, da ist ein Geschäft
	mit traditioneller schottischer Bekleidung aus Streichgarn.
Verkäuferin	Kann ich Ihnen helfen?
Clare	Wir suchen Kilts.
Verkäuferin	Hier drüben, bitte.
Peter Hoffmann	Du meine Güte! Ich wusste nicht, dass es so viele
	verschiedene Farben gibt.
Verkäuferin	Jeder Clan benutzt seine eigenen Muster und Farbtöne.
	Welche Größe haben Sie?
Clare	Oh, es ist nicht für Peter.
Peter Hoffmann	Es ist für meine Mutter.
Verkäuferin	Ich verstehe. Also, welche Größe und Farbe möchten Sie?
Peter Hoffmann	Also, meine Mutter hat die deutsche Größe 40.
Verkäuferin	Einen Moment,
	ich habe hinter dem Tresen eine Umrechnungstabelle.
	Das wäre Größe 14 in britischer Größe.
Peter Hoffmann	Gut. Haben Sie den blauen da in Größe 14?
Verkäuferin	Ja, haben wir, aber welche Länge wollen Sie?
Peter Hoffmann	Oh, ich weiß nicht.
	Vielleicht könntest du ihn anprobieren, Clare.
	Du bist ungefähr so groß wie meine Mutter,
	aber viel schlanker, natürlich.
Clare	Ja, das mache ich gerne.
	Da, er hat genau die richtige Länge.

Clerk	Next, please.
Peter Hoffmann	Good morning.
Clerk	Yes, please?
Peter Hoffmann	I would like to send this parcel to Germany. How much would that be?
Clerk	Please place it on the scales here. Thank you. That weighs two kilos. That will be £ 11.09.
Peter Hoffmann	How long will that take?
Clerk	It can take up to ten days.
Peter Hoffmann	Oh, dear! That's too long. Isn't there a quicker way?
Clerk	Well, you could send it by Airsure. That would only take two days.
Peter Hoffmann	And how much is that?
Clerk	That would be £ 19.82.
Peter Hoffmann	OK. I'll do that.
Clerk	Then I need you to fill in this document and attach it to the parcel.
Peter Hoffmann	How much are post cards to Germany?
Clerk	50 pence.
Peter Hoffmann	And a letter?
Clerk	The same – 50 p.
Peter Hoffmann	In that case I would like five 50p stamps, please.
Clerk	That will be £22.32.
Peter Hoffmann	Thank you.
Clerk	You are welcome. Next, please.

Now listen and repeat.

70

Angestellter	Der nächste, bitte.
Peter Hoffmann	Guten Morgen.
Angestellter	Ja, bitte?
Peter Hoffmann	Ich möchte dieses Päckchen nach Deutschland schicken? Wie viel würde das kosten?
Angestellter	Bitte legen Sie es auf die Waage hier. Danke. Das wiegt zwei Kilo. Das macht £ 11,09.
Peter Hoffmann	Wie lange wird das dauern?
Angestellter	Es kann bis zu zehn Tagen dauern.
Peter Hoffmann	Oje! Das ist zu lange. Gibt es keine schnellere Möglichkeit?
Angestellter	Tja, Sie könnten es mit Airsure schicken. Das würde nur zwei Tage dauern.
Peter Hoffmann	Und wie viel kostet das?
Angestellter	Das wären £ 19.82.
Peter Hoffmann	OK. Das mache ich.
Angestellter	Dann müssen Sie mir dieses Formular ausfüllen und es am Päckchen anbringen.
Peter Hoffmann	Wie viel kosten Postkarten nach Deutschland?
Angestellter	50 Pence.
Peter Hoffmann	Und ein Brief?
Angestellter	Dasselbe – 50 Pence.
Peter Hoffmann	In dem Fall hätte ich gerne fünf Briefmarken à 50 Pence, bitte.
Angestellter	Das macht £ 22,32.
Peter Hoffmann	Danke schön.
Angestellter	Gern geschehen. Der nächste, bitte.

Clare	I'm quite hungry.
Peter Hoffmann	So am I.
Clare	How about a pub lunch?
Peter Hoffmann	That sounds interesting.
	I didn't know pubs served lunch.
Clare	Yes, they do. You can eat in most pubs.
	The choice isn't as wide as in a restaurant, though.
Peter Hoffmann	Look, here is the "Flying Scotsman".
	Shall we go in?
Peter Hoffmann	What would you like, Clare?
Clare	A shandy, please.
Bartender	Yes? What will it be?
Peter Hoffmann	A pint of bitter and half a pint of shandy, please.
Bartender	Here you are, sir.
Peter Hoffmann	What have you got to eat?
Bartender	We have got mushroom or onion soup, Scotch eggs,
	steak & kidney pie, haggis, roast lamb or pork
	with boiled potatoes or chips and ham sandwiches.
Peter Hoffmann	What is haggis?
Bartender	Oh, it is a typical Scottish dish.
Peter Hoffmann	Oh, I would like to try that. What about you Clare?
Clare	The lamb for me, please.
	Are you sure you want to try the haggis?
Peter Hoffmann	Yes, why not? Cheers!
Clare	Cheers!
Bartender	Here you are. Hope you enjoy it.
Peter Hoffmann	Thank you. Yuck! It tastes disgusting.
	I don't like it.
Clare	Neither do I.
	It is made from sheep's offal, you know.
Peter Hoffmann	And you did warn me.
	I'll have to order something else.
	Yours looks safe. I'll get myself the same.

Now listen and repeat.

Clare	Ich bin ziemlich hungrig.
Peter Hoffmann	Ich auch.
Clare	Wie wäre es mit einem Mittagessen im Pub.
Peter Hoffmann	Das klingt interessant.
	Ich wusste nicht, dass Pubs Mittagessen anbieten.
Clare	Ja, tun sie. Man kann in den meisten Pubs essen.
	Allerdings ist die Auswahl ist nicht so groß wie in einem Restaurant.
Peter Hoffmann	Schau, hier ist der „Flying Scotsman".
	Wollen wir hineingehen?
Peter Hoffmann	Was möchtest du, Clare?
Clare	Einen Radler / ein Alster(wasser).
Gastwirt	Ja bitte? Was darf es sein?
Peter Hoffmann	Einen Pint Bitterbier und einen halben Pint Radler bitte.
Wirt	Bitte schön, mein Herr.
Peter Hoffmann	Was haben Sie zu essen?
Gastwirt	Wir haben Pilz- oder Zwiebelsuppe, hart gekochte Eier in Wurstbrät, Rindfleisch-Nieren-Pastete, Haggis*, gebratenes Lamm oder Schwein mit Kartoffeln oder Pommes frites, und Schinkenbrote.
Peter Hoffmann	Was ist Haggis?
Gastwirt	Oh, es ist ein typisches schottisches Gericht.
Peter Hoffmann	Oh, das möchte ich probieren. Was ist mit dir, Clare?
Clare	Für mich das Lamm, bitte.
	Bist du sicher, dass du Haggis probieren möchtest?
Peter Hoffmann	Ja, warum nicht? Prost!
Clare	Prost!
Gastwirt	Bitte schön. Guten Appetit.
Peter Hoffmann	Danke schön. Igitt! Das schmeckt ekelhaft.
	Das mag ich nicht.
Clare	Ich auch nicht.
	Es wird aus Schafsinnereien gemacht, weißt du.
Peter Hoffmann	Und du hast mich gewarnt. Ich werde etwas anderes bestellen müssen.
	Deins sieht ungefährlich aus.
	Ich werde mir das Gleiche holen.

Schafsinnereien im Schafsmagen

Jack	Are you sure this is going to work, Duncan?
Duncan Black	Well, the guy has to turn up sooner or later in this office to get the missing sketches for the Super 8 machine.
Peter Hoffmann	Why is that?
Duncan Black	Well, for security reasons. Only parts of the construction plans for the machine are in Manchester, the other part is here.
Jack	Yes, that is true, but maybe he has already made copies of your plans, Duncan.
Duncan Black	I don't think so. If he had already made them, he would have disappeared quickly, as he did in Manchester.
Peter Hoffmann	That makes sense.
Jack	If only I had realised what he was up to I could have reacted sooner.
Duncan Black	Don't worry, Jack, we will catch him tonight.
Peter Hoffmann	But why should he strike tonight?
Duncan Black	For two reasons: first of all it is the annual staff party and there will be a lot of people about, so the spy will feel secure.
Peter Hoffmann	I see. And the second reason?
Duncan Black	Well, it is a long weekend and if the thief manages to get the plans this Friday, he will have plenty of time to get away.
Jack	Clever, but not clever enough for us.
Duncan Black	That is right. We have plain clothes policemen and policewomen all over the building. And there are two hidden cameras in my office. So all we have to do is wait.
Peter Hoffmann	How will we know if he is there?
Duncan Black	The police have installed an alarm. So, when he comes out, he will be trapped.

Now listen and repeat.

172

Jack	Bist du sicher, dass das funktionieren wird, Duncan?
Duncan Black	Nun ja, der Typ muss früher oder später in diesem Büro auftauchen, um die fehlenden Zeichnungen für die Super-8-Maschine zu holen.
Peter Hoffmann	Warum das?
Duncan Black	Tja, aus Sicherheitsgründen. Es sind nur Teile der Konstruktionspläne für die Maschine in Manchester, der andere Teil ist hier.
Jack	Ja, das ist wahr, aber vielleicht hat er schon Kopien eurer Pläne gemacht, Duncan.
Duncan Black	Das glaube ich nicht. Wenn er schon welche gemacht hätte, wäre er schnell verschwunden, wie er es in Manchester gemacht hat.
Peter Hoffmann	Das macht Sinn.
Jack	Wenn ich doch nur begriffen hätte, was er vorhatte, dann hätte ich früher reagieren können.
Duncan Black	Macht dir keine Sorgen, Jack, wir werden ihn heute Abend erwischen.
Peter Hoffmann	Aber warum sollte er heute Abend zuschlagen?
Duncan Black	Aus zwei Gründen: Erstens ist heute die jährliche Betriebsfeier und es werden viele Leute da sein, sodass sich der Spion sicher fühlen wird.
Peter Hoffmann	Ich verstehe. Und der zweite Grund?
Duncan Black	Also, es ist ein langes Wochenende, und wenn der Dieb es schafft, die Pläne diesen Freitag zu bekommen, hat er genug Zeit, um davonzukommen.
Jack	Schlau, aber nicht schlau genug für uns.
Duncan Black	Das ist richtig. Wir haben Polizisten und Polizistinnen in Zivil im ganzen Gebäude. Und in meinem Büro sind zwei versteckte Kameras. Also, alles, was wir zu tun haben, ist warten.
Peter Hoffmann	Wie werden wir wissen, dass er da ist?
Duncan Black	Die Polizei hat einen Alarm installiert. Wenn er dann herauskommt, sitzt er in der Falle.

176	Mr Jackson	Mr Hoffmann, Peter, we are so grateful to you. You saved the company's most valuable asset – the plans for the machine.
	Peter Hoffmann	It was a pleasure. What happens now?
	Mr Jackson	Well, as you know, the man was arrested and now our lawyers are dealing with the case.
	Peter Hoffmann	Good. I'm glad to hear that.
	Mr Jackson	We would like to show our gratitude by presenting you with this cheque.
	Peter Hoffmann	Oh, I can't possibly accept that.
	Mr Jackson	I insist. And we are offering you a post in our company when you have finished your studies in Germany.
	Peter Hoffmann	Oh! I don't know what to say. You are very kind.
	Mr Jackson	We hope you found your time with us useful and worthwhile.
	Peter Hoffmann	Yes, thank you. I have enjoyed my stay very much.
	Mr Jackson	I am glad to hear that. We hope to see you here again soon.

(*at the airport*)

Peter Hoffmann	Thank you very much for bringing me to the airport.
Janet	It's no trouble at all.
Peter Hoffmann	And thank you, too, for making my stay so interesting.
Jack	It was a pleasure having you and it was you who made the stay so interesting.
Peter Hoffmann	You will come and visit me in Germany, won't you?
Janet	Yes, we'd love to.
Peter Hoffmann	Promise you will or I will be very disappointed.
Jack & Janet	We promise.
Jack	Oh, and say hello to our mutual friend, Martina Glass.
Peter Hoffmann	Yes, I'll do that.

 Now listen and repeat.
177

Herr Jackson	Herr Hoffmann, Peter, wir sind Ihnen so dankbar. Sie haben den größten Vermögenswert der Firma gerettet – die Pläne für die Maschine.
Peter Hoffmann	Gern geschehen. Was passiert jetzt?
Herr Jackson	Tja, wie Sie wissen, wurde der Mann verhaftet, und nun befassen sich unsere Rechtsanwälte mit dem Fall.
Peter Hoffmann	Gut. Ich bin froh, das zu hören.
Herr Jackson	Wir möchten Ihnen unsere Dankbarkeit zeigen, indem wir Ihnen diesen Scheck überreichen.
Peter Hoffmann	Oh, das kann ich unmöglich annehmen.
Herr Jackson	Ich bestehe darauf. Und wir bieten Ihnen eine Position in unserer Firma an, nachdem Sie ihr Studium in Deutschland beendet haben.
Peter Hoffmann	Oh! Ich weiß nicht, was ich sagen soll. Sie sind sehr freundlich.
Herr Jackson	Wir hoffen, dass Ihre Zeit mit uns nützlich und lohnenswert war.
Peter Hoffmann	Ja, vielen Dank. Ich habe meinen Aufenthalt sehr genossen.
Herr Jackson	Ich freue mich, das zu hören. Wir hoffen, Sie hier bald wieder zu sehen.

(am Flughafen)

Peter Hoffmann	Vielen Dank, dass ihr mich zum Flughafen gebracht habt.
Janet	Nicht der Rede wert.
Peter Hoffmann	Und auch vielen Dank dafür, dass ihr meinen Aufenthalt so interessant gemacht habt.
Jack	Es war ein Vergnügen, dich hier zu haben, und du warst es, der den Aufenthalt so interessant gemacht hat.
Peter Hoffmann	Ihr werdet mich doch in Deutschland besuchen kommen, nicht wahr?
Janet	Ja, das würden wir gerne.
Peter Hoffmann	Versprecht mir, dass ihr kommt / kommen werdet, sonst werde ich sehr enttäuscht sein.
Jack & Janet	Wir versprechen es.
Jack	Oh, und grüße unsere gemeinsame Freundin Martina Glass.
Peter Hoffmann	Ja, das werde ich machen.

Vokabular

In der rechten Spalte neben der Übersetzung finden Sie einen Verweis auf das Kapitel, in dem Wörter und Wendungen das erste Mal vorkommen

English	Deutsch	
a	ein, -e, -er	1
AA	ADAC	29
able	fähig, imstande	27
about	ungefähr	1
(to) accept	akzeptieren	28
accommodation	Unterkunft	8
acre	Morgen (Maßeinheit)	30
across	hin-, her-, über	18
(to) act	schauspielern	26
activity	Aktivität	14
actually	eigentlich	15
address	Adresse	23
afraid: I'm ~	leider, es tut mir leid	8
after	nach	5
afternoon	Nachmittag	8
again	wieder	17
agent	Makler/-in	9
ages	Ewigkeit	17
ago	vor X Jahren	14
(to) agree	zustimmen	26
ahead	vor, voraus, voran	18
aids	Aids	14
air	Luft	29
airport	Flughafen	36
alarm	Alarm	35
all	alle, -s	3
all for	dafür sein	26
almost	fast, beinahe	6
along	entlang	12
already	schon	35
also	auch	15
always	immer	10
am	vor 12.00 Uhr mittags	19
America	Amerika	1
American	amerikanisch, Amerikaner/-in	7

an	ein, -e, -er (vor vokalischem Anlaut)	2
and	und	3
ankle	Knöchel	14
annual	jährlich, -e, -es	35
any	(irgend) einer; einige	6
anything	(irgend) etwas, alles	7
anyway	ohnehin	4
anywhere	irgendwo	24
apartment	Wohnung	8
April	April	24
arm	Arm	14
around	rundherum	3
(to) arrest	festnehmen	36
arrival	Ankunft	3
arrive	ankommen	9
as	als	13
as ... as	so ... wie	7
as soon as	sobald	6
(to) ask	fragen	11
asset	Aktivposten, Gut	36
assistant	Assistent, Helfer	3
at	an, auf, bei, für	4
at the same time	zur selben Zeit, gleichzeitig	25
atmosphere	Atmosphäre, Stimmung	20
(to) attach	anhängen	33
away	weg	35
back	zurück	17
bacon	Speck	10
bad	schlecht, schlimm, arg	14
bag	Tasche	29
bank	Bank	18
basement	Souterrain	15
bath	Bad	9
(to) be	sein	8
beard	Bart	24
beautiful	schön	11

because	weil	7
bed	Bett	9
bed & breakfast	Pension, Privatunterkunft	8
before	bevor	6
beg	bitten, flehen	10
begin	beginnen	21
behind	hinter	32
Belgium	Belgien	31
(to) believe	glauben	8
best	am Besten	4
better	besser	7
big	groß	30
bigger	größer	7
birth	Geburt	24
birthday	Geburtstag	32
bitter	dunkles Bier	13
black	schwarz	16
blanket	Decke	32
blue	blau	16
blueprints	Blaupausen	21
boarding house	Pension	10
body	Körper	14
boiled potatoes	gekochte Kartoffeln	34
book	Buch	2
(to) book: booked out	buchen, ausgebucht	27
booking	Buchung	27
boot	hier: Kofferraum	29
bother	lästig	2
bottle	Flasche	13
boutique	Boutique	15
(to) break	brechen	14
break in	Einbruch	21
breakdown	Autopanne	29
breakfast	Frühstück	9
bring	bringen	22
British	britisch	16
brother	Bruder	4
buffet	Büfett	22
(to) build	bauen	30
building	Gebäude	30
bus	Bus	10
business class	Business Klasse	2
busy	beschäftigt	25

but	aber	1
buy	kaufen	15
by	bei, an, neben, bis, von	4
by the way	übrigens	3
bye	Tschüss	17
cake	Kuchen	13
call	anrufen	3
camera	Kamera	35
camping	Zelten	27
(to) can	können	2
Canadian	Kanadier	1
capacity	Kapazität	30
car	Auto	4
car park	Parkhaus	4
card	Karte	28
care for	interessiert sein an, etw oder jmd mögen	13
case: in this ~	in diesem Fall	28
cash	Bargeld	28
(to) catch	fangen	35
category	Kategorie	28
certain	sicher	7
certainly	sicherlich	5
chance	Chance, Gelegenheit	23
(to) change	verändern	7
changing of the guard	Wachablösung	20
changing rooms	Umkleidekabinen	16
charge	Gebühr	28
cheaper	billiger	16
(to) check	überprüfen	8
cheers	Prost	34
cheese	Käse	15
cheque	Scheck	36
Cheshire	Cheshire (Grafschaft)	15
chicken Korma	Hühnchen Korma	13
children	Kinder	15
Chinese	chinesisch	12
chips	Pommes Frites	34
choice	(Aus-)wahl	34
civil servant	Beamter, Beamtin	25
clan	Clan	32
class	Kurs, Klasse	25

clever	schlau, klug	7	darker	dunkler	16
(to) close	schließen	21	date	Datum	24
clothes	Kleider	7	day	Tag	4
clothing	Kleidung	15	(to) deal with	sich befassen, handeln	36
club	Klub, Verein	14	delicious	lecker	13
coach	Reisebus	19	delighted	entzückt	17
coat	Mantel	5	department	Abteilung	15
coffee	Kaffee	13	department store	Kaufhaus	15
coincidence	Zufall	4	description	Beschreibung	21
colour	Farbe	16	design	Design	30
colouring	Färbung	32	desk	Schreibtisch	24
(to) come	kommen	2	dessert	Nachtisch	13
come in	hereinkommen	6	detail	Detail	17
Come on!	Komm schon!	29	detective	Detektiv	20
company	Firma	1	development	Entwicklung	21
competitors	Konkurrenz	7	different	andere, -r, -s	20
completely	vollkommen, völlig	27	direct	direkt	19
comprehensive insurance	Vollkasko- versicherung	28	(to) disappear	verschwinden	35
computer	Computer	7	disappoint	enttäuschen	36
conditions	Konditionen, Bedingungen	25	disease	Krankheit	14
(to) confirm	bestätigen	31	disgusting	ekelhaft	34
construction	Konstruktion, Bau	35	dish	Gericht	13
contact	Kontakt	23	(to) do	machen	5
contagious	ansteckend	14	document	Dokument	33
Continental	Kontinental	10	double	Doppel-	9
conversion table	Umrechnungstabelle	32	down	hinunter, runter	7
cooking	hier: Küche	12	downhill	bergab	30
copies	Kopien	24	(to) draw up	zeichnen, entwerfen	30
(to) copy	kopieren, nachmachen	7	drawer	Schublade	21
could	Pret. von *can*	5	(to) drink	Getränk, trinken	13
counter	Theke, hier: Kasse	15	(to) drive	fahren	28
course	Gang (Essen)	13	dungarees	Latzhosen	15
(to) cover	abdecken (Gebiet)	30	during	während	2
credit	Kredit	28	each	jede, -r, -s	16
crossing	Kreuzung, Übergang	18	early	früh	19
cup	Tasse	13	(to) earn	verdienen	25
curry	Curry, Indisches Essen allg.	12	eat	essen	10
			economy	Wirtschaft	30
(to) cut	schneiden	7	eggs	Eier	10
CV	Lebenslauf	24	eight	acht	10
damage	Schaden	28	either	entweder	16
dark	dunkel	16	else: Anything ~?	ansonsten; Sonst noch etwas?	24
dark blue	dunkelblau	16	e-mail	E-Mail	31

(to) employ	anwenden, einstellen, beschäftigen	30
end	Ende	7
engaged	hier: besetzt	5
engine	Motor	29
engineer	Ingenieur	30
England	England	6
English	englisch	1
English breakfast	englisches Frühstück	10
enjoy	genießen	6
enough	genug	21
especially	besonders, vor allem	12
espionage	Spionage	21
estate agent	Immobilienmakler/-in	8
Europe	Europa	1
even	sogar	19
evening	Abend	19
ever	jemals	23
every	jede, -r, -s	11
everybody	jedermann, alle	25
everyone	jedermann, alle	25
everywhere	überall	20
excellent	ausgezeichnet	1
except	außer	31
excuse: Excuse me, please.	Entschuldigen Sie, bitte.	1
exist	existieren, bestehen	21
(to) expect	erwarten	30
expensive	teuer	16
eye	Auge	24
factory; ~ floor	Fabrik; Fabrikhalle	7
fair	blond	24
(to) fall off	herunterfallen	14
family	Familie	4
fan belt	Keilriemen	29
fantastic	phantastisch	4
fare	Fahrgeld	19
fashion	Mode	15
father	Vater	4
fax	Fax	31
(to) feed	hier: einführen	7
feel	fühlen	35
festival	Fest	26

few	einige, wenige	29
fight	Kampf	26
(to) fill in	hier: ausfüllen	14
film	Film	20
(to) find	finden	
(to) find out	herausfinden	12
fine	fein, prima	3
(to) finish	fertig, beenden	6
first	erst, -e, -er, -es	4
(to) fit	passen	7
five	fünf	10
(to) fix	reparieren	29
flag	Fahne	20
(to) flash	blinken	18
flat	Wohnung	8
flight	Flug	2
floor	Geschoss, Etage	5
(to) fly	fliegen	19
(to) follow	folgen	21
fond: be ~ of sb	jdn gern haben, lieben	12
food	Essen, Lebensmittel	12
food hall	Lebensmittelabteilung	15
foot	Fuß (Maßeinheit)	7
foot	Fuß	14
for	für	2
(to) forget	vergessen	21
fork	Gabel	13
form	Formular	14
formal	förmlich	22
four	vier	28
fourth	vierte, -er, -es	5
fracture	Knochenbruch	14
France	Frankreich	23
free	frei, umsonst	9
French Canadian	Französisch-Kanadier/-in	1
frequently	öfter	11
Friday	Freitag	19
fried; ~ egg	gebraten; Spiegelei	10
friend	Freund/-in	4
friendly	freundlich	8
Fringe	Fringe (Rand)	26
from	von	1

fruit	Obst	13	(to) hand	überreichen	20
fully	völlig, vollkommen	27	handsome	ansehnlich, stattlich, schön	24
fun	Spaß	25	(to) happen	geschehen	23
funnily	komischer-, lustigerweise	24	hardly	kaum	24
gallon	Gallone (Maßeinheit)	29	(to) have	haben, besitzen, bekommen	2
game	Spiel	14	(to) have to	etw. müssen	12
German	Deutsch	1	have: to ~ guests	jdn beherbergen	36
Germany	Deutschland	3	hazard lights	Warnblinkanlage	29
(to) get	erhalten, bekommen, kriegen	15	he	er	5
(to) give	geben	8	headquarter	Zentrale	5
give up	aufgeben	30	health	Gesundheit	14
glad	froh, erfreut	23	(to) hear	hören	14
(to) go	gehen	6	height	Größe	32
(to) go along; ~ with sth	entlang gehen; mit etwas einverstanden sein	18	helmet	Helm	7
			(to) help	helfen	2
good	gut	4	hepatitis	Hepatitis, Leberentzündung	14
Good afternoon.	Guten Tag.	8	her	ihr, -e, -en	4
Good evening.	Guten Abend.	27	here	hier	1
good grief	Mensch, ach du Schande	31	(to) hesitate	zögern	6
			(to) hide	verstecken	35
Good morning.	Guten Morgen.	2	him	ihn, ihm, den, dem (-jenigen)	6
Goodbye!	Auf Wiedersehen!	6	himself	(er, ihn, ihm, sich) selbst	14
goodness	meine Güte	32			
gram	Gramm	15	hire	mieten	28
grateful	dankbar	4	his	sein, -e, -en	4
gratitude	Dankbarkeit	36	holiday	Urlaub	1
great	großartig	3	home; at ~	heim; zu Hause	10
green	grün	7	homespun	handgemacht, in Handarbeit hergestellt	32
group	Gruppe	25			
guard	Wächter	20	honest	ehrlich	26
guest	Gast	27	(to) hope	hoffen	6
guesthouse	(Hotel-)Pension	27	hospital	Krankenhaus	14
guy	Typ, Kerl	35	hospitality	Gastfreundlichkeit	17
had	siehe have	6	host	Gastgeber	20
had better	sollte besser	23	hostess	Gastgeberin	20
haggis	schottisches Gericht aus Schafsinnereien	34	hot	heiß	29
hair	Haar(-e)	24	hotel	Hotel	8
hairdresser's	Friseursalon	15	hour	Stunde	19
half	halb, -e, -er, -es	13	house	Haus	8
half: ~ a lager	ein kleines Bier	13	how	wie	5
ham	Schinken	34	how about	wie wäre es mit	16
hand	Hand	2			

how are you	wie geht es dir	17
how do feel about	wie denkst du über	26
How do you do?	Angenehm. / Sehr erfreut.	3
how many	wieviel, -e	10
how much	wieviel	15
human resources director	Personalleiter/-in	4
hungry	hungrig	34
(to) hurt	verletzen	14
I	ich	1
idea	Idee	7
if	wenn, falls	6
(to) imagine	sich vorstellen	25
immediately	sofort	8
important	wichtig	24
impressive	beeindruckend	20
(to) improve	verbessern	1
in	in, an, auf, bei	1
in fact	eigentlich	17
in order to	um … zu …	29
inch	Zoll (Maßeinheit)	7
included	inklusive	28
Indian	indisch	12
industrial	industriell	21
industry	Industrie	6
informal	formlos, zwanglos	22
information	Information, Auskunft	15
insist (on)	bestehen auf	36
(to) inspect	inspizieren, untersuchen	12
install	einsetzen	35
instead	anstatt	13
insurance	Versicherung	28
interesting	interessant	4
(to) interrupt	unterbrechen	14
into	in … hinein	7
(to) introduce	vorstellen	12
introduction	Bekanntmachung	6
investor	Investor	7
invitation	Einladung	22
(to) invite	einladen	22
is	ist	1
it	es (auch: er, sie)	1

(to) join	teilnehmen, Mitglied werden	25
(to) joke	scherzen	20
juice	Saft	13
just	gerade, genau	8
keen: be ~ on	auf etw scharf sein	12
(to) keep	hier: aufbewahren	24
kilt	Schottenrock	32
kind	nett	17
knife	Messer	13
knit	stricken	32
(to) know	wissen	4
lager	Lagerbier	13
lamb	Lamm(-fleisch)	34
land	Land	30
landlady	Wirtin, Vermieterin	8
landlord	Wirt, Vermieter	8
large	groß, weit	8
last	letzte, -r, -s	14
late	spät	19
later (on)	später	29
lawyer	Rechtsanwalt; -anwältin	36
(to) leave	verlassen	10
left	links	14
leisure	Freizeit-	14
length	Länge	7
less	weniger	16
(to) let	lassen	7
letter	Brief	4
licence	Lizenz, Zulassung, (Führer-)Schein	28
lift	Aufzug	5
light	hier: (Blink-)Licht	18
light blue	hellblau	16
(to) like	mögen	2
like; Do you ~ …?	mögen; Magst Du?	10
likely	wahrscheinlich	24
line	hier: Leitung	5
litre	Liter	29
little	klein	7
(to) live	wohnen, leben	4
long	lang	16
loo	Klo, Toilette	4
(to) look (at)	(an-)schauen	4

(to) look for	etw suchen	2	mine	mein	4
(to) look forward to	sich auf etw freuen	9	minute	Minute	8
looks as though	sieht aus als ob	29	(to) miss	fehlen	21
lose	verlieren	23	missing	vermisst, abhanden	31
lot	viel	3	mistake	Fehler	5
(to) love	lieben, mögen	10	mix	Mischung, Gemisch	20
lovely	herrlich, schön	11	mixture	Mischung, Gemisch	13
luck	Glück	2	model	Modell	7
luggage	Gepäck	2	moment	Moment	9
lunch	Mittagessen	12	Monday	Montag	9
machine	Maschine	7	month	Monat	17
made from	besteht aus	34	more	mehr	12
magazine	Zeitschrift	2	morning	Morgen	11
main	Haupt-	13	most	meist, -en, -es	20
(to) make	machen	21	mother	Mutter	32
(to) manage	handhaben, organisieren, es schaffen	35	motorbike	Motorrad	14
			Mr	Herr	2
manual	Hand-, manuell	7	Mrs	Frau (verheiratet)	9
many	viel, -e, -es	20	Ms	Frau (ohne Nennung des Familienstands)	9
Market Square	Marktplatz	18			
material	Material	30	much	viel	9
matter: What's the ~?	Was ist los?	6	mushroom	Pilz	34
			music	Musik	22
(to) may	dürfen	5	(to) must	müssen	17
May	Mai	9	mutual	gegenseitig, wechselseitig	36
maybe	vielleicht	14			
me	mich, mir	3	my	mein, -e, -en, -s	1
(to) mean	meinen, bedeuten	14	myself	ich selbst, mir, mich	14
(to) measure	messen	7	mysterious	mysteriös	21
mechanic	Mechaniker	29	mystery	Geheimnis	24
(to) meet	treffen	4	name	Name	2
meet: Nice to ~ you	Angenehm. / Sehr erfreut.	3	naan bread	Naanbrot	13
			navy blue	marineblau	16
meeting	Sitzung, Besprechung	9	near	nahe	12
			necessary	nötig	22
melon	Melone	13	need	brauchen	6
men's	Männertoilette	5	neighbour	Nachbar	22
(to) mention	erwähnen	18	neither	weder … noch	30
mentor	Mentor, Lehrer	23	never	nie	7
metal	Metall	7	nevertheless	nichtsdestotrotz	30
metre	Meter	7	new	neu	31
might	Pret. von may, vielleicht	7	news	Nachrichten	31
			newspaper	Zeitung	2
mileage	hier: freie Kilometer	28	next	nächste, -r, -s	32
mind: (I) don't ~	(Es) macht (mir) nichts aus	26	next to	neben	7

nice	nett, schön	5
night	Nacht	9
no	nein	1
nobody	niemand	21
noise	Geräusch	29
nor	noch	30
normal	normal	19
normally	normalerweise	28
north	Norden	6
not	nicht	1
not at all	überhaupt nicht	15
nothing	gar nichts	6
(to) notice	bemerken	20
now	jetzt	4
number	Nummer	8
nylons	Nylonsstrumpfhosen	29
o'clock	Uhr	10
object	Objekt	26
occasion	Anlaß	22
of	von, bei, aus, um	1
of course	natürlich	2
off we go	los geht's, fahren wir	4
offal	Innereien	34
(to) offer	anbieten	8
office	Büro	21
official	offiziell	27
often	oft	10
oh dear	oje	8
oil	Öl	29
OK	OK	10
old	alt	10
on	an, auf, bei, nach	1
one	ein, -e, -er, -s	3
ones	diejenige, -n, -s	16
onion	Zwiebel	34
only	nur	2
open	offen	21
(to) operate	bedienen (eine Maschine)	7
operate	hier: funktionieren	12
opposite	gegenüber	18
option	Option, Möglichkeit	19
or	oder	8
orange	Apfelsine, Orange	13

(to) order	bestellen	13
other	andere, -r, -s	16
our	unser, -e	4
ourselves	wir selbst, uns	14
outsider	Außenseiter	26
over	über, hin-, herüber	20
over there	da drüben	3
overall	Schutzanzug	7
own	eigen, -e, -er, -es	27
pair	Paar	15
paperwork	Papierarbeit	25
parcel	Paket	33
pardon: ~ me.	Entschuldigen Sie.	10
part	Teil	14
party	Party, Fest	22
passport	Reisepaß	2
past	nach (Uhrzeit)	10
patent	Patent	7
pattern	Muster	32
(to) pay	bezahlen	25
pence	Pence	33
people	Leute	12
per	pro	28
perfect	perfekt	12
(to) perform	vorführen	25
perhaps	vielleicht	14
person	Person	24
personnel	Personal	24
personnel director	Personalleiter/-in	3
phone	anrufen	5
photo	Foto	24
(to) pick up	abholen	4
pint	Pinte (Maßeinheit)	34
pity	schade	16
place	hier: Einrichtung	8
plain clothes	hier: Polizisten in Zivilkleidung	35
plan	Plan	30
plane	Flugzeug	1
plant	Werk	30
play	spielen	14
(to) play	Theaterstück	26
please	bitte	2
pleased	erfreut, zufrieden	5

pleasure: My ~.	Bitte schön. / Es war mir ein Vergnügen.	4
plenty	genug	35
pm	nach 12.00 Uhr mittags	19
poached egg	pochiertes Ei	10
police	Polizei	35
policeman	Polizist	35
policewoman	Polizistin	35
policy	Politik	7
pork	Schweinefleisch	34
possible	möglich	7
post	Post	36
postcard	Postkarte	33
post office	Postamt	33
pound	Pfund (Maßeinheit)	15
pound	Pfund Sterling	33
practise	üben	25
(to) prefer	bevorzugen	9
(to) present	präsentieren	23
private	privat	31
probably	wahrscheinlich	4
problem	Problem	4
(to) produce	produzieren	7
production line	Fertigungsanlage	7
production site	Produktionsstandort	6
programme	Programm	4
(to) promise	versprechen	36
protective (suit)	Schutz-(anzug)	7
proud	stolz	7
(to) provide	(zur Verfügung) stellen	22
pub	Kneipe	26
(to) put	setzen, legen, stellen	2
puzzled	perplex	6
quarter	viertel	10
quicker	schneller	19
quickly	schnell	35
quiet	ruhig	24
quite	ziemlich	20
rate	Preis, Gebühr	28
(to) rationalize	hier: rationalisieren, einsparen	30
(to) react	reagieren	35
(to) read	lesen	2

ready	fertig	5
(to) realize	merken, sich klar machen	30
really	in der Tat	2
reason	Grund	35
(to) recognize	erkennen	20
(to) recommend	empfehlen	8
records	Unterlagen	24
red	rot	13
regional manager	regional/-e Vertriebsleiter/-in	30
(to) remember	sich erinnern	4
reservation	Reservierung	8
restaurant	Restaurant, Gaststätte	12
return	Rückfahrkarte	19
(to) return: ~ hospitality	sich revanchieren, wiedergeben	17
rice	Reis	13
right	korrekt, in Ordnung	3
right	richtig	4
right	rechts	14
right now	jetzt, in diesem Moment	12
(to) ring	anrufen	17
river	Fluß	8
rivet	Bolzen, Niete	7
road	Straße	12
roast lamb	geschmortes Lammfleisch	34
rod	Stab	7
room	Zimmer	9
round	Tour, Runde (Wachschutz)	21
row	Reihe	1
Royal Infirmary	Krankenhaus	14
(to) run	laufen, fahren	11
safe	sicher	23
salary	Gehalt	25
same	gleich, -e, -er, -es	11
sandwich	belegtes Brot	34
satisfied	zufrieden	26
Saturday	Samstag	14
(to) save	sparen	29
(to) save	retten	36
saw	Pret. von *see*	20

(to) say	sagen	1
scales	Waage	33
scene	Szene, Akt im Theaterstück	26
Scotch	schottisch, Whisky	34
Scotland	Schottland	6
Scottish	schottisch	32
Scottish Tourist Board	Schottische Fremdenverkehrszentrale	27
seat	Sitz(platz)	1
second	zweite, -r, -s	15
secondary	hier: Sekundarstufe	25
secure	sichern	35
security	Sicherheits-	21
(to) see	sehen	1
(to) see: I ~.	Ich verstehe.	25
(to) seem	(er-)scheinen	10
selection	Auswahl	13
(to) sell	verkaufen	7
(to) send	schicken	27
sense	Sinn	21
seriously	ernsthaft	20
servant	Bediensteter	25
(to) serve	bedienen	34
service	hier: direkte Zugverbindung	19
service manager	Service-Leiter/-in	31
(to) settle (in)	(ein-)gewöhnen	12
seven	sieben	10
several	einige	19
(to) shall	sollen	22
shandy	Radler, Alsterwasser	34
she	sie	4
sheep	Schaf	34
shop	Geschäft	32
(to) shop	einkaufen	16
short	kurz	31
(to) shorten	kürzen	26
shorts	Shorts	15
should	Pret. von shall	16
shoulder	Schulter	14
shouldn't	sollte nicht	23
(to) show	(herum-) zeigen, führen	6
shower	Dusche	9

shown	Partizip von show	6
side	Seite	15
sight	Sehenswürdigkeit	20
(to) sign	unterschreiben	14
silly	dumm	17
similar	ähnlich	6
since	seit	6
sir	Herr	2
sister	Schwester	4
situation	Situation	30
six	sechs	17
size	Größe	7
sketch	Skizze	35
skirt	Rock	32
(to) sleep	schlafen	11
slight	kleines	12
slimmer	schlanker	32
slowly	langsam	12
small	klein	4
so	so	1
so far	bisher	6
(to) solve	lösen (ein Rätsel)	24
some	einige	7
somebody	jemand	21
somehow	irgendwie	21
something	etwas	13
sometimes	manchmal	11
somewhere	irgendwo	23
soon	bald, früh	36
sooner	eher, früher	35
sorry	Entschuldigung	2
(to) sound	klingen	8
soup	Suppe	13
(to) speak	sprechen	9
special	spezial	22
(to) spell	buchstabieren	9
sports	Sport-	15
(to) spot	sichten	31
spy	Spion/-in	31
staff	Angestellte, Belegschaft	35
stage	Bühne	25
stamp	Briefmarke	33
(to) start	anfangen	10

starter	Vorspeise	13
station	Bahnhof	17
stay	Aufenthalt	6
steak & kidney pie	Rindfleischpastete	34
(to) steal	stehlen	24
stop	(Bus-) Haltestelle	10
story	Geschichte	31
straight	gerade(aus)	18
strange	merkwürdig	23
stranger	Fremder	18
street	Straße	8
(to) strike	zuschlagen	35
studies	Studium	36
subsidiary	Filiale, Zweigstelle	27
successful	erfolgreich	7
suddenly	plötzlich	23
(to) suggest	vorschlagen	13
(to) suit	stehen, gefallen	8
(to) suit	passen, recht sein	12
suitcase	Koffer	3
super	super	17
supersaver	Sparticket	19
sure	sicher	5
(to) surprise	überraschen	6
suspect	vermuten	14
sweater	Pullover	32
sweet	süß, hier: Dessert	13
swollen	geschwollen	14
syphilis	Syphilis	14
(to) take	nehmen, fahren, mitnehmen	5
(to) talk	reden	31
tall	groß	7
taller	größer	7
tartan	kariert, Schottenmuster	32
(to) taste	schmecken	20
tax office	Finanzamt	25
teacher	Lehrer/-in	25
team	Team, Mannschaft	25
telephone	Telefon	27
(to) tell	sagen	5
ten	zehn	10
terrible	schrecklich	26
than	als	7

(to) thank	sich bedanken	1
thank you	danke schön	2
thanks	danke	30
that	der, die, das (jenige), welche	3
the	der, die, das	1
the front	die Front (eines Gebäudes), vorne	2
theatre	Theater	25
theft	Diebstahl	28
their	ihr, -e	4
them	sie, ihnen	7
then	dann, damals, da, denn, also	2
there	da, dort, darin	3
these	diese	3
they	sie, welche	4
thickness	Dicke	7
thief	Dieb/-in	35
thing	Ding, Gegenstand	26
(to) think	denken, meinen	6
third	dritte, -r, -s	9
thirty	dreißig	33
this	diese, -r, -s	1
those	die, jene	3
though	obwohl	29
thousands	Tausende	20
three	drei	10
through	durch	26
ticket	Fahrkarte	2
tights	Strumpfhose	6
time	Zeit	6
tired	müde	26
to be tired of	etw leid sein	26
to	zu, gegen, nach, an, in, auf	1
today	heute	8
together	zusammen	10
toilet	Toilette	5
tomorrow	morgen	8
tonight	heute Abend	9
too	zu, allzu, auch, noch dazu	4
tour	Führung	7
tourist	Tourist	20
traditional	traditionell	32

traffic	Verkehr	18
traffic light	Verkehrsampel	18
train	Zug	19
trainee	Praktikant/-in	1
trap	Falle	35
trapped	gefangen	35
travel	reisen	17
travel agent's	Reisebüro	18
traveller	Reisende/r	2
trip	Reise	20
trolley	(Gepäck-)Wagen	3
trouble: It's no ~.	Das macht keine Umstände.	17
true	wahr	1
(to) try	versuchen, anprobieren	7
Tuesday	Dienstag	9
(to) turn up	auftauchen	35
(to) turn; ~ a corner	wenden; um die Ecke biegen	18
turning	Abzweigung, Biegung, Straßenecke	18
twenty	zwanzig	9
twist	verstauchen	14
two	zwei	8
type	Art, Sorte	28
typical	typisch	23
tyre	Reifen	29
under	unter	2
(to) understand	verstehen	30
unfortunate	unglücklich	8
unleaded	bleifrei	29
unless	es sei denn, außer	21
until	bis	8
up	hoch, hinauf	4
us	wir	24
(to) use	benutzen, gebrauchen	7
useful	nützlich	36
usually	gewöhnlich	10
valid	gültig	19
valuable	wertvoll	36
VAT (Value Added Tax)	Mehrwertsteuer	28
very	sehr	4

very sorry	untröstlich, es tut mir leid	8
(to) visit	besuchen	17
visit	Besuch	17
(to) wait	warten	29
waiver fee	Freibetrag	28
(to) walk	gehen	11
(to) want	wollen	6
warm	warm	11
(to) warn	warnen	34
warning light	Warnlicht	29
(to) watch	zusehen, ansehen	7
water	Wasser	29
(to) wave	winken	20
way: by the ~	übrigens	4
we	wir	2
(to) wear	tragen (Kleidung)	7
week	Woche	32
weekend	Wochenende	17
(to) weigh	wiegen	33
welcome	Willkommen	15
well	also	4
what	was	1
what kind of	was für ein, -e, -er, -s	24
when	wann	9
where	wo	4
whether	ob	31
which	welche, -r, -s	7
while	während	29
white	weiß	13
who	wer	9
whole	ganz, -e, -r, -es	20
why	warum	6
wide	breit	13
wife	Ehefrau	22
(to) will	wollen	8
wine	Wein	13
with	mit	1
woman	Frau	24
(to) wonder	sich wundern, sich fragen	24
wonderful	wunderbar	11
work	arbeiten	7
worker	Arbeiter/-in	7
world	Welt	4

(to) worry; Don't ~.	sich sorgen; Mach' dir keine Sorgen	35
worthwhile	der Mühe wert, lohnend	36
would: ~ like	würden, möchten	2
(to) write	schreiben	14
wrong	falsch, inkorrekt	9
x-ray	Röntgenaufnahme	14
year	Jahr	24
yellow	gelb	16
yes	ja	1
yet	noch, jetzt noch, bis jetzt, schon	6
you	du	1
young	jung	23
your	euer (e), dein(e), Ihre	1
yours	deines, eures, Ihres	29
yuck	(inf) igitt	34
zebra crossing	Zebrastreifen	18

Deutsch	English	
abdecken (Gebiet)	(to) cover	30
Abend	evening	19
aber	but	1
abholen	(to) pick up	4
Abteilung	department	15
Ach du Schande	good grief	31
acht	eight	10
ADAC	AA	29
Adresse	address	23
ähnlich	similar	6
Aids	aids	14
Aktivität	activity	14
Aktivposten	asset	36
akzeptieren	(to) accept	28
Alarm	alarm	35
alle, -s	all	3
als	as, than	7, 13
also	well, then	2, 4
alt	old	10
am Besten	best	4
Amerika	America	1
Amerikaner/-in	American	7
amerikanisch	American	7
an	at, on	1, 4

anbieten	(to) offer	8
andere, -r, -s	different, other	16, 20
anfangen	(to) start	10
Angenehm.	Nice to meet you. / How do you do?	3
anhängen	(to) attach	33
ankommen	arrive	9
Ankunft	arrival	3
Anlass	occasion	22
ausprobieren	(to) try	7
anrufen	call, phone, (to) ring	3, 5, 17
ansehen	(to) watch	7
ansehnlich	handsome	24
ansonsten	else: Anything ~?	24
anstatt	instead	13
ansteckend	contagious	14
anwenden	(to) employ	30
April	April	24
arbeiten	work	7
Arbeiter/-in	worker	7
Arm	arm	14
Art	type	28
Assistent	assistant	3
Atmosphäre	atmosphere	20
auch	also, too	4, 15
auf	at, on, in, to	1, 4
auf etw scharf sein	keen: be ~ on	12
Auf Wiedersehen!	Goodbye!	6
aufbewahren	(to) keep	24
Aufenthalt	stay	6
aufgeben	give up	30
auftauchen	(to) turn up	35
Aufzug	lift	5
Auge	eye	24
aus	of	1
ausfüllen	(to) fill in	14
ausgezeichnet	excellent	1
Außenseiter	outsider	26
außer	except	31
Auswahl	selection	13
Auto	car	4
Autopanne	breakdown	29

Bad	bath	9	bitte	please	2
Bahnhof	station	17	Bitte schön.	My pleasure.	4
bald	soon	36	bitten	beg	10
Bank	bank	18	blau	blue	16
Bargeld	cash	28	Blaupausen	blueprints	21
Bart	beard	24	bleifrei	unleaded	29
Bau	construction	35	blinken	(to) flash	18
bauen	(to) build	30	blond	fair	24
Beamter, Beamtin	civil servant	25	Boutique	boutique	15
bedeuten	(to) mean	14	brauchen	need	6
bedienen	(to) serve	34	brechen	(to) break	14
bedienen (eine Maschine)	(to) operate	7	breit	wide	13
			Brief	letter	4
Bediensteter	servant	25	Briefmarke	stamp	33
beeindruckend	impressive	20	bringen	bring	22
beenden	(to) finish	16	britisch	British	16
beginnen	begin	21	Bruder	brother	4
bei	by, at, on, in, of	4	Buch	book	2
Bekanntmachung	introduction	6	buchen, ausgebucht	(to) book: booked out	27
Belegschaft	(to) staff	35			
belegtes Brot	sandwich	34	buchstabieren	(to) spell	9
Belgien	Belgium	31	Buchung	booking	27
bemerken	(to) notice	20	Büfett	buffet	22
benutzen	(to) use	7	Bühne	stage	25
bergab	downhill	30	Büro	office	21
beschäftigt	busy	25	Bus	bus	10
Beschreibung	description	21	Business Klasse	business class	2
besetzt	engaged	5	Cheshire (Grafschaft)	Cheshire	15
besitzen	(to) have	2	chinesisch	Chinese	12
besonders	especially	12	Clan	clan	32
besser	better	7	Computer	computer	7
bestätigen	(to) confirm	31	da drüben	over there	3
bestehen auf	insist (on)	36	da	there, then	2, 3
besteht aus	made from	34	dafür sein	all for	26
bestellen	(to) order	13	damals	then	2
Besuch	visit	17	dankbar	grateful	4
besuchen	(to) visit	17	Dankbarkeit	gratitude	36
Bett	bed	9	danke	thanks	30
bevor	before	6	danke schön	thank you	2
bevorzugen	(to) prefer	9	dann	then	2
bezahlen	(to) pay	25	darin	there	3
Biegung	turning	18	Das macht keine Umstände.	It's no trouble.	17
billiger	cheaper	16			
bis	until, by	8, 4	Datum	date	24
bisher	so far	6	Decke	blanket	32

deines	yours	29	ein, -e, -er	a	1
denken	(to) think	6	ein, -e, -er (vor vokalischem Anlaut)	an	2
denn	then	02	ein, -e, -er, -s	one	3
der, die, das	the	1	(irgend)ein, -e, -r	any	6
der, die, das (jenige), welche	that	3	Einbruch	break in	21
Design	design	30	einführen	hier: (to) feed	7
Detail	detail	17	einige	several, some, any, few	6, 7, 19, 29
Detektiv	detective	20			
Deutsch	German	1	einkaufen	(to) shop	16
Deutschland	Germany	3	einladen	(to) invite	22
Dicke	thickness	7	Einladung	invitation	22
die Front (eines-Gebäudes)	the front	2	Einrichtung	place	8
Dieb/-in	thief	35	einsetzen	install	35
Diebstahl	theft	28	einstellen	(to) employ	30
diejenige, -n, -s	ones	16	ekelhaft	disgusting	34
Dienstag	Tuesday	9	E-Mail	e-mail	31
diese	these	3	empfehlen	(to) recommend	8
diese, -r, -s	this	1	Ende	end	7
Ding	thing	26	England	England	6
direkt	direct	19	englisch	English	1
direkte Zugverbindung	hier: service	19	englisches Frühstück	English breakfast	10
Dokument	document	33	entlang	along	12
Doppel-	double	9	entlang gehen	(to) go along	18
dort	there	3	Entschuldigen Sie, bitte.	excuse: Excuse me, please.	1
drei	three	10	Entschuldigen Sie.	Pardon me.	10
dreißig	thirty	33	Entschuldigung	sorry	2
dritte, -r, -s	third	9	enttäuschen	disappoint	36
du	you	1	entweder	either	16
dumm	silly	17	entwerfen	(to) draw up	30
dunkel	dark	16	Entwicklung	development	21
dunkelblau	dark blue	16	entzückt	delighted	17
dunkler	darker	16	er	he	5
dunkles Bier	bitter	13	erfolgreich	successful	7
durch	through	26	erfreut	pleased	5
dürfen	(to) may	5	erhalten	(to) get	15
Dusche	shower	9	erkennen	(to) recognize	20
Ehefrau	wife	22	ernsthaft	seriously	20
ehrlich	honest	26	erst, -e, -er, -es	first	4
Eier	eggs	10	erwähnen	(to) mention	18
eigen, -e, -er, -es	own	27	erwarten	(to) expect	30
eigentlich	actually, in fact	15, 17	es	it	1
			es schaffen	(to) manage	35
ein kleines Bier	half a lager	13	es sei denn, außer	unless	21

essen	eat	10
Essen	food	12
Etage	floor	5
es tut mir leid	very sorry	18
etw leid sein	be tired of	26
etw oder jmd mögen	care for	13
etw. müssen	(to) have to	12
etw suchen	(to) lock for	2
etwas	something	13
(irgend) etwas	anything	7
euer (e, s)	your(s)	1, 29
Europa	Europe	1
Ewigkeit	ages	17
existieren	exist	21
Fabrik(halle)	factory; ~ floor	7
fähig	able	27
Fahne	flag	20
fahren	(to) drive, (to) run, (to) take	5, 8, 11, 28
Fahrgeld	fare	19
Fahrkarte	ticket	2
Falle	trap	35
falsch	wrong	9
Familie	family	4
fangen	(to) catch	35
Farbe	colour	16
Färbung	colouring	32
fast	almost	6
Fax	fax	31
fehlen	(to) miss	21
Fehler	mistake	5
fein	fine	3
fertig	ready	5
Fertigungsanlage	production line	7
Fest	festival	26
festnehmen	(to) arrest	36
Filiale	subsidiary	27
Film	film	20
Finanzamt	tax office	25
finden	(to) find	
Firma	company	1
Flasche	bottle	13
fliegen	(to) fly	19

Flug	flight	2
Flughafen	airport	36
Flugzeug	plane	1
Fluß	river	8
folgen	(to) follow	21
förmlich	formal	22
Formular	form	14
Foto	photo	24
fragen	(to) ask	11
Frankreich	France	23
Französisch-Kanadier/-in	French Canadian	1
Frau	woman	24
Frau (ohne Nennung des Familienstands)	Ms	9
Frau (verheiratet)	Mrs	9
frei	free	9
Freibetrag	waiver fee	28
freie Kilometer	mileage	28
Freitag	Friday	19
Freizeit-	leisure	14
Fremder	stranger	18
Freund/-in	friend	4
freundlich	friendly	8
Fringe (Rand)	Fringe	26
Friseursalon	hairdresser's	15
froh	glad	23
früh	early, soon	9, 19, 36
früher	sooner	35
Frühstück	breakfast	9
fühlen	feel	35
(Führer-)Schein	licence	28
Führung	tour	7
fünf	five	10
funktionieren	operate	12
für	for, at	2, 4
Fuß	foot	14
Fuß (Maßeinheit)	foot	7
Gabel	fork	13
Gallone (Maßeinheit)	gallon	29
Gang (Essen)	course	13
ganz, -e, -r, -es	whole	20
gar nichts	nothing	6
Gast	guest	27

93

Gastfreundlichkeit	hospitality	17
Gastgeber	host	20
Gastgeberin	hostess	20
Gebäude	building	30
geben	(to) give	8
Gebühr	charge	28
Geburt	birth	24
Geburtstag	birthday	32
gefangen	trapped	35
gegen	to	1
gegenseitig	mutual	36
gegenüber	opposite	18
Gehalt	salary	25
Geheimnis	mystery	24
gehen	(to) go, (to) walk	6, 11
gekochte Kartoffeln	boiled potatoes	34
gelb	yellow	16
Gelegenheit	chance	23
genau	just	8
genießen	enjoy	6
genug	enough, plenty	1, 21, 35
Gepäck	luggage	2
gerade(aus)	straight	18
gerade	just	8
Geräusch	noise	29
Gericht	dish	13
Geschäft	shop	32
geschehen	(to) happen	23
Geschichte	story	31
geschmortes Lammfleisch	roast lamb	34
geschwollen	swollen	14
Gesundheit	health	14
Getränk	drink	13
(ein-)gewöhnen	(to) settle (in)	12
gewöhnlich	usually	10
glauben	(to) believe	8
gleich, -e, -er, -es	same	11
Glück	luck	2
Gramm	gram	15
groß	big, tall, large	7, 8, 30
großartig	great	3

Größe	height, size	7, 32
größer	bigger, taller	7
grün	green	7
Grund	reason	35
Gruppe	group	25
gültig	valid	19
gut	good	4
Guten Abend.	Good evening.	27
Guten Morgen.	Good morning.	2
Guten Tag.	Good afternoon.	8
Haar(-e)	hair	24
haben	(to) have	2
halb, -e, -er, -es	half	13
(Bus-) Haltestelle	stop	10
Hand	hand	2
handeln	(to) deal with	36
handgemacht	homespun	32
handhaben	(to) manage	35
Haupt-	main	13
Haus	house	8
(zu) Hause	home; at ~	10
heiß	hot	29
helfen	(to) help	2
hellblau	light blue	16
Helm	helmet	7
Hepatitis	hepatitis	14
herausfinden	(to) find out	12
hereinkommen	come in	6
Herr	Mr, sir	2
herrlich	lovely	11
herüber	across	18
herunterfallen	(to) fall off	14
heute	today	8
heute Abend	tonight	9
hier	here	1
hinter	behind	32
hinunter	down	7
hoch	up	4
hoffen	(to) hope	6
hören	(to) hear	14
Hotel	hotel	8
Hühnchen Korma	chicken Korma	13
hungrig	hungry	34
ich	I	1

94

ich selbst	myself	14
Ich verstehe.	I see.	25
Idee	idea	7
igitt	yuck	34
ihn, ihm	him	6
ihr, -e	their	4
ihr, -e, -en	her	4
Ihr(es)	your(self)	34
immer	always	10
Immobilienmakler/-in	estate agent	8
in der Tat	really	2
in diesem Fall	in this case	28
in diesem Moment	right now	12
in … hinein	into	7
in	in, to	1
indisch	Indian	12
Industrie	industry	6
industriell	industrial	21
Information	information	15
Ingenieur	engineer	30
inklusive	included	28
Innereien	offal	34
inspizieren	(to) inspect	12
interessant	interesting	4
interessiert sein an	care for	13
Investor	investor	7
irgendwie	somehow	21
irgendwo	anywhere, somewhere	23, 24
ist	is	1
ja	yes	1
Jahr	year	24
jährlich, -e, -es	annual	35
jdn beherbergen	have: to ~ guests	36
jdn gern haben	fond: be ~ of sb	12
jede, -r, -s	each, every	11, 16
jedermann, alle	everybody, everyone	25
jemals	ever	23
jemand	somebody	21
jene	those	3
jetzt	now	4
jung	young	23
Kaffee	coffee	13
Kamera	camera	35
Kampf	fight	26
Kanadier	Canadian	1
Kapazität	capacity	30
Karte	card	28
Käse	cheese	15
Kategorie	category	28
kaufen	buy	15
Kaufhaus	department store	15
kaum	hardly	24
Keilriemen	fan belt	29
Kinder	children	15
Klasse	class	25
Kleider	clothes	7
Kleidung	clothing	15
klein	little, small	4, 7
kleines	slight	12
klingen	(to) sound	8
Klo	loo	4
Klub	club	14
Kneipe	pub	26
Knöchel	ankle	14
Knochenbruch	fracture	14
Koffer	suitcase	3
Kofferraum	boot	29
komischerweise	funnily	24
Komm schon!	Come on!	29
kommen	(to) come	2
Konditionen	conditions	25
Konkurrenz	competitors	7
können	(to) can	2
Konstruktion	construction	35
Kontakt	contact	23
Kontinental	Continental	10
Kopien	copies	24
kopieren	(to) copy	7
Körper	body	14
korrekt	right	3
Krankenhaus	hospital, Royal Infirmary	14
Krankheit	disease	14
Kredit	credit	28
Kreuzung	crossing	18
Küche	cooking	12
Kuchen	cake	13
Kurs	class	25

kurz	short	31	Maschine	machine	7
kürzen	(to) shorten	26	Material	material	30
Lagerbier	lager	13	Mechaniker	mechanic	29
Lamm(-fleisch)	lamb	34	mehr	more	12
Land	land	30	Mehrwertsteuer	VAT (Value Added Tax)	28
lang	long	16			
Länge	length	7	mein	mine	4
langsam	slowly	12	mein, -e, -en, -s	my	1
lassen	(to) let	7	meine Güte	goodness	32
lästig	bother	2	meinen	(to) mean	14
Latzhosen	dungarees	15	meist, -en, -s	most	20
laufen	(to) run	11	Melone	melon	13
leben	(to) live	4	Mentor	mentor	23
Lebenslauf	CV	24	merken	(to) realize	30
Lebensmittel	food	12	merkwürdig	strange	23
Lebensmittel-abteilung	food hall	15	messen	(to) measure	7
			Messer	knife	13
lecker	delicious	13	Metall	metal	7
Lehrer/-in	teacher	25	Meter	metre	7
leider	I'm afraid	8	mich, mir	me	3
Leitung	line	5	mieten	hire	28
lesen	(to) read	2	Minute	minute	8
letzte, -r, -s	last	14	Mischung	mix, mixture	13, 20
Leute	people	12			
(Blink-)Licht	light	18	mit	with	1
lieben	(to) love, (to) be founf of sb	10, 12	mit etw einverstanden sein	(to) go along with it	18
links	left	14	mitnehmen	(to) take	5
Liter	litre	29	Mittagessen	lunch	12
Lizenz	licence	28	möchten	would like	2
lohnend	worthwhile	36	Mode	fashion	15
los geht's	off we go	4	Modell	model	7
lösen (ein Rätsel)	(to) solve	24	mögen	(to) like, (to) love	2, 10
Luft	air	29	möglich	possible	7
machen	(to) do, (to) make	5, 21	Moment	moment	9
			Monat	month	17
(Es) macht (mir) nichts aus	mind: (I) don't ~	26	Montag	Monday	9
			Morgen	morning	11
Mai	May	9	morgen	tomorrow	8
Makler/-in	agent	9	Morgen (Maßeinheit)	acre	30
manchmal	sometimes	11	Motor	engine	29
Männertoilette	men's	5	Motorrad	motorbike	14
Mantel	coat	5	müde	tired	26
manuell	manual	7	Musik	music	22
marineblau	navy blue	16	müssen	(to) must	17
Marktplatz	Market Square	18			

Muster	pattern	32	oft	often	10
Mutter	mother	32	öfter	frequently	11
mysteriös	mysterious	21	ohnehin	anyway	4
Naanbrot	naan bread	13	oje	oh dear	8
nach	after, on, to	1, 5	OK	OK	10
nach (Uhrzeit)	past	10	Öl	oil	29
nach 12.00 Uhr mittags	pm	19	Option	option	19
Nachbar	neighbour	22	Orange	orange	13
Nachmittag	afternoon	8	Paar	pair	15
Nachrichten	news	31	Paket	parcel	33
nächste, -r, -s	next, by	4, 7, 32	Papierarbeit	paperwork	25
Nacht	night	9	Parkhaus	car park	4
Nachtisch	dessert	13	Party	party	22
nahe	near	12	passen	(to) fit, (to) suit	7, 12
Name	name	2	Patent	patent	7
natürlich	of course	2	Pence	pence	33
neben	next to	7	Pension	boarding house, bed & breakfast	8, 10
nehmen	(to) take	5	(Hotel-)Pension	guesthouse	27
nein	no	1	perfekt	perfect	12
nett	kind, nice	5, 17	perplex	puzzled	6
neu	new	31	Person	person	24
nicht	not	1	Personal	personnel	24
nichtsdestotrotz	nevertheless	30	Personalleiter/-in	human resources director, personnel director	3, 4
nie	never	7	Pfund (Maßeinheit)	pound	15
niemand	nobody	21	Pfund Sterling	pound	33
Niete (techn.)	rivet	7	phantastisch	fantastic	4
noch	nor, yet, too	4, 6, 30	Pilz	mushroom	34
Norden	north	6	Pinte (Maßeinheit)	pint	34
normal	normal	19	Plan	plan	30
normalerweise	normally	28	plötzlich	suddenly	23
nötig	necessary	22	pochiertes Ei	poached egg	10
Nummer	number	8	Politik	policy	7
nur	only	2	Polizei	police	35
nützlich	useful	36	Polizist	policeman	35
Nylonsstrumpfhosen	nylons	29	Polizisten in Zivilkleidung	plain clothes	35
ob	whether	31	Polizistin	policewoman	35
Objekt	object	26	Pommes Frites	chips	34
Obst	fruit	13	Post	post	36
obwohl	though	29	Postamt	post office	33
oder	or	8	Postkarte	postcard	33
offen	open	21	Praktikant/-in	trainee	1
offiziell	official	27			

präsentieren	(to) present	23	Schaden	damage	28
Preis	rate	28	Schaf	sheep	34
privat	private	31	(an-)schauen	(to) look (at)	4
pro	per	28	schauspielern	(to) act	26
Problem	problem	4	Scheck	cheque	36
Produktionsstandort	production site	6	(er-)scheinen	(to) seem	10
produzieren	(to) produce	7	scherzen	(to) joke	20
Programm	programme	4	schicken	(to) send	27
Prost	cheers	34	Schinken	ham	34
Pullover	sweater	32	schlafen	(to) sleep	11
Radler (Getränk)	shandy	34	schlanker	slimmer	32
rationalisieren	(to) rationalize	30	schlau	clever	7
reagieren	(to) react	35	schlecht	bad	14
rechts	right	14	schließen	(to) close	21
Rechtsanwalt; -anwältin	lawyer	36	schlimm	bad	14
			schmecken	(to) taste	20
recht sein	(to) suit	12	schneiden	(to) cut	7
reden	(to) talk	31	schnell	quickly	35
regional/-e Vertriebsleiter/-in	regional manager	30	schneller	quicker	19
			schon	already, yet	6, 35
Reifen	tyre	29	schön	beautiful, hand-some, lovely, nice	5, 11, 24
Reihe	row	1			
Reis	rice	13			
Reise	trip	20	Schottenmuster	tartan	32
Reisebüro	travel agent's	18	Schottenrock	kilt	32
Reisebus	coach	19	schottisch	Scottish, Scotch	32, 34
reisen	travel	17			
Reisende/r	traveller	2	Schottische Frem-denverkehrszentrale	Scottish Tourist Board	27
Reisepass	passport	2			
reparieren	(to) fix	29	schottisches Gericht aus Schafsinnereien	haggis	34
Reservierung	reservation	8			
Restaurant	restaurant	12	Schottland	Scotland	6
retten	(to) save	36	schrecklich	terrible	26
richtig	right	4	schreiben	(to) write	14
Rindfleischpastete	steak & kidney pie	34	Schreibtisch	desk	24
Rock	skirt	32	Schublade	drawer	21
Röntgenaufnahme	x-ray	14	Schulter	shoulder	14
rot	red	13	Schutzanzug	overall	7
Rückfahrkarte	return (ticket)	19	schwarz	black	16
ruhig	quiet	24	Schweinefleisch	pork	34
rundherum	around	3	Schwester	sister	4
Saft	juice	13	sechs	six	17
sagen	(to) say, (to) tell	1, 5	sehen	(to) see	1
Samstag	Saturday	14	Sehenswürdigkeit	sight	20
schade	pity	16	sehr	very	4
			sein	(to) be	8

sein, -e, -en	his	4
seit	since	6
Seite	side	15
Sekundarstufe	secondary	25
(er, ihn, ihm, sich) selbst	himself	14
Service-Leiter/-in	service manager	31
setzen	(to) put	2
Shorts	shorts	15
sich auf etw freuen	(to) look forward to	9
sich bedanken	(to) thank	1
sich befassen	(to) deal with	36
sich erinnern	(to) remember	4
sich fragen	(to) wonder	24
sich klar machen	(to) realize	30
sich revanchieren	(to) return hospitality	17
sich sorgen; Mach' dir keine Sorgen	(to) worry; Don't ~.	35
sich vorstellen	(to) imagine	25
sich wundern	(to) wonder	24
sicher	certain, safe, sure	5, 7, 23
Sicherheits-	security	21
sicherlich	certainly	5
sichern	secure	35
sichten	(to) spot	31
sie	she	4
sie, ihnen	them	7
sie, welche	they	4
sieben	seven	10
sieht aus als ob	looks as though	29
Sinn	sense	21
Situation	situation	30
Sitz(platz)	seat	1
Sitzung	meeting	9
Skizze	sketch	35
so	so	1
so … wie	as … as	7
sobald	as soon as	6
sofort	immediately	8
sogar	even	19
sollen	(to) shall	22
sollte besser	had better	23
sollte nicht	shouldn't	23
sonst noch etwas?	anything else?	24

Souterrain	basement	15
sparen	(to) save	29
Sparticket	supersaver	19
Spaß	fun	25
spät	late	19
später	later (on)	29
Speck	bacon	10
spezial	special	22
Spiegelei	fried egg	10
Spiel	game	14
spielen	play	14
Spion/-in	spy	31
Spionage	espionage	21
Sport-	sports	15
sprechen	(to) speak	9
Stab	rod	7
(jmdm) stehen	(to) suit	8
stehlen	(to) steal	24
(zur Verfügung) stellen	(to) provide	22
stellen	(to) put	2
stolz	proud	7
Straße	road, street	8, 12
stricken	knit	32
Strumpfhose	tights	6
Studium	studies	36
Stunde	hour	19
super	super	17
Suppe	soup	13
süß	sweet	13
Syphilis	syphilis	14
Szene	scene	26
Tag	day	4
Tasche	bag	29
Tasse	cup	13
Tausende	thousands	20
Team	team	25
Teil	part	14
teilnehmen	(to) join	25
Telefon	telephone	27
teuer	expensive	16
Theater	theatre	25
Theaterstück	(to) play	26
Theke	counter	15

Toilette	toilet	5
Tour (Wachschutz)	round	21
Tourist	tourist	20
traditionell	traditional	32
tragen (Kleidung)	(to) wear	7
trinken	(to) drink	13
treffen	(to) meet	4
Tschüss	bye	17
Typ	guy	35
typisch	typical	23
üben	practise	25
über	over	20
überall	everywhere	20
Übergang	crossing	18
überhaupt nicht	not at all	15
überprüfen	(to) check	8
überraschen	(to) surprise	6
überreichen	(to) hand	20
übrigens	by the way	3
Uhr	o'clock	10
um	of	1
um … zu …	in order to	29
Umkleidekabinen	changing rooms	16
Umrechnungstabelle	conversion table	32
umsonst	free	9
und	and	3
ungefähr	about	1
unglücklich	unfortunate	8
uns	ourselves	14
unser, -e	our	4
unter	under	2
unterbrechen	(to) interrupt	14
Unterkunft	accommodation	8
Unterlagen	records	24
unterschreiben	(to) sign	14
Urlaub	holiday	1
Vater	father	4
verändern	(to) change	7
verbessern	(to) improve	1
verdienen	(to) earn	25
vergessen	(to) forget	21
verkaufen	(to) sell	7
Verkehr	traffic	18
Verkehrsampel	traffic light	18
verlassen	(to) leave	10

verletzen	(to) hurt	14
verlieren	lose	23
vermisst	missing	31
vermuten	suspect	14
verschwinden	(to) disappear	35
Versicherung	insurance	28
versprechen	(to) promise	36
verstauchen	twist	14
verstecken	(to) hide	35
verstehen	(to) understand	30
versuchen	(to) try	7
viel, -e, -es	lot, much, many	3, 9, 20
vielleicht	maybe, perhaps	14
vier	four	28
vierte, -er, -es	fourth	5
viertel	quarter	10
völlig	fully, completely	27
Vollkasko-versicherung	comprehensive insurance	28
von	from, by, of	1, 4
vor 12.00 Uhr mittags	am	19
vor X Jahren	ago	14
vor(aus)	ahead	18
vorführen	(to) perform	25
vorschlagen	(to) suggest	13
Vorspeise	starter	13
vorstellen	(to) introduce	12
Waage	scales	33
Wachablösung	changing of the guard	20
Wächter	guard	20
(Gepäck-)Wagen	trolley	3
(Aus-)wahl	choice	34
wahr	true	1
während	during, while	2, 29
wahrscheinlich	likely, probably	4, 24
wann	when	9
warm	warm	11
Warnblinkanlage	hazard lights	29
warnen	(to) warn	34
Warnlicht	warning light	29
warten	(to) wait	29
warum	why	6

was	what	1
was für ein, -e, -er, -s	what kind of	24
Was ist los?	What's the matter?	6
Wasser	water	29
weder … noch	neither	30
weg	away	35
weil	because	7
Wein	wine	13
weiß	white	13
weit	large	8
welche, -r, -s	which	7
Welt	world	4
wenden; um die Ecke biegen	(to) turn; ~ a corner	18
wenige	few	29
weniger	less	16
wenn	if	6
wer	who	9
Werk	plant	30
wertvoll	valuable	36
Whisky (schottisch)	Scotch	34
wichtig	important	24
wie	how	5
wie denkst du über	how do feel about	26
wie geht es dir	how are you	17
wie wäre es mit	how about	16
wieder	again	17
wiegen	(to) weigh	33
wieviel, -e	how much, how many	10, 15
Willkommen	welcome	15
winken	(to) wave	20
wir	us, we	2, 24
wir selbst	ourselves	14
Wirt	landlord	8
Wirtin	landlady	8
Wirtschaft	economy	30
wissen	(to) know	4

wo	where	4
Woche	week	32
Wochenende	weekend	17
wohnen	(to) live	4
Wohnung	apartment, flat	8
wollen	(to) want, (to) will	6, 8
wunderbar	wonderful	11
würden	would	2
Zebrastreifen	zebra crossing	18
zehn	ten	10
zeichnen	(to) draw up	30
(herum-) zeigen	(to) show	6
Zeit	time	6
Zeitschrift	magazine	2
Zeitung	newspaper	2
Zelten	camping	27
Zentrale	headquarter	5
ziemlich	quite	20
Zimmer	room	9
zögern	(to) hesitate	6
Zoll (Maßeinheit)	inch	7
zu	too, to	4
Zufall	coincidence	4
zufrieden	satisfied, pleased	5, 26
Zug	train	19
zur selben Zeit	at the same time	25
zurück	back	17
zusammen	together	10
zuschlagen	(to) strike	35
zusehen	(to) watch	7
zustimmen	(to) agree	26
zwanglos	informal	22
zwanzig	twenty	9
zwei	two	8
zweite, -r, -s	second	15
Zwiebel	onion	34

101

Unregelmäßige Verben

Infinitiv	Präteritum	Partizip	
be	was	been	sein
become	became	become	werden
begin	began	begun	beginnen
break	broke	broken	(zer)brechen
bring	brought	brought	bringen
build	built	built	bauen
buy	bought	bought	kaufen
catch	caught	caught	fangen
come	came	come	kommen
cost	cost	cost	kosten
cut	cut	cut	schneiden
do	did	done	tun
drink	drank	drunk	trinken
drive	drove	driven	fahren
eat	ate	eaten	essen
fall	fell	fallen	fallen
feed	fed	fed	füttern
feel	felt	felt	fühlen
fight	fought	fought	kämpfen
find	found	found	finden
fly	flew	flown	fliegen
forget	forgot	forgotten	vergessen
get	got	got	bekommen; werden
give	gave	given	geben
go	went	gone	gehen
grow	grew	grown	wachsen
have	had	had	haben
hear	heard	heard	hören
hit	hit	hit	schlagen; treffen
hold	held	held	halten
hurt	hurt	hurt	verletzen
keep	kept	kept	behalten
know	knew	known	wissen
lead	led	led	führen
learn	learnt/learned	learnt/learned	lernen
leave	left	left	verlassen
let	let	let	lassen
lie	lay	lain	liegen
lose	lost	lost	verlieren
make	made	made	machen
mean	meant	meant	meinen; bedeuten
meet	met	met	treffen; kennenlernen

pay	paid	paid	bezahlen
put	put	put	setzen, stellen, legen
read	read	read	lesen
ring	rang	rung	klingeln
run	ran	run	laufen
say	said	said	sagen
see	saw	seen	sehen
sell	sold	sold	verkaufen
send	sent	sent	senden, (ver)schicken
show	showed	shown	zeigen
shut	shut	shut	(ver)schließen
sing	sang	sung	singen
sit	sat	sat	sitzen
sleep	slept	slept	schlafen
speak	spoke	spoken	sprechen
spell	spelt/spelled	spelt/spelled	buchstabieren
spend	spent	spent	ausgeben; verbringen
stand	stood	stood	stehen
steal	stole	stolen	stehlen
swim	swam	swum	schwimmen
take	took	taken	(mit)nehmen; (hin-, weg)bringen
teach	taught	taught	unterrichten, lehren
tell	told	told	erzählen
think	thought	thought	denken
understand	understood	understood	verstehen
wake up	woke up	woken up	aufwachen; aufwecken
wear	wore	worn	(Kleidung, Brille) tragen
win	won	won	gewinnen
write	wrote	written	schreiben